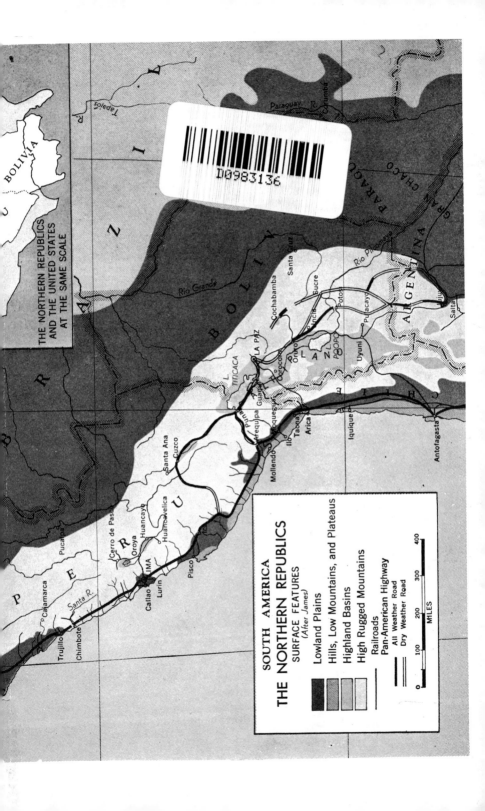

THE AMERICAN FOREIGN POLICY LIBRARY

SUMNER WELLES, EDITOR
DONALD C. MCKAY, ASSOCIATE EDITOR

The United States and South America
The Northern Republics

THE
UNITED STATES
AND
South America
The Northern Republics

By

Arthur P. Whitaker

GREENWOOD PRESS, PUBLISHERS
WESTPORT, CONNECTICUT

Library of Congress Cataloging in Publication Data

Whitaker, Arthur Preston, 1895-
    The United States and South America, the northern
republics.

    Reprint of the ed. published by Harvard University
Press, Cambridge, in series: "The American foreign
policy library.
    Bibliography: p.
    1. South America. 2. United States--Foreign rela-
tions--South America. 3. South America--Foreign rela-
tions--United States. I. Title. II. Series: The
American foreign policy library.
F2216.W45 1974   918'.03'3   73-21493
ISBN 0-8371-6411-7

MAPS PREPARED UNDER THE CARTOGRAPHIC
DIRECTION OF ARTHUR H. ROBINSON

033300

CONTENTS

PART II

Wartime Developments

PART III

Retrospect

Contents

PART IV

Prospect

MAPS

INTRODUCTION

This volume that Professor Arthur P. Whitaker has written upon the republics of Bolivia, Colombia, Ecuador, Peru, and Venezuela is an outstanding contribution toward the enlightenment of public opinion in the United States with regard to certain of the more important aspects of our foreign policy. It offers the reader a comprehensive survey, political, social, cultural, and economic, of these neighboring countries that now lie by air only a few hours from our doors.

I may individually disagree in a few cases with Professor Whitaker's estimates of individuals or with the conclusions he has reached upon political and social developments in the countries of which he writes. But his book is written with the authority derived from the intimate knowledge of these countries and of their peoples obtained by Professor Whitaker during the years when he has traveled in them, and when he has worked and taught in their centers of learning. The picture he gives us is presented with sympathy and with understanding. It should help every citizen of the English-speaking democracies of the New World better to understand the nature of the problems that these near-by peoples are now confronting, and better to appreciate the forces which are shaping their national destinies.

No citizen of this country should any longer fail to recognize how important to our own welfare and security are the friendship and coöperation of the peoples of these five republics of South America. It has, unfortunately, been the tendency in this country, and for that matter in some of the largest of the other South American republics, to think of these five states, in whose establishment as independent republics Bolívar played so decisive a part, as small and relatively unimportant members of the American family of nations. Nothing, of course, could be more directly contrary to fact. It is true that their populations are as yet not great, although they are already equal to or larger than the populations of many of those European nations which have for so long played an important part in world affairs. But their territories are vast. Many of the sparsely populated areas within their frontiers are admirably suited for the resettlement of those millions of Europeans who wish to find new homes across the seas. Latin America is already a region of the earth where the rate of population increase reaches its highest level. There can be little question that if these republics encourage desirable immigration by such legislation as that now under consideration in several of them the population of every one of them will increase at a far more rapid rate during the coming generation.

They possess natural resources of the utmost value to the world's economy, and of especial value to the economy of the United States. The minerals produced in Bolivia and Peru, and the oil of Venezuela and Colombia are increasingly essential to the productive capacity of this country, and the agricultural products which they all export are finding a growing market here.

From the strategic standpoint the coöperation of these countries is vital to our own safety. Had it not been for the wholehearted support which they gave us after Pearl Harbor, and for the air and naval facilities they granted us within their territory, the United States would have confronted almost insuperable obstacles in protecting the Panama Canal and in helping to prevent areas within the southern part of the Western Hemisphere from serving as a base from which an Axis attack could have been launched against this country.

For lack of accurate information, we are often inclined here in the United States to underestimate the extent of the progress already made by the peoples of these countries toward political stability and the establishment of truly democratic institutions. This progress, it is true, has sometimes been halted by those social upheavals that are inevitable in times of economic distress when so large a percentage of the nationals of these countries are still subjected to a pitifully low standard of living. But during the past few years liberal democratic governments have been freely elected in every one of these five nations. The prospects for the consolidation of institutions under which economic as well as political security may be guaranteed are brighter than they have ever been before.

Nor can we afford to overlook the fact that it is in these republics where many of the most noteworthy accomplishments in the realm of Latin American culture, and particularly in the field of literature, have been produced. We have still much to learn of the cultural standards attained by our neighbors. Fortunately, some of the more noteworthy books that have been written in recent years in these five republics are now available in English language editions. But we do not yet in general possess more than a rudimentary appreciation of the value to us of the culture of these American Republics.

The Bolivarian countries represent an ever more important part of the inter-American system. That hemispheric association of sovereign partners is in turn becoming an increasingly essential factor in safeguarding the security and prosperity of the United States, and in strengthening the United Nations. These five countries have long been among those American republics that have been more a name than a living reality to the average man and woman in the United

States. Professor Whitaker's book will do much to make them a reality to those who read these pages. It will make it far easier for all of us to comprehend why political and economic coöperation, and friendship and mutual understanding, between the United States and these five sister states are of vital importance to the people of the United States.

Sumner Welles

PREFACE

The famous Liberator Simón Bolívar was mainly instrumental in founding the five republics of northwestern South America discussed in this volume—Venezuela, Colombia, Ecuador, Peru, and Bolivia. They are therefore often called the Bolivarian countries. This term is open to some objections, which will be explained below in Chapter 1; but it is a handy designation and, for lack of a better one, will be freely used in this volume.

These five countries have failed to fulfill Bolívar's high hopes at the time of their founding; he himself was completely disillusioned about them for some time before his death in 1830. Since then they have made marked progress along many lines; but they are still among the smallest nations in the world (the largest of them, Colombia, has fewer inhabitants than Pennsylvania), and, as their own writers never tire of pointing out, in the economic sense they are still living in the colonial period. Weak individually, they have little cohesion as a group. Why then is it important for the student of American foreign policy to understand the behavior of their governments and peoples?

The reasons are numerous, though not always flattering to those countries. From the military point of view, they are quite as important to the United States as the Balkan states are to the Soviet Union. The Panama Canal is within easy bombing range from all of them except Bolivia, and two of them have extensive coast lines along the Caribbean, a primary defense zone of the United States. They are, moreover, leading producers of strategic materials, such as tin, platinum, vanadium, copper, and oil. They also play an essential role in the peace-time economy of the United States, as a source of supply of raw materials and foodstuffs (more coffee is imported into the United States from Colombia than from any other country in the world except Brazil), and as a field for investment. From the point of view of international politics, it is a matter of considerable moment to the United States how their five votes are cast in Pan-American conferences and in the General Assembly of the United Nations; and their views may affect the votes of the other fifteen Latin-American states as well, because of the long-established and apparently growing sense of Latin-American solidarity.

The foregoing considerations have been presented from the point of view of the United States, but most of them serve equally well to show that the five Bolivarian countries are important in any broad view of world affairs, and the point can be reinforced by many other considerations. Thus, their five votes in inter-American and United Nations meetings are obviously a matter of interest not only to the United States but to all the states concerned. So also are the opportunities which they offer for foreign business enterprise and the stand which their several governments take on the crucial issues of international trade policy that have divided the great powers since the close of World War II. They play a prominent role in that rivalry of the great powers over Latin America which was largely in abeyance during the war but has now broken out in full force again. Which of the suitors they will favor is by no means a foregone conclusion. Since 1920 there has been a net improvement in their relations with the United States, and at least three of them (Colombia, Peru, and Venezuela) have developed democratic institutions and practices which in some respects bear a close resemblance to those of this

country. But, quite aside from the fact that Yankeephobia
is by no means dead among them, there is a widespread
feeling in all these countries that at several crucial points
the policies and practices of the United States are not suited
to their particular needs. The other foreign powers that
have retained or recently gained considerable influence in
the area—Great Britain, France, Spain, and the Soviet Union
—do not neglect the opportunity to turn this situation to
their own advantage.

Moreover, in one of the newest and potentially most significant fields of international action—the promotion of
social welfare—the Bolivarian countries offer both a challenge and an opportunity. The challenge lies in their woefully low standard of living; the opportunity, in their potential capacity to absorb emigration from more thickly
populated countries. Because of the inhospitable character
of large parts of their territory, this capacity is not nearly
so great as their present low rates of population density
might lead one to expect; but it is still not negligible.
Finally, three of them (Ecuador, Bolivia, and Peru) present
the problem of national minorities in a form all but unique
among the nations of Europe and America: the existence of
a body of several million unassimilated Indians—including
in each case about half the total population of the country
—who are political ciphers and cultural aliens in their own
land. Guatemala is the only country in the Atlantic world
where this problem is encountered on anything like the
same scale.

If we are to understand the peoples of these five South
American republics, it is essential to know the physical
environment in which their cultural heritage has been developed, and to follow the national pattern in studying the
environment. The geographical factor is even more important among them than in the United States and Europe.
This is mainly because nature is so much more violent in all

these five countries, and constantly threatens to overwhelm
man; but partly also because society here is relatively backward in the modern technology that gives man the upper
hand over nature in other parts of the world.

To stress the national pattern in a discussion of these countries may seem a paradox, and a rather silly one at that, in
view of their relatively low degree of national unity. Yet
while they are not closely integrated within their respective boundaries, they are sharply divided from each other.
Their leaders think and act in national terms, and each
country constitutes a distinct economic entity, whose economic ties are very largely with Europe and the United
States, not with the other members of the group.

Accordingly, Part I of this volume gives a brief survey
of this area—first as a whole, then by countries—mainly in
terms of the physical environment and the kind of people
it has produced. It is hoped that even this bird's-eye view
will help the reader understand why these people and their
governments act as they do. How they have acted, particularly in the recent past, is the subject of Parts II and III,
which give some indication of the course they may be expected to follow in the near future. The principal problems
in relation to which their course will have to be steered are
described in Part IV.

Topically, emphasis is laid upon the factors which seem
most important from the point of view of international
relations, particularly upon the political and economic pat-
terns that have emerged as a result of the interplay between
the local environment and the impact of foreign interests
and influences. Geographically, attention is focused mainly
on Colombia and Peru, as the leading nations of this area;
but the others will not be neglected, and from time to time
some special problem will require the limelight to be turned
on one or another of them.

I began the preparation of this volume in 1945, but it is

based in large part upon study, discussions, and observation of an earlier period. As a result, a complete list of the persons to whom I am indebted in one way or another would be not only inordinately long but (mainly because of a faulty memory) impossible to compile. For example, when I visited Peru, Ecuador, and Colombia in 1941 and Colombia and Venezuela in 1946, I made it a practice to discuss the domestic and foreign affairs of those countries with people of all shades of opinion. In Peru and Colombia this was all the easier for me to do because I was rash enough to give public lectures on the foreign policy of the United States in both those countries (at the Catholic University and San Marcos University, Lima, in 1941, and at the National University and the National Library, Bogotá, in 1946). Fancying myself a scholar with some knowledge of Latin America as well as of American foreign policy, I tried in these lectures to give a scholarly, impartial account of the subject in terms comprehensible to my Latin-American audiences. The passages in which I criticized the course of my country's government met with warm approval; those in which I defended it provoked loud dissent, which was freely expressed to me personally. Both reactions were grist to my mill, and led to many discussions that enriched my knowledge and helped clarify my opinions.

The names of some of the persons to whom I am thus indebted were recorded in the diaries I kept on these two trips, but others which seem equally important in retrospect were omitted and some of them cannot now be recalled. So it seems best to omit them all; though I think it fitting to make a blanket acknowledgment to the six young *Colombianos* who took my seminar on American foreign policy at the National University of Colombia in the 1946 summer session (the first such session ever held at that University). There was a wide variety in their ages (which ranged from 18 to 28), in their training, background, and opinions, and in the degree of help they gave me; they were all alike, however, in their high degree of intelligence, seriousness, and good will. My association with them was perhaps the pleasantest and most stimulating experience of an exceptionally interesting summer in northern South America.

Similarly, this book is in part the product of information acquired and opinions formed in discussions with my associates in the Department of State while I was working on Latin-American affairs as an officer of the Department in 1943 and 1944. Obviously, their names cannot be given here. It might be added parenthetically that no secret information obtained at that time is revealed in the following pages, though it is inevitably reflected in some of the opinions expressed or implied in them.

Otherwise, the best preparation that I had for writing this volume came from work over a period of five years (1942–1946), as editor of the annual survey *Inter-American Affairs* and as author of the chapters on Pan-American politics and diplomacy in these five volumes. Not only did the Bolivarian countries bulk large in the story told in these volumes, but they and the other American states were discussed in a broad perspective which was well adapted to the purpose of the present volume and the series of which it forms a part. This perspective was described in the foreword of the first of these annual surveys, in which it was stated that their purpose was to bring out the international significance of developments in the several American nations, not as a means of promoting "hemispheric isolationism" but on the contrary in order to "show, among other things, how the Americas are united by living bonds to other parts of the world, especially Europe." Such a perspective is essential for an understanding of the international role of the Bolivarian countries. To have been employing it for several years past in writing about Latin

America at large was a useful preparation for writing about this particular group of Latin-American states. And I wish to add here another blanket acknowledgment—to the other contributors to *Inter-American Affairs*, whose chapters on economic, social, and other developments of the period covered have been helpful to me in many ways.

For nonconfidential information and advice given recently in response to my requests, I am indebted to the following United States government officials: George Wythe, of the Department of Commerce; Alvin C. Loosely, of the Tariff Commission; and Roland D. Hussey and Harley Notter, of the Department of State. I am also grateful for the advice I have received from the Editor and the Associate Editor of this series.

Philadelphia   A. P. W.
April 30, 1947

PART I

LANDS AND PEOPLES

1. The "Bolivarian" Countries

1. RESEMBLANCES

On a map of South America our five northwestern republics form a gigantic C. Beginning at the boundary of British Guiana, the top of the letter is formed by Venezuela, which fronts on the Caribbean. The line then bends from west to south in Colombia, which faces both the Caribbean and the Pacific; continues southward through the Pacific states of Ecuador and Peru; and turns eastward again to its termination in landlocked Bolivia, whose easternmost frontier reaches almost halfway across the continent. The open space within the letter is occupied by the northwestern territory of Portuguese-speaking Brazil, which has a common frontier with all of these Spanish-speaking states except Ecuador. Their combined area, some 1,800,000 square miles, is more than double that of the United States east of the Mississippi; but if the populations of the two groups were exchanged, the five republics' 27,000,000 inhabitants would provide replacements for only New York, New Jersey, and Pennsylvania. The other states east of the Mississippi would have no inhabitants at all.

These five countries have much in common. In all of them there are large areas of both tropical lowland and temperate-to-cold highland; but the bulk of the population is concentrated in a few cities and in rural clusters which, though numerous, occupy less than half the national territory. Economic and other ties with Europe are very strong; the cultural influence of France has been great ever since the eighteenth century, and Spanish is not only the official language in all of them but also the mother tongue of the majority of their inhabitants. All are overwhelmingly Roman Catholic.

The resemblances between their several economic, social, and political systems are numerous and important. Mineral production and foreign commerce bulk large in their national economies, and manufactures are beginning to develop, but the great majority of their people are engaged in agriculture, many of them in subsistence agriculture. All these countries have always maintained at least the form of republican government under written constitutions modeled to some extent upon that of the United States but have actually been torn by frequent civil war and revolutions and dominated for long periods by dictators or oligarchies. The latter are built up around a core of great landowners, for everywhere landownership is concentrated in a small fraction of the population, though the degree varies from country to country, and is lowest in Colombia. These oligarchies are still influential; but (again in all five countries in varying degrees) the impact of foreign business enterprise and ideologies has promoted the rise of rival elements in the present century—a new plutocracy, a stronger middle class, and the first labor organizations.

Everywhere the larger cities have been transformed, mainly since 1920, in spirit as well as in the externals of modernity, such as large office buildings with elevator service, congested automobile traffic, broadcasting stations, and newspapers publishing the latest reports of the world's great newsgathering agencies. But even in the cities the benefits of material progress have not been equally distributed, and in all of these countries the rural districts have shared in them little if at all. Compared with the United States, the standard of living is very low, the birth and death rate high.

Illiteracy is widespread, ranging from about 56 per cent in Colombia to 80 per cent in Bolivia. All have one or more universities, but these are in nearly all cases aggregations of professional schools served by part-time faculties. For advanced training in the social sciences, the humanities, engineering, and several other subjects, it is still necessary for the student to go abroad.

Despite these unfavorable conditions, all five countries have produced leaders of international reputation in many fields. To give only a few examples from the present century, these include the poets José Santos Chocano of Peru and Guillermo Valencia of Colombia; the novelists Rómulo Gallegos of Venezuela, José Eustasio Rivero of Colombia, Ciro Alegría of Peru, Jorge Icaza of Ecuador, and Alcides Argüedas of Bolivia; the historians Caracciolo Parra-Pérez of Venezuela, Francisco García Calderon and Jorge Basadre of Peru, and the journalist-historian Germán Arciniegas of Colombia; the essayists Luis López de Mesa of Colombia and José Carlos Mariátegui and Luis Alberto Sánchez of Peru; the biologist Carlos Monge of Peru; the surgeon J. M. Montoya-Flórez of Colombia; and, in politics and international affairs, Alberto Ulloa, Víctor Andrés Belaunde, and Víctor Raúl Haya de la Torre of Peru, Eduardo Santos, Alfonso López, and Alberto Lleras Camargo of Colombia, Alberto Ostria Gutiérrez and Fernando Guachalla of Bolivia, Ponce Borjas of Ecuador, and (again) Caracciolo Parra-Pérez of Venezuela. All of these men, and others besides, have demonstrated a high order of talent that would have enabled them to make their mark anywhere in the world. Yet the fact remains that, outside a small, favored circle in each country, the general cultural level is low in all these countries; and even the cultural élite are still very susceptible to the influence of more advanced nations, particularly France.

If, as their people complain, all these countries are also

colonial in an economic sense, they are no less dependent in a military sense, for not one of them could hope to defend itself successfully against one of the great powers even if the latter did not have the atomic bomb. In this sense the mechanization of warfare has made them even more vulnerable, and an even more truly dependent area, than was the case in their colonial period. In 1740 Britain suffered a major disaster in the repulse of a large expedition sent out under Admiral Vernon * to take Cartagena (in present Colombia). Barring the intervention of a third power, it is almost inconceivable that a comparable British expedition two centuries later could have failed to take Cartagena or any other city on this coast.

Our five countries share many of these traits with the rest of Spanish America. To distinguish them as a unique group, they are often called the "Bolivarian countries" because, as already stated, they constitute that part of America which won its independence from Spain a century and a quarter ago under the leadership of Simón Bolívar. Often called the George Washington of Spanish America, Bolívar was a statesman as well as a soldier, and he left a strong imprint upon the national institutions and policies of these five countries. His political legacy is still a living force among some of them—a kind of South American counterpart of the Napoleonic legend in France. In order to stress the idea of their solidarity still more strongly, they are sometimes referred to as the "Bolivarian bloc."

2. DIFFERENCES

The unity or solidarity of the Bolivarian countries is, however, much more apparent than real. So far in their

* For whom Mount Vernon was named. George Washington's elder brother Lawrence was a member of Admiral Vernon's expedition against Cartagena.

history the centripetal forces at work among them have been far outweighed by the factors making for disunity. The strongest of these is the geographical barrier of the Andes, which has discouraged trade and travel among them and made it difficult for them to maintain even their national unity. Despite this handicap they have succeeded in maintaining it for more than a century, but their very success has built up a second barrier to Bolivarian solidarity—the political barrier of nationalism. In fact, the Bolivarian tradition is weak in Peru and Bolivia, where Bolívar was always regarded as a foreigner, and strong only in the Liberator's native Venezuela and neighboring Colombia and Ecuador.

These three states once formed a single republic called Gran Colombia, which Bolívar was mainly instrumental in founding and of which Peru and Bolivia were not a part. Though Gran Colombia broke up in 1830 and has never been reconstituted, the idea of Grancolombian unity has never died out. In recent years it has been given wide publicity and a modest measure of practical effect. If there is anything in this area that deserves to be called a bloc, it is the Grancolombian bloc of these three states. Yet in one important respect—the ethnic composition of its people, half of whom are Indians—Ecuador belongs not in this bloc but with Peru and Bolivia. Similarly, a special relationship, rooted in historical and other factors, exists between the latter two; but the tie is not a strong one.

In short, we are dealing here with five separate national states, which guard their several sovereignties as jealously in their relations with one another as with the rest of the world. Economically, too, they are five distinct entities; indeed, in this respect each of them has much stronger ties with Europe and the United States than with the other four members of the group.

Their political diversity was suggested long ago by

Bolívar, who called Venezuela a barracks, Colombia a debating society, and Ecuador a convent. We might round out the picture by calling Bolivia half barracks and half company store, and Peru a Society of Colonial Dames. The differences between these countries have persisted despite the common experiences already mentioned—ranging from civil war and dictatorship to the recent impact of the industrial age—which might have been expected to break them down. Each country still retains its own individuality, which is becoming ever more sharply defined. Colombia is the most orderly and democratic, Bolivia and Ecuador the least so; and Peru and Venezuela occupy different positions between these two extremes. The explanation lies in the fact that the same force produced different effects because of differences in the national environments upon which it acted. What these environmental differences were will be made clearer in the following chapters of this section.

Nor does the fragmentation of the group stop here. Even within their own borders only one of them, Colombia, has achieved a degree of national unity approaching that of the United States, the countries of Western Europe, and some of the other Latin-American states, such as Argentina and Uruguay; and even Colombia did not achieve it until the present century. The internal weakness of these countries was due partly to the fact that, in contrast with the European states, their national governments were set up before they were nations; partly to differences in race and language and certain other factors, all of which will be discussed in due course; but most of all to their inhospitable landscape. Three-fourths of their total area consists of tropical jungle, deserts drier than the Sahara, and the massive multiple ranges of the Andes. In each country nature seems to have placed these with a view to making national integration as difficult as possible.

In no other comparable area in the world is the influence

of physical environment on the development of human society better illustrated than in this one; and there is none that better deserves the hackneyed epithet "land of contrasts," whether in regard to environment or society. Drought and flood, torrid heat and subarctic cold, rags and riches, exquisite refinement and sodden brutishness—such antitheses could be multiplied indefinitely; and they describe not the fringe of life in this area, but its very fabric. They are best explained in terms of geographical conditions, and they determine the behavior of the peoples of the area in their relations not only with one another but also with the outside world.

Bolivia is often called the Switzerland of America. The comparison is a good one in the sense that the part of the country where most of the people live is a mass of rugged mountain ranges and high plateaus. But the same epithet could be applied equally well to our five republics as a whole, with the proviso that they would have to be described as a vaster Switzerland with the addition of a seacoast and a tropical hinterland. For their total area is more than one hundred times as large as that of Switzerland and falls into three main zones: a narrow coastal strip along the Caribbean and the Pacific; a wide band of mountains—the Andes—and its intermontane valleys and plateaus; and, finally, a broad expanse of plain and jungle stretching out from the eastern foothills of the Andes across the upper basins of the Orinoco, Amazon, and La Plata rivers.

The second zone alone—that of the Andes—dwarfs Switzerland's total area (about 16,000 square miles) and highest mountain peaks (15,210 feet). From the southernmost country of our group, Bolivia, the Andes run northward through the other four for a total distance of more than 2500 miles, with a varying width that averages about 200 miles. They thus cover an area of more than 500,000 square miles. They are half as high again as the Alps. Their two highest peaks (one in Bolivia, the other in Peru) exceed 22,000 feet, and at least fifteen others (in Bolivia, Peru, Ecuador, and Colombia) range from 17,000 to more than 21,000 feet. It is in this Andean zone and the coastal zone that the overwhelming majority of the inhabitants of these five countries live; and there is a definite preponderance in favor of the former. An approximate idea of the distribution is given by the location of the five national capitals. Three of these are high up in the Andes: La Paz, Bolivia, at an altitude of 12,000 feet (which makes it the highest capital in the world); Quito, Ecuador, at 9350 feet; and Bogotá, Colombia, at 8700 feet. All three are remote from the seacoast, in time if not also in space; the closest, Quito, is more than twelve hours' journey by rail from the nearest seaport, Guayaquil. On the other hand, Caracas, Venezuela, at an altitude of 3400 feet, is only twenty miles by automobile highway (an hour's ride) from the seaport of La Guaira; and Lima, Peru, at a paltry 500 feet, has the country's principal port, Callao, virtually in its suburbs.

The third zone is the tropical hinterland east of the Andes. Hot, jungle-covered, and difficult of access, a large part of it is still a closed book to what we fondly call civilized man, though four hundred years have passed since this country was first traversed by a European, the Spaniard Francisco de Orellana, who made the journey from Quito across the continent to the mouth of the Amazon in 1539–1541. The sparse population of this hinterland includes primitive Indian tribes. White men pass up and down the rivers and live in towns and settlements along their banks, but seldom penetrate into the interior. Since Orellana's time many of them have been drawn to this area by the traditional quest of the age of the Spanish conquerors, "glory, gold, and God," or by their modern variants, rubber and scientific knowledge; but the rewards have very seldom been sufficient to hold them long. And yet the region has had an irresistible fascination for statesmen and entrepreneurs, not only of South America but of other lands; it has long been the subject of international boundary disputes and other controversies, which have several times led to the brink of war and even over it. For reasons which will be discussed later, there is a widespread belief that the long-delayed development of at least a considerable part of this dark country is at hand. Up to the present, however, it has been important mainly as a source of international friction, and it is from this point of view that it will be discussed in the following pages.

The tripartite division of our five countries into coastal, Andean, and transmontane zones is a reasonably accurate description of the group as a whole; but, when they are considered separately, only two of these countries—Colombia and Peru—will be found to correspond exactly to it. As for the other three, Bolivia has no seacoast; Ecuador has relatively little land east of the Andes; and the majority of Venezuela's population is found neither on a coastal plain nor in mountain fastnesses, but in rolling hills and interior lowlands. Even Colombia and Peru, which both conform to the general pattern, differ greatly from each other in detail.

Also, as the following table shows, the total area and population of the group are very unequally divided among its five members, and there are wide discrepancies in their population density and rate of growth. For purposes of comparison, figures for the United States and the whole of South America are included in the table on page 12.*

In area, the largest of our five republics, Peru, is nearly five times the size of the smallest, Ecuador. The only two which are approximately equal are Bolivia and Colombia,

* This table combines data in table 2 and table 4 in *Demographic Status of South America*, by Halbert L. Dunn, Hope Tisdale Eldridge, and Nora P. Powell (Department of Commerce, Bureau of the Census, *Vital Statistics—Special Reports*, Vol. 23, No. 3, September 18, 1945).

Area	Population (1941)	Area in square miles	Population per square mile	Average annual increase	
				Per cent	Period
Bolivia	3,495,450	416,040	8.4	2.3	1900–1942
Colombia	9,387,930	439,828	21.3	2.4	1918–1938
Ecuador	3,085,871	103,415	29.8	2.1	1930–1943
Peru	7,132,626	482,258	14.8	1.3	1930–1940
Venezuela	3,951,371	352,150	11.2	2.0	1926–1941
Five Northern Republics	27,043,248	1,793,291	15.1 *	2.0 *	(as above)
South America (all)	91,995,732	6,871,454	13.4	2.0 *	—— †
United States	133,202,873	2,977,128	44.7	1.2	1920–1940

* Figure not given in original tables (see footnote in text).
† Varying periods of from ten to thirty-six years since 1900; no terminal date earlier than 1936.

each of which is more than half as large again as Texas; yet the difference between even these two equals the combined areas of Massachusetts, Connecticut, and New Hampshire. Colombia, which ranks second, is smaller than Peru by the area of these three New England states together with New Jersey, Delaware, and Maryland.

The discrepancies in population are not quite so great, but they are still very wide. Ecuador, which again stands at the foot of the list, has less than one third as many inhabitants as Colombia, which heads it. Peru stands second with a population nearly twice as large as that of its nearest competitor; and the combined population of Peru and Colombia is more than 60 per cent larger than that of the other three countries —a fact which goes far to explain the preponderance of the first two in this group of states.

Population density is greatest in the country with the smallest population, Ecuador, where there were 29.8 inhabitants per square mile in 1940, as compared with 48 per square mile in the United States. But in Ecuador, as in the other four countries as well, the vast majority of the people (more than 90 per cent) live in only half its total area—that is, in the coastal and mountain zones which constitute the effective national territory in all five of our countries. The other half of their area, the tropical hinterland, contains only 6.5 per cent of the population. As a result, the density of population in the effective national territory is twice as great as the figures in our table indicate. On this basis Colombia has a density rate (47 per square mile) which is virtually the same as that of the United States. This situation has obvious advantages, but these are sometimes outweighed by the disadvantages—for example, as both Bolivia and Ecuador have found to their cost, remote and uninhabited territories invite foreign pressure and are hard to hold.

Without going behind the figures in the table we may note that in population density our five countries approximate closely both the extremes and the average for the whole of South America. The rate for Bolivia (8.4 per square mile) is the lowest except for Paraguay (6.9), whereas Ecuador (29.8) is exceeded only by Uruguay (30.3); and the average for our group is 15.1, compared with 13.4 for the whole continent. But the story is a very different one when we come to the question of urbanization, for a comparison based on figures for about 1940 relating to cities having a population of 100,000 or more showed that all the other South American countries were more highly urbanized than the five in our group. For the latter, the urban percentage ranged from 7 to 10; for the rest, it ranged from 11.5 in Paraguay up to about 33 each for Argentina and Uruguay, which latter are more urban than the United States.

One of the most important facts about the population of South America is its exceptionally rapid rate of increase. It is growing more rapidly than the United States—faster, indeed, than any other continent for which data are available. As a group, our five republics are growing at the same rapid rate as the rest of South America; but there are some important differences among them. The rate of increase is lowest in Peru, where it is barely above that of the United States; it is highest in Colombia, where it is double that of the United States. Already the most populous country in the group, Colombia, bids fair to leave the others far behind in the next half century.

Qualitatively, too, there are striking differences among the peoples of these five countries, though in this respect three of them form a distinct group, and in all five the differences are less wide in the ruling classes than lower down the social scale. These ruling classes are all Spanish-speaking. They are also preponderantly European in both culture and racial origin. There are exceptions, but they do not alter the general rule that in all these countries the upperclass world is a white man's world. In all of them except Colombia, however, only about 10 or 15 per cent of the population are actually white. In Ecuador, Peru, and Bolivia about 35 per cent are *mestizos* (persons of mixed white and Indian blood); and about 50 per cent are Indians.

Many of the Indians still cling to the remnants of their native culture that survived the Spanish conquest. Their tenacity in this respect is illustrated by the fact that even today, after more than four centuries of domination by Spanish-speaking peoples, they have not yet adopted the language of their masters. The three languages spoken by most of them are Aymara (in Bolivia and Peru), Quechua (in Peru and Ecuador), and Jíbaro (in Ecuador). Among other survivals are their native songs, dances, and dress; and in large areas even their communal land system has withstood repeated efforts to introduce a regime of private property. These Indians, the largest single group in each of these three countries, are thus separated from the ruling classes by a cultural abyss. The mestizos do not bridge it, for most of them flock to the white man's world, where the rewards are richer. A few devoted "Indianists"—white as well as mestizo and Indian—have attacked the problem, and they are steadily gaining reinforcements; but so far they have met with little success. This need not surprise us, for the difficulty of the task is appalling.

In Colombia and Venezuela, too, there are many mestizos, but the unmixed Indian element is insignificant, and the proportion of Negroes and mulattoes (persons of mixed white and Negro blood) is much higher. Exact data are impossible to obtain, but there can be no question about the central fact, which is that the cultural schism which afflicts Bolivia, Peru, and Ecuador has no counterpart in either Venezuela or Colombia. The latter has achieved a much higher degree of cultural and social integration than any of its neighbors. This has proved an important source of strength to Colombia, but at the same time it has heightened the element of national diversity that characterizes the group.

Many other illustrations of this diversity could be given, but in order not to labor the point we shall offer only two. Both are of an economic character and thus help round out the picture. Per capita national income ranges from a high of $200 a year in Venezuela down to $34 in Bolivia and Ecuador. Colombia and Peru, with $75 and $62 respectively, stand far above the latter two, but even farther below Venezuela. In per capita value of foreign trade, Venezuela again stands at the head of the list, with a rate about ten times as high as that of Ecuador, which again stands at the foot. In this case Bolivia moves up to second place because of its heavy exports of tin ore, but not far ahead of Peru and Colombia; all three are widely separated from the extremes represented by the other two.

In short, from whatever point of view the observer approaches the northern republics of South America, he soon finds that the first essential to an understanding of the group is an acquaintance with its individual members.

2. Bolivia: Tin

1. THE MINING COMPLEX

Our survey of the individual countries of northern South America begins again with Bolivia, which was the starting point of our comparison of the whole group with Switzerland. For our purposes it is appropriate to take Bolivia first, since its role in international affairs has been important, though largely passive and sacrificial. Also, Bolivia is the southern terminus of the wide band of unmixed Indian peoples—the living ruins of the Inca empire—which continues northward through Peru and Ecuador, and is a prime factor in the domestic affairs and foreign relations of all three countries.

Bolivia bears little resemblance to Switzerland except that both are landlocked and mountainous. Even here a reservation must be entered: only two-fifths of Bolivia is mountainous; the rest, lying east of the Andes in the upper Amazon and Plata basins, is tropical lowland. But in the human sense, the mountains are Bolivia, for here live more than four-fifths of the country's population of some 3,500,-000. As if to make their isolation still more complete, they are concentrated in the midst of the rugged Andes, which attain their maximum width (400 miles) and almost their maximum height (some 22,000 feet) in Bolivia. There are two main areas of concentration. The first is the *altiplano*, a broken plateau averaging about 12,000 feet above sea level, which is cold and bleak, but contains most of the country's mines and Indians, its national capital and largest city, La Paz, and its third largest city, Oruro. The other main area consists of the high eastern valleys, about 8000 feet above sea level, where agriculture flourishes, where the majority of the country's white population lives,* where society has been Europeanized and the Indians reduced to peonage or tenancy on large estates, and where some of the chief provincial cities are found. Among these are Cochabamba, the second largest city and a center of intense political activity, and Sucre, a charming old Spanish colonial city, once the national capital and still a leading cultural center, which has borne four names since it was founded as many centuries ago.

In both areas the population is overwhelmingly rural. La Paz, the only large city, had about 300,000 inhabitants in 1942; Cochabamba had 60,000, Oruro 50,000, and Sucre 40,000. This situation helps to explain the high rate of illiteracy (about 80 per cent) and the low ratio of enrollment in schools to population of school age (about 1 to 4), for the rural school system is sketchy.

Bolivia has not always been landlocked. It once had a seacoast, on the Pacific, but this was lost to Chile in the War of the Pacific (1879-1883). Ever since then the desire to break out again has been an obsession with the Bolivians— national claustrophobia, some writers have called it. But the realization of the desire seems unlikely in the extreme, for Bolivia is hemmed in by strong neighbors—Chile, Peru, Brazil, and Argentina—and by Paraguay, which, though weak, can usually count on Argentine support; and Bolivia herself is weak. Indeed, if we must find an Old World counterpart for Bolivia, we should compare it not to Switzerland but to the Turkey which was called the "sick man of Europe" in the nineteenth century, or the Poland which

* According to the census of 1900, the last which shows racial distribution.

was partitioned by its neighbors, first in the eighteenth century and again in the twentieth.

Some forty years ago an outspoken Bolivian writer, Alcides Argüedas, hit the nail on the head by giving the title "A Sick People" (*Pueblo enfermo*) to a book in which he diagnosed the condition of the country at that time. The title would serve equally well for a book about its present condition. Bolivia is sick not merely in the sense that many of its inhabitants are physically diseased and undernourished: the whole body politic seems to be wracked by an ancient and incurable malady. One symptom of this condition is the frequency with which the country has been torn by domestic violence; another, the sadistic cruelty that has often marked these outbreaks.

As a result of this inner weakness, the country has suffered more at the hands of foreign powers than has any other state in Latin America. Its neighbors have stripped it of nearly half the territory it claimed when its independence was established in 1825.* The same year marked the beginning of that foreign interference in its domestic affairs which has continued unabated to the present day. Its first constitution was written by a Venezuelan, Simón Bolívar, the Liberator; its first president was Bolívar's lieutenant,

---

* Most of Bolivia's territorial losses have occurred since 1900. These are shown by the following table (adapted from U. S. Department of Commerce and others, *Bolivia: Summary of Biostatistics*, 1945, p. 40), which includes the confirmation to Chile in 1904 of the coastal zone occupied by it since the War of the Pacific:

Year	Area in square miles ceded by Bolivia to bordering countries	Bordering countries increased in area
1903	72,859	Brazil
1904	34,749	Chile
1909	96,525	Peru
1925	4,146	Argentina
1928	669	Brazil
1938	90,757	Paraguay
Total	299,705	

Antonio José de Sucre; and the reader hardly needs to be reminded that the country also took its very name from the Venezuelan Liberator.

The mineral resources of Bolivia are rich and varied, but they have contributed to its undoing. Two of these minerals have been the axis of Bolivian economic development ever since the Spanish conquest—silver in the colonial and early national period, tin since the close of the nineteenth century. Bolivia has been rich in both minerals not merely by South American standards, but by any standard. The dream of El Dorado was realized—though in silver, not gold—when in 1546 the Spaniards discovered Potosí, a veritable mountain of the precious metal. Other rich deposits were soon discovered in the same region, and for a century and a half Bolivia rivaled Mexico as the world's largest producer of silver, which was poured out in such quantities as to bring about a price revolution all over Europe. Silver still ranks high in Bolivia's national economy, though since 1900 it has yielded first place to tin. Bolivia's production of tin does not hold the world preëminence formerly enjoyed by its silver, for in normal times the output of the tin mines of British Malaya and the East Indies is far greater; but these are the only countries that do surpass it, and when they were overrun by Japan in World War II, Bolivian tin became of vital importance to the war effort of the United Nations. Together with silver and other minerals, tin has fastened on Bolivia what we may call its mining complex.

That these minerals have yielded some important advantages to the country is not open to question. They have enabled it to pay for its imports from abroad, which include most of its manufactured goods and a large part of the food consumed in its cities; they now make up about 90 per cent of its exports, tin alone accounting for about 70 per cent. They also pay most of the cost of running the national government (about 60 per cent of its annual revenue is derived from taxes on tin), and are responsible for the fact that Bolivia's rail connections with the outside world are, by South American standards, exceptionally good. The capital of much more populous Colombia, Bogotá, has only one rail connection with the coast, and even that is not quite continuous; the Bolivian capital, La Paz, has four. Three of these run to ports of Chile and Peru on the Pacific, and the fourth links it with the Atlantic at Buenos Aires, thus forming one of the only two transcontinental rail routes in South America (the other runs from Buenos Aires to Santiago, Chile). All of them were built to serve the foreign commerce made possible by Bolivia's mineral exports. Finally, the exploitation of the country's mineral resources provides jobs for many Bolivians, and at peak production the tin industry alone gives direct employment to about 100,000 persons (one in every 35 of the population).

On the other hand, Bolivia has suffered greatly from its mining complex. This has made it an extreme example of the one-sided, unstable economies so common in Latin America, and has increased its dependence upon foreigners, not only for capital (mainly from New York and London), but also for food (mainly from Argentina). The mining complex has also promoted the spirit of speculative and exploitative enterprise, to the detriment of sound economic development of the country's resources, and has intensified the division of the people of Bolivia into two distinct and alien groups, the one Indian and the other European.

In connection with the latter point, it should be emphasized that the majority of the Bolivian people are not engaged in mining or any related activity, such as transportation, but in subsistence agriculture. They do not produce for the market, whether at the mines, in the cities, or abroad, but only for themselves. Conversely, they are not consumers of manufactured goods, either those imported from abroad, or the few (such as furniture, glassware, and processed foods) produced by Bolivia's own handful of factories. They do not exert a stabilizing influence on what is known as the national economy—the economy dominated by mining and foreign trade; in fact, they do not influence it at all, for they are almost as completely separated from it as if they lived on another planet.

Now these are the same Indians who, as we have already seen, constitute a distinct cultural and racial group in Bolivia, Ecuador, and Peru, and number about half the population in each country. The chasm separating the Indian half from the Europeanized other half has reached its widest point in Bolivia because it is here that the degree of separation between their two economic systems has been rendered most complete through the increasing domination of one of them—the "national" economy—by the tin industry, which at the top requires heavy capital outlay, international connections, and great technical skill and managerial ability. At the bottom of the industry Indians have always been employed as laborers in the mines and in related occupations, and the number so employed has greatly increased in recent years. But the two economic systems have not thereby been brought appreciably closer together, for while these Indians remain at the mines they live as aliens in a white man's world and when they return to their villages they revert completely to their native way of life.

An Indian may even, by a miracle, win great success in the white man's world, but when he does he is lost to his own. A case in point is the famous one of Simón Patiño, the humble Indian miner who became the leading tin magnate of Bolivia and was long reputed to be the richest living South American, but who for many years before his death in April 1947 made his home at the Waldorf-Astoria Hotel in New York City. His reason for leaving Bolivia has been explained by a story to the effect that when he first made his pile he had himself put up for membership in the best club of his native town, Cochabamba—and was blackballed, though he could have bought up the club, all its members, and the whole town, without making a dent in his bank account. The story may be apocryphal, but it gives a true picture of the difficulty facing any Bolivian Indian, no matter how successful, who tries to gain acceptance in the white man's world of his own country. It should be added that the story had a happy ending, for Patiño became an ambassador and his daughters married into the bluest-blooded families of Europe.

The profits from the tin industry have gone mainly to absentee owners, either absentee Bolivians, such as Patiño, or foreigners—even the Patiño interests are controlled in part by New York and London bankers. In so far as the country has benefited, the benefits have been monopolized by the Europeanized, urban part of it; almost none have trickled through to the other half, the Indian's world of subsistence agriculture, and of ignorance, squalor, and disease. What little progress has been made by the first of these two halves of a divided nation has therefore increased the gap between the two. For the Indian's half has remained stationary, still clinging to the remnants of a culture shattered by the Spanish conquerors four centuries ago, and comprehending the white man's half less and less as the latter has taken on the trappings of finance capitalism and the machine age.

2. PARTITIONS

Another result of Bolivia's internal situation has been its passive and sacrificial role in its external relations. For our present purpose, the point is best illustrated by Bolivia's grievous territorial losses, to which reference has already been made. The two worst were suffered as a result of defeat in war: the loss of its seacoast to Chile in the War

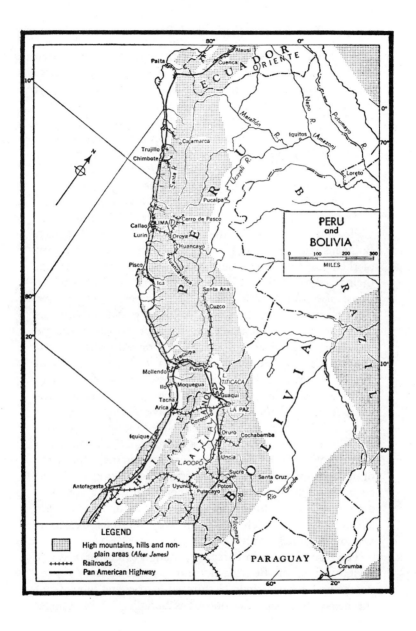

LEGEND

High mountains, hills and non-plain areas (*After James*)

++++++ Railroads

——— Pan American Highway

PERU and BOLIVIA

0   100   200   300
MILES

of the Pacific (1879–1883) and of the disputed Gran Chaco
area to Paraguay in the Chaco War of 1932–1935; but there
were also peaceful cessions, to Brazil (the Acre territory,
in the Amazon basin, in 1902), to Argentina (on the upper
Paraguay, in 1904), and to Peru (in northern Bolivia, in
1909). Some of these losses involved disputed territory to
which Bolivia did not have a clear title, and some of the
cessions brought compensation in the form of aid in building Bolivia's railroads. But the price was a high one at best;
each amputation gave a shock to the Bolivian body politic.

The greatest shocks came from the loss of its seacoast to
Chile and its defeat in the Chaco War with Paraguay.
Bolivians still yearn—and sometimes clamor—for the return
of their *terra irredenta*. But for their feebleness as a nation,
their irredentism would be one of the gravest threats to the
peace of South America. As it is, their resentment against
Chile is one of the reasons why they have gravitated towards
the orbit of Argentina in recent years. Other reasons are the
increasing dependence of their cities on Argentine wheat
and the growing weight of Argentina in the scale of South
American power politics since the last quarter of the nineteenth century. Brazil's efforts in the past decade to challenge Argentine influence in Bolivia have not met with much
success; but there has been a definite reorientation of Bolivia's foreign contacts from west to east since the nineteenth
century, when its relations with Peru formed the main theme
of its foreign policy, the two countries seeking time and
again throughout the century either to annex or dominate
each other or to form some kind of union. It was their
alliance of 1873 which paved the way for their disastrous
war of 1879–1883 with Chile.

The territory lost to Paraguay, though extensive, was not
a vital part of the Bolivian domain; but the country's manpower and national morale suffered a grievous blow from
the heavy casualties, the notorious bungling of its leaders,

and the ultimate defeat. The political consequences, both domestic and international, of this disaster were still apparent in the Bolivian revolution of 1943, which will be discussed below in Chapter 7. Here, it is enough to say that the disaster intensified certain elements in the Bolivian scene which had been familiar for many years past—militarism, domestic strife, and the weakness of the country's international position; but it also strengthened the hand of organized labor and made the country more susceptible to the influence of Nazi-Fascist agents and ideas. As it happened, the Axis incursion into Latin America was just getting into full swing as the Chaco War came to a close.

3. Peru: One Country, Two Cultures

1. THE EUROPEAN WORLD

With one highly important exception, the land-and-people pattern of Peru is very much like that of Bolivia. About half * of the population of Peru (seven million in 1940) consists of unmixed Indians, most of whom cling tenaciously to the languages and customs of the Inca Empire in the days before the Spanish conquest. From one-tenth to one-seventh are whites of European (overwhelmingly Spanish) origin, who constitute the ruling class. The remainder (about one-third or two-fifths) are mestizos, except for a sprinkling of Negroes and Japanese (about 30,000 each). Likewise, the two zones which constitute Bolivia—the rugged Andes, with its high valleys and tableland, and the eastern tropical plain and jungle—continue northward through Peru and contain the bulk of its national territory. But, unlike Bolivia, Peru has a seacoast, and herein lies one of the chief reasons why its

* Forty-six per cent, according to the census of 1940, which, though probably the most accurate ever taken in Peru, is admittedly only approximate in this and other respects. It does not distinguish between whites and mestizos, who according to it comprise 52 per cent of the population. Its general character is indicated by the fact that the figure it gives for the total population of Peru, 7,023,111, was a composite of the following items:

Enumerated population	6,207,967
Calculated for omissions	465,144
Estimated for jungle tribes	350,000

national history has been a happy one compared with that
of its southern neighbor.

A closer examination would show that there are important
differences both within the major geographic zones of Peru,
as of Bolivia, and also between the Peruvian and Bolivian
segments of two of these zones, the Andes and the eastern
lowlands. For example, the Andes are only about 200 miles
wide in most of Peru, as compared with 400 miles in Bolivia;
and the eastern lowlands of Peru, unlike those of Bolivia,
can be reached by continuous navigation from the sea—up
the Amazon to Iquitos, 2000 miles inland. In both countries
the unity of each zone is broken by natural barriers (desert,
ravine, jungle) and in many cases there is more intercourse
between zones than among the various subdivisions of each.
Thus, Lima has closer ties with Huancayo and Cerro de
Pasco in its Andean hinterland than with the important
sugar-planting district of Trujillo on the coast of northern
Peru. This is only partly due to the fact that a railroad links
Lima with this hinterland, but not with Trujillo; for the tie
antedated the railroad, and was indeed one of the reasons
why it was built. The recent improvement of transportation
facilities (such as the construction of trunk highways along
the coast and between ranges of the Andes) has altered this
situation somewhat, but has by no means revolutionized it.

Yet, while such shadings are important and should be kept
in mind, a clear-cut distinction between the three major
zones corresponds so closely to the realities of Peruvian life
that it provides the best approach for such a brief discussion
as this one must be. And two of these zones are so much
like their continuations in Bolivia that most of what has been
said about the latter can be understood to apply to them.
Let us, then, look briefly at the land and people of each of
these three zones.

The coast line of Peru extends some 1200 miles along the
Pacific from about 5° to 18° south latitude. Throughout

this distance the coastal plain is narrow. Most of it is arid and, despite its location within the tropics, all but the northernmost tip is kept cool by the great Humboldt or South American current, which sweeps up from the Antarctic. Never more than a few miles inland, the parched foothills of the Andes extend at some points to the very water's edge. The intervening strips of coastal plain are miniature Saharas, whose drifting sands force road crews to wage incessant battle to keep the highways open. The traveler from the northern United States might fancy himself at home in midwinter on a country road, in a world of snow fences and snowplows, except that in Peru the enemy is not snow but sand and the fight goes on the whole year round. But this desert of coastal plain and adjacent valleys is sprinkled with oases which lie along the banks of the many little rivers that tumble down from the steep western ranges of the Andes. These rivers are the only important source of water supply, for the average annual rainfall along this coast ranges from two or three inches down to zero. The water, used mainly for irrigation, is carefully conserved, and doled out with an eye-dropper. Little if any of it is permitted to escape to the sea. Thus, even by the time it has reached Lima, still several miles inland, the Rimac "river" has become a dry bed.

Yet these oases produce most of the agricultural exports of Peru—cotton, sugar, and rice; and the volume of production is considerable. For example, more cotton is grown in Peru than in any other Latin American country except Brazil. The coastal area is also the seat of the country's important petroleum industry (the fourth largest in Latin America), of its few but flourishing factories, and of its most ambitious enterprise in the field of hydroelectric power, the Santa Corporation, which is a kind of Peruvian counterpart of the Tennessee Valley Authority.

Most important of all, the national metropolis, Lima, lies

in this area, only five air miles from the sea. Lima is the political capital of Peru, the main focus of its economic and cultural life, and the largest city in all our five Bolivarian countries. Its population of half a million in 1946 placed it slightly ahead of its nearest rival in this group, Bogotá, Colombia; and its seaport and virtual suburb, Callao, is the second largest city in Peru (population about 85,000 in 1946). The third city, Arequipa in southern Peru, is only one-seventh the size of Lima–Callao. In no other country of our group is the disparity between the metropolis and the largest provincial city so great as in Peru. As a result, national political power is concentrated in Lima to an exceptionally high degree; in the national economy its preponderance is exceeded in only one aspect—foreign commerce—and by only one other city in our group of countries—Guayaquil, Ecuador.

Lima is also unique in the sense that it is by far the most Spanish and the least Indian metropolis in all the preponderantly Indian countries of Latin America. In the capitals of other countries of this kind, pure-blooded Indians, clad in their distinctive garb and speaking not Spanish, but their own tongue, are met at every turn. In Lima, such an apparition would cause a traffic jam of sightseers. There are many Indians in the city, but they have adopted—at least in externals such as speech and clothing—the protective coloration of the white man's way of life.

That way, in Lima, is Spanish, and has been so from the beginning. Unlike most of the other leading cities in Indo-America (such as Mexico City, Bogotá, and Quito), Lima was not founded on the site of an old Indian city or in the midst of a teeming Indian population. Such a place was available to Pizarro and his companions in Cuzco, ancient capital of the Inca Empire, high up in the Andes; but they preferred the more easily defensible and accessible site of Lima, down by the sea. There, in 1535, the Spaniards built a new city of their own, and it is still largely theirs despite four centuries of infiltration by Indians, mestizos, Negroes, Italians, and Japanese. Despite the fact, also, that a large part of the economic life of Lima and all Peru is controlled by foreign capital and business enterprise, mainly from the United States and Great Britain, as represented by such giants as W. R. Grace & Co. and the Cerro de Pasco Corporation (United States), the International Petroleum Corporation (United States and Canada), and the Peruvian Corporation (Britain). The principal non-Spanish influence has been that of France, which has been strong throughout the national period and has been exerted mainly through cultural channels. The intimacy of this long-standing tie is illustrated by the fact that the Peruvian Francisco García Calderón's *Latin America: Its Rise and Progress,* to give it its English title—one of the best interpretations of the development of Latin America from the pen of any Latin American—was first published (1912) in French, in Paris, and with an introduction written by Raymond Poincaré.

The alternative name by which Lima has long been known, "City of the Kings" (*Ciudad de los Reyes*), is a reminder of its colonial past. It was so called not because Inca kings or emperors had lived here, for none had; or even because Lima was for nearly three centuries the seat of the Spanish viceroys, who lived in regal pomp and whose jurisdiction for many years extended over the whole of Spanish South America; but because the city was founded during the feast of the Epiphany, which commemorates the journey of the three "Kings" (*reyes*) or wise men to the infant Jesus in Bethlehem.

The colonial tradition survives in many other parts of Spanish America as well, but in Lima it assumes a special form, for here it is more specifically a viceregal tradition. The chief literary monument to Lima's viceregal period consists of Ricardo Palma's long and entertaining series of anecdotes entitled *Tradiciones peruanas* ("Peruvian traditions"). The chief social and political monument to that period is the oligarchy; for the viceregal tradition is both aristocratic and authoritarian. It connotes not only the dominance of a small group—about twenty-five—of the "best" families in Lima and the control of the rest of the country by the capital, but also (as in Buenos Aires) leadership of the countries which, now independent, were a part of the viceroyalty in the late colonial period. The tradition has been vigorously maintained by the oligarchy, the core of which is composed of great landowners enjoying the social prestige of descent from colonial bigwigs and reinforced by recruits from the new plutocracy that began to appear about the middle of the nineteenth century. With occasional interruptions, the oligarchy's control of the country was almost complete until very recently. Democratic forms were usually observed, but political power was confined to a small minority and the great "national" issues, such as liberalism versus conservatism, and civilian versus military control of the government, actually represented only factional differences within the ruling class.

Only a fundamental change in the social and economic fabric of Peru could seriously weaken the hold of the oligarchy. This has been taking place, mainly since World War I, under the stimulus of foreign economic penetration. For our present purpose, the main result has been the growth of a large and influential middle class in Lima, and the formation, here and elsewhere, of labor organizations, which, though still few and small, are not negligible. As will be related in Chapter 7, these new elements finally succeeded in ousting the oligarchy from control of the national government in the election of 1945, which was the most democratic in the history of Peru. Even this election, however, was democratic only in a limited sense, for the Indian half of the people took almost no part in it.

2. THE INDIAN WORLD

The Indian problem has not by any means been neglected by Peruvian writers. In fact, though the Indianist movement of the twentieth century has reached its apogee in Mexico, some of its chief pioneers were Peruvians. Foremost among these was Manuel González Prada (1848–1918), who, though a member of one of the "traditional" families of Lima, devoted his exceptional literary talent in both prose and verse to protesting against the oppression of the Indians. "His defense of the native," says Pedro Henríquez-Ureña, "is the first since the Hispanic American nations won their independence that assumes a systematic form and becomes a program." Both the protest and the program have been continued and broadened by Peruvians of the present generation, such as Víctor Raúl Haya de la Torre, founder of the now powerful APRA party, and Ciro Alegría, who is best known in the United States for his novel *Broad and Alien Is the World* (*El mundo es ancho y ajeno*), which deals with this theme. Peruvian scholars, too, have made important contributions to the study of the condition of the country's Indians from pre-Inca times to the present. Nevertheless, Indianism in Peru still remains largely literary and academic, and little progress towards the solution of the problem has been made since González Prada opened his campaign.

When we turn our attention to the country's other two zones we understand at once why the Indians took so little part even in the unprecedentedly democratic election of 1945 and will doubtless continue to play a passive part in the nation's political life for many years to come. For it is these two zones—the Andes and the eastern lowlands—that contain the bulk of the Indian half of the population of Peru, and these Indians are and must long remain political ciphers. Most of them are disqualified from voting by the literacy test; and, even if they enjoyed the suffrage, they would be unable to use it effectively because of the cultural chasm which separates them from the white man and renders his ways, including his political institutions and practices, unintelligible to them.

The great majority of the Indians live in the Andean zone, which contains more than half the population of Peru and produces most of its foodstuffs and livestock, as well as the minerals for which it is famous. In Peru the Andes consist of two main ranges, the Eastern and Western Cordilleras, and the highland population is densest in the chain of high valleys lying between them at an altitude of about 9000 to 12,000 feet. Though most of these mountaineers are rural and Indian, there are several cities and large towns. The whites of the zone live in these; but so do many Indians and mestizos. Among these cities are Arequipa, whose population of 80,000 in 1945 made it the third largest city in Peru, and whose comparatively low altitude of 8000 feet barely qualifies it for inclusion in this zone; Cuzco, ancient capital of the Inca Empire and present archaeological capital of South America; Cajamarca, where Pizarro betrayed and murdered the Inca Atahualpa after collecting from his subjects the richest ransom of which history has any record; Huancayo, famous for its weekly Indian fairs; and near-by Oroya, site of a large copper-smelting plant belonging to the Cerro de Pasco Corporation.

Oroya is also an important junction on one of the two railroads that link the Andean zone with the seacoast. One of these, the highest standard-gauge railroad in the world, climbs in six hours from coastal Lima to the point where it crosses the western Andes at 15,665 feet shortly before arriving at Oroya, from which one branch leads south to Huancayo and another north to the Cerro de Pasco mines. The other railroad runs from Mollendo on the coast to Arequipa, and thence to Cuzco and La Paz, Bolivia. Both roads were planned and partly built by an enterprising Yankee, Henry Meiggs, a native of up-state New York, in one of Peru's boom periods about 1870.

The Andean zone presents the extremes of antiquity and modernity in a profusion and close juxtaposition hardly to be matched elsewhere in South America—llama and airplane, communal village and giant corporation, temples to the Inca sun-god and up-to-date smelting plants, plaintive piping of an Indian song centuries old, and radio programs originating in Europe and the United States. Old and new run in parallel lines that seldom meet. Though most of the Indians serve the white man in one capacity or another, as farmer, miner, or domestic servant, they give only their service; their culture, such as it is—truncated by conquest and atrophied by long subjection—remains their own.

From this point of view, Peru stands in striking contrast to Mexico and Bolivia. In Mexico, Indians have long played an important part in national affairs, both in civil war and peace; a rising tide of Indianism has enriched the cultural life of the nation in the present century; and the mestizos far outnumber the pure Indians. In Bolivia, no such development has yet occurred; but in almost every part of the settled area, including the zone which contains the national capital, white and Indian populations are interspersed in a geographical propinquity so close that the time cannot be distant when the cultural wall between them will be broken down. In Peru, on the other hand, the bulk of the Indians live in an isolation which is geographical as well as cultural. Their highland area constitutes a kind of colony of lowland Lima, focus of white Peru. Too alien and too remote to participate effectively in the white man's world, they influence it mainly because they constitute a potential threat to its culture and even (though they seem a thoroughly beaten race) to its peace and security. A natural defensive reaction to this threat helps explain the strength of Hispanicism in white Peru, particularly in Lima, principal custodian of the viceregal tradition.

The third zone, east of the mountains, is even more definitely Indian and colonial; but it is a colony that Lima can hope to make over in its own image if the transportation problem can be solved. For, despite its great extent (it embraces half the total area of Peru), even its Indian population is very sparse, and any important development of its considerable resources is likely to come from, and make it a part of, the white man's world.

Whatever its future may be, most of this remote region is at present wilderness. Extending from the eastern foothills of the Andes, it bends down the upper Amazon basin in a broad salient between Colombia and Brazil. Iquitos is the largest of the few towns in this whole vast area. All of them cling timidly to the river banks, for most of the region is covered with jungle, and in all but a small part of it the rivers are the only highways—or were before the air age, which began here only recently. Yet the soil is rich, the forests are extensive, and there is also oil.

Many Peruvians have long had faith in the future of this tropical frontier. It flourished during the rubber boom at the beginning of this century and then fell into a decline which lasted about twenty years. Since 1930 the national government has made vigorous efforts to develop and extend it. These helped bring on two major international crises, with Colombia and Ecuador. During World War II the development of the region was further stimulated by the quest for rubber and otherwise. Swamps were drained, colonization fostered, and, most important of all, new transportation routes to this remote area were established. Formerly, its principal town, Iquitos, could be reached from Lima only by a one or two months' sea voyage via Cape Horn or the Panama Canal and then two thousand miles up the Amazon. Now it can be reached in four hours by plane from Lima, and the two are also connected by a combination highway-and-river route via Tingo María and Pucallpa, which was opened in 1943.

The national center of gravity still lies on the Pacific coast, in Lima, and will probably remain there for a long time to come. Of all the five countries in our group, however, Peru has been much the most active in developing its tropical hinterland; and it is the only one that has made a sustained effort to exploit all the major areas within its boundaries. These efforts and activities have evoked the cry of "imperialism" from its neighbors, especially from Ecuador, and have played an important part in shaping the course of its foreign relations.

4. Ecuador: A Tale of Two Cities

Ecuador lies in the shadow of its two much larger neighbors, Peru and Colombia. It marks the northern terminus of that long belt of mountain-dwelling Indians which we have already followed from Bolivia up through Peru. Since it also contains a ruling class which is largely Spanish in origin, its people resemble those of Bolivia and Peru in most essentials. Where they differ, the explanation lies largely in the physical environment. Out of this environment has grown the rivalry between the two cities, almost exactly equal in size, about which most of the nation's life revolves—highland Quito, the national capital, and the seaport of Guayaquil. Their rivalry has been a constant source of weakness to Ecuador, whose international position could hardly have been strong in any case, since its population (three million in 1941) is less than half as large as that of Peru and less than one-third as large as that of Colombia.

Also the smallest of our five countries in area, Ecuador is less than one-fourth as large as either Peru or Bolivia. It contains the three familiar zones of seacoast, mountains, and tropical hinterland; but in only one of these zones, the mountains, is its resemblance to either Peru or Bolivia at all close. And the geographical distribution of its population is unique, as is the strategic value of its Galápagos Islands.

The seacoast of Ecuador is not only much shorter than that of Peru; it is also hot and humid, whereas most of Peru's seacoast is temperate and arid, for the cold Humboldt current swings far out into the Pacific from the northern coast of Peru well before it reaches the southernmost tip of Ecuador. Moreover, most of the coastal zone of Ecuador is considerably broader than that of Peru, and it contains one distinctive feature of great importance to the economic life of the country: the broad and fertile lowlands along the Guayas River and its branches, which run in a roughly north-south direction and are flanked on the east by the Andes and on the west by a hilly belt that extends to the Pacific. The Guayas flows to the sea past the port of Guayaquil. Partly for this reason, Guayaquil dominates both the economic life of the coast and the maritime commerce of the whole country to an even greater degree than does Lima-Callao in Peru.

East of the Andes the contrast is even more striking. This part of Ecuador, known as the Oriente, has a population density (4.5 inhabitants per square mile) which, while low, is larger than that of the corresponding parts of Bolivia and Peru; but the latter are potentially much more valuable because the Oriente is far smaller, has less geographical unity, and is even more difficult of access. The area of the Oriente is just under 50,000 square miles; Bolivia and Peru each have approximately five times as much territory east of the Andes.

Under the terms of the boundary agreement of 1942 with Peru,* the Oriente was confined to the foothills of the Andes and to the upper reaches of several small rivers which do not communicate with each other until long after they have left Ecuadorian territory. They are, moreover, merely tributaries of the Marañón River, which is in turn a tributary of the Amazon. Yet the Oriente's only outlet is by way of these rivers, which pass through a vast expanse of territory belonging to Peru, Colombia, and Brazil before they reach the Atlantic. There is no city or river port worthy of the

* For the conclusion of this agreement, see below, Chap. 9.

name in this area; the nearest port, five hundred miles away, is Peruvian Iquitos, from which it is another 2000 miles to the mouth of the Amazon.

Nor does any railroad or first-class highway connect the Oriente with the rest of the national territory west of it across the Andes. Ecuadorians complain that the boundary agreement of 1942 blasted their hopes for the development of the Oriente; but it is not easy to see how this small, poor, and divided nation could have found the means to develop any considerable part of Amazonia. That is a task requiring money, men, and technical skill on a scale far beyond the reach of Ecuador.

Sixty per cent of the country's inhabitants live in the intermediate mountain zone, but this populous region forms only a thin band across the map of Ecuador, for the broadening of the coastal area north of Peru is matched by the narrowing of the Andes. Their two-hundred-mile width in Peru is maintained through the southernmost third of the country, but shrinks in the remaining two-thirds to a mere one hundred miles, which is only one-fourth their breadth in Bolivia. But their peaks continue to thrust up to the same dizzy heights (the altitude of Chimborazo, in the center, is 20,600 feet, and that of Cotopaxi, in the north, 19,300) and are interspersed with high valleys in which most of the population of the country's mountain zone is concentrated. Again, as in Peru and Bolivia, the bulk of the mountaineers are Indians who are wedded to ancient customs and languages; are engaged in the same occupations—farming, stock-raising, and mining; and are dominated by the same kind of ruling class—one that clusters about a core of great land-owning families who carry on the traditions of the Spanish colonial period.

In the heart of this highland area, at an altitude of 9350 feet, lies the nation's capital, Quito, which serves as a counterpoise to the commercial metropolis and largest city, lowland Guayaquil. Therein lies another difference between Ecuador and its southern neighbors, for Peru has no Quito and Bolivia has no Guayaquil. The difference is an important one. Though they are almost equal in population—in 1943, Guayaquil had 185,000 inhabitants, Quito 180,000—the opposing thrusts of these rival cities have not maintained a national balance. Rather, their rivalry has been a disturbing factor in national affairs throughout the country's history. They are much the largest cities in Ecuador, containing together about 12 per cent of its population. Each dominates its own section, thereby bringing to a dangerously sharp focus the antagonism between highland and lowland.

Their rivalry proceeds mainly from the fact that they are approximately equal in strength and sharply differentiated from each other and that the bonds between them are few and weak. The highlands have the edge in population, the lowlands in foreign commerce. Economic production and political power are about equally divided between them. Quito has greater cultural prestige, mainly in the field of *belles lettres;* but Guayaquil is not far behind, though its chief interest lies in practical present-day problems, as befits a bustling commercial city. Its outlook is also more liberal and forward-looking. Quito is still famous mainly as a treasure-house of Spanish colonial architecture; many of its colonial buildings, such as the Convent of San Francisco and the richly ornamented Jesuit Temple, are among the finest anywhere in Latin America. Guayaquil, on the other hand, is a monument to modern public health and sanitation, which since 1915 have revolutionized living conditions in this former plague spot—with important aid, it should be noted, from the Rockefeller Foundation.

Except for variations in rainfall, there are no seasonal changes in either section; but the coastal zone is hot and the mountains are cool. For example, Quito, lying within a few miles of the equator, but nearly two miles above sea

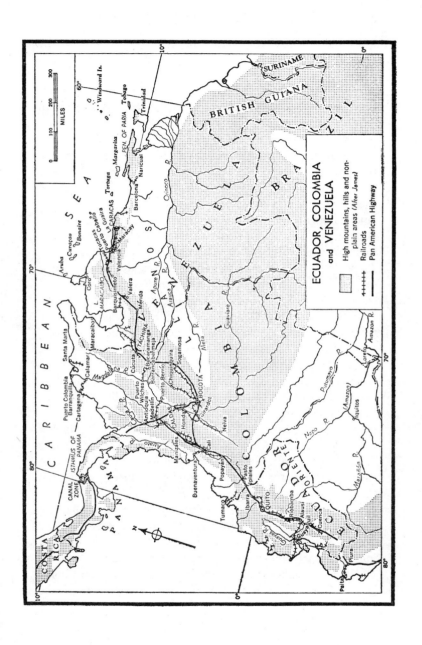

ECUADOR, COLOMBIA
and VENEZUELA

High mountains, hills and non-
plain areas *(After James)*

+++++ Railroads

—— Pan American Highway

level, has a mean temperature of 55° every month in the year; at Guayaquil, which is one hundred miles farther from the equator but stands only forty feet above sea level, the average temperature is more than twenty degrees higher, but the range is still small—from 76° in coolest months to 80° in the warmest. The average annual rainfall at both places is moderate.

Similar conditions exist in each of the sections dominated by these two cities; and the differences between them could be multiplied. Probably the most important differences are the ethnic and economic. The large Indian mass of the highland population, wedded to its ancient culture, has no counterpart in the lowlands, where its place is taken by mestizos and mulattoes. The country's identifiable Negroes (4 per cent of the total population) are also concentrated exclusively in the lowlands. Foreign trade is more important to this region than to the mountain zone. Aside from the fact that it contains Guayaquil, it exports a large part of its principal products (cacao, balsa wood, "Panama" hats, coffee, and rice). The highlanders, too, export the greater part of their mineral production (mainly gold, silver, and petroleum), but the vast majority of them are engaged in raising foodstuffs (cereals, vegetables, and livestock) for domestic consumption.

Only one railroad and one good highway, both running from Guayaquil to Quito, connect these two sections. Their lines of communication run mainly north and south within each zone, and from them to foreign countries. Thus the Guayas basin ties a large part of the lowland people to Guayaquil and through it to the foreign nations that are their best customers. Similarly, the highland settlements within the Andes are linked together by a chain of high intermontane valleys and plateaus, the northernmost of which merges almost imperceptibly into the southern highlands of Colombia around Pasto. The completion of the

Pan-American highway through Ecuador (a short section in the extreme south remains to be built) may accentuate the sectional pattern of the country still more sharply, for this highway follows a mountain route all the way through Ecuador, leaving Guayaquil far to one side.

The fundamental disunity of the country is best illustrated by the position of its Galápagos Islands, officially known as the *Archipiélago de Colón* (Columbus Archipelago). Lying six hundred miles west of the mainland in the Pacific, they are barren as well as remote. Their only important natural resource consists in the giant tortoises and rich marine life that abound in their waters; this is one of the richest tuna fishing areas in the world. But even as a fisherman's paradise these islands cannot support a large population. In 1941 they had only 2100 inhabitants. Like the Oriente, they have never formed a part of the effective national territory of Ecuador. Their importance lies mainly in their strategic value in relation to the defense of the Panama Canal.

In conclusion, it should be pointed out that Ecuador lacks the great natural resources of Bolivia, Peru, and many other Latin-American countries, and that one of its chief sources of wealth from far back in the colonial period—cacao—suffered disastrously from blight and foreign competition early in the present century, and has never recovered. In per capita value of foreign trade, it stands far below the other four countries in our group; in illiteracy and disease it shares the primacy with Bolivia. Its small group of élite has produced some of the ablest exponents of Latin-American thought, such as those nineteenth-century giants, Gabriel García Moreno, conservative and clerical; his sworn enemy, Juan Montalvo, a liberal in the Spanish tradition, who, by the way, was no admirer of the United States or of democracy as practiced here; and Eloy Alfaro, the country's outstanding anticlerical liberal at the turn of the century. In the present century, too, its writers have won an enviable place in the world of letters.

Nevertheless, considered as a whole, Ecuador is one of the most backward countries in Latin America culturally and socially, as well as one of the weakest politically. In this respect, too, it must be bracketed with Bolivia, for it, too, has been unable either to play an effective part in international affairs, or even to protect the integrity of its territory, and has looked to stronger neighbors for protection—in recent years, to Colombia—but without much success. If it now constitutes a less serious international danger spot than Bolivia, it does so mainly because its smaller size and relative poverty in easily exploitable natural resources offer less temptation to its neighbors. Both countries, of course, now enjoy a large measure of protection against wars of aggression by virtue of the guarantees recently set up by the inter-American system and the United Nations.

5. Colombia: A Nation of City States

1. THE TRANSPORTATION PROBLEM

Colombia is unique or exceptional in several respects. It stands almost in the exact center of the twenty Latin-American states and is the only country in South America that fronts on both the Atlantic and the Pacific. It has the largest and most rapidly growing population of all the five republics in our group (9,429,000 in 1942) and contains no alien cultural groups of any importance: the few Indians live on the periphery and the many mestizos and Negroes have been assimilated to the culture of the white man. It also has the highest degree of concentration of population in the coastal and mountain zones (98.6 per cent), and consequently the lowest in the tropical hinterland, which contains more than half the total area of Colombia, but only one in every seventy of its inhabitants. Its economy is one of the most highly diversified in Latin America, for important contributions to the national wealth are made by its mills and factories (led by textiles), as well as by its oil wells, mines (gold, silver, platinum, and emeralds), and agriculture (coffee, sugar, and subsistence farming). Finally, it leads the Bolivarian group in literacy and educational facilities, and all the South American countries in political stability—it is the only one that came through the world crisis of 1929–1945 without either a dictatorship or a revolution.

The physical environment has left a strong imprint upon the national character of Colombia and has made it a nation of city states. Throughout the country, nature has broken the habitable areas into small fragments and raised up formidable obstacles to intercourse among them. The effective national territory, where nearly 99 per cent of the people live, extends from the eastern range of the Andes westward and northward to the Pacific and the Caribbean. Most of this part of the country is mountainous, and a considerable part of the lowland area is covered with jungle. Though somewhat lower than in the countries to the south, the Andes are still high and rugged in Colombia and they spread out into three ranges which, together with a separate fourth range along most of its Pacific coast, measure some four hundred miles across. Several peaks, including Tolima near the center of the settled area, reach an altitude of over 16,000 feet. The road connecting the national capital, Bogotá, with the thickly settled Cauca valley and the Pacific port of Buenaventura, crosses the central range of the Andes at 10,000 feet. Bogotá itself stands in yet another range—the eastern—at an altitude of 8700 feet.

Save for the Magdalena, the rivers of Colombia have not given much help in overcoming these natural obstacles to travel and transportation. Even the Magdalena, though nearly a thousand miles long, is highly unsatisfactory because of its shallowness and tortuous course and the hazards to health involved in even a short trip between its miasmal, insect-infested banks. The Magdalena has been extensively used as a commercial highway from early colonial times, but only because there was no alternative. Its long tributary, the Cauca, which flows past several of the largest provincial cities, is even shallower and more frequently broken by rapids.

The country's other large river, the Atrato, which flows into the Caribbean just east of the Isthmus of Panama, was once urged as a route for an interoceanic canal, which was to be cut from its head of navigation through the few remaining miles to the Pacific; but little use is made of the Atrato, for it passes through a thinly settled region, much of which is jungle and marsh. Extending northward into and across the Isthmus, and becoming ever more difficult, this terrain has so far proved an impassable barrier to overland communication between Colombia and the Canal Zone. No road has ever crossed it. This is the widest of several gaps still remaining in the Pan-American Highway, and will probably be the last filled. For all practical purposes, then, Colombia's (and South America's) land link with Central and North America might as well not exist—might better not, from the point of view of Colombia, for it only further complicates her transportation problem by impeding communication between her Caribbean and Pacific coasts.

The difficulty of this problem has had a profound effect upon the development of Colombia. For one thing, it has been partly responsible for the country's neglect of its tropical hinterland, for practically all of the government's revenues have gone to meet the urgent needs of the already settled area in the mountains and on the coast. For another, it lies at the root of the strongly marked regionalism of Colombia, which has been concentrated in the chief cities of each region and has shaped the nation's history from colonial times to the present century. To be sure, for more than half a century Colombia has had one of the most highly centralized governments in Latin America; but this system had to be adopted precisely because the centrifugal tendencies of the several regions were so powerful that only an exceptionally strong central government could keep them from flying apart. The secession of Panama from Colombia in 1903 was an extreme expression of this regional spirit. which the people of Panama, as well as other regions of

Colombia, had expressed many times before, in one form or another. The difference was that in 1903 foreign influences encouraged local leaders to carry the centrifugal tendency to the extreme of secession, and then assured their success.

Great improvement in the transportation facilities of Colombia has been made in the past quarter century, especially through the use of the airplane. The first commercial airline in America was established in Colombia in 1920. By 1945 the country was covered with a network of airways serving small, remote towns as well as the principal cities. An enormous saving in travel time resulted. The journey from Bogotá to Barranquilla, principal port on the Caribbean, was cut from a week or ten days, via the Magdalena, to three hours; that from Bogotá to Cali or Medellín, from a full day to one hour and ten minutes. Similar improvements were made in air service to foreign countries. In fact, the airplane has worked wonders in expediting the movement of passengers and goods that can afford to pay the price. To this extent, it is doubtful whether any country in the world has benefited more from the coming of the air age.

Up to the present, however, most of the freight has not been able to pay the price of air transport, and has had to stick to land and water routes. Here progress has been slow. Since 1920 this has consisted mainly in the improvement and extension of automobile highways, and yet even in 1946 nearly all of these were still essentially local roads. According to European or North American standards, very few of them were first class for more than thirty or forty miles outside the principal cities. In this respect even Peru was ahead of Colombia. In railroad lines, most of which were built between 1860 and 1920, Colombia had made even less progress by 1946. Barranquilla and the other Caribbean ports were still not connected with Bogotá or any other city of the interior by rail; and the one line connecting

Bogotá with the Cauca valley and Buenaventura, Colombia's only important port on the Pacific, was still broken at the central range of the Andes, which had to be crossed by the highway over the Quindío Pass. Service on the Magdalena was no better than a generation earlier, and possibly worse, as the river boats were suffering from the loss of revenue which resulted from the diversion of passenger traffic to the air lines.

Consequently, while the condition mainly responsible for the vigorous regionalism of Colombia has been weakened in the past half century, it has not been destroyed, and regionalism is still a vitally important factor in the national life of the country. Since the four principal regions are fairly equal in population, and since elections are fairly free and honest, political power is much more widely diffused in Colombia than in the other four Bolivarian countries—than in Peru, where Lima holds a heavy preponderance; Ecuador, where there is a duel between Quito and Guayaquil; and Bolivia and Venezuela, where the high frequency of dictatorship has greatly retarded the development of political regionalism.

2. REGIONS

In short, Colombia is the sum of its regions, which are in effect city states; and national policy, foreign as well as domestic, represents in the long run a compromise among their several interests and points of view. They differ widely from one another, economically and socially as well as politically. Space does not permit a careful examination of them, but it will pay us to glance briefly at the four principal regions and the cities that dominate them. These are the highland region (Bogotá); the mid-Cauca valley (Medellín and Manizales); the upper Cauca valley (Cali and Popayán); and the Caribbean coast (Barranquilla, Cartagena, and Santa

Marta). For a short time in the nineteenth century some of
them were actually independent republics, and during most
of the rest of the century they either exercised autonomy
or were fighting to obtain it. National union was not finally
established until 1886, and even after that it took the shock
of the country's last and most destructive civil war (1899–
1903) and the secession of Panama (1903) to bring about
the general abandonment of what we in the United States
call the extreme states' rights doctrine.

Until the advent of the air age in 1920, Bogotá, perched
up in the innermost range of the Andes near the eastern
fringe of settlement, was one of the most inaccessible cities
in America. Though it was a viceregal capital in the late
colonial period and has been the national capital almost
ever since the independence of Colombia * was established
under Bolívar's leadership, it strongly reflects the character of the isolated highland region of which it is the metropolis. Indeed, with the end of the Spanish domination and
the wars of independence, which had prodded it into taking
a larger view, it relapsed into a narrow provincialism which
continued to prevail for three-quarters of a century and has
not yet entirely disappeared.

Throughout most of its history the Bogotá region has
been marked by some unusual if not unique features. It
contains the only group of thickly settled high basins in
Colombia. Until recently its economy was based largely on
agricultural production for the home market; commerce,
industry, and mining played a very minor part in it; and
much of its prosperity has been due to the fact that it has
always been an important seat of government. Its people are
overwhelmingly Spanish and mestizo. Although class dis-

---

* Simplifying a complex problem of history and terminology, we
may say that Colombia was first a part of Gran Colombia; after this
disintegrated in 1830, it took the name of New Granada (which it had
borne as a colonial viceroyalty); and assumed its present name in 1863.

tinctions are still sharp, it possesses cultural and social homo-geneity in an exceptionally high degree, for the pure Indians and their culture disappeared at an early date. Yet people in the rest of Colombia still regard the Bogotanos as abnormally secretive and suspicious and attribute these traits to Indian influence.

While the cultural pattern is thoroughly Spanish, French influences have been strong here ever since the period of the eighteenth-century Enlightenment; but the same can be said of Spain itself, with which Bogotá maintained contact even in the period of its greatest isolation. Indeed the vigor and integrity with which Spanish traditions have been carried on in this region are remarkable; better Spanish is spoken and written here than almost anywhere else in the world outside Spain itself. Until the rise of organized labor after 1930, social tension was lower than in the rest of Colombia, partly because of the patriarchal system which characterized the region. Life in Bogotá was not Arcadian. In fact, in the latter half of the nineteenth century it was one of the most turbulent cities in Latin America; but this was largely the result of personal or factional rivalries within the ruling class and did not alter the essential features of the pattern, which was provincial, patriarchal, civilian, Spanish, Catholic, and as liberal as it was possible to be within this framework.

Though many of these features still survive, the regional pattern has been broken down by the revolution which since 1920 has made Bogotá the real as well as the titular capital of the nation. Foreign business enterprise has played an important part in the process. So have the final victory of nationalism over federalism, which was not sealed until the beginning of the present century, and the great expansion of the area of government activity which has taken place in Colombia, as in many other countries, in recent years and has led to a great increase in the number of government office holders, especially in the national capital. The air age also has stimulated its growth.

As a result, Bogotá has become not only by far the largest city in Colombia, but its commercial and cultural capital as well. Its communications with the rest of the country, though still inadequate except by air, are far better than before. Large corporations, such as the Tropical Oil Company, maintain headquarters, with large staffs, at the seat of government even when their field of operations lies elsewhere. The only Colombian newspapers that have a nationwide circulation—*El Tiempo*, Liberal, and *El Siglo*, Conservative—are both published in Bogotá; and for ambitious authors generally, this city has become almost indispensable as a place not only of publication but of residence as well.

These are only a few of the most important reasons why the population of Bogotá more than doubled in thirty years, growing from 200,000 in 1915 to almost half a million in 1946. The difference is qualitative as well as quantitative. For one thing, as a leading Colombian writer, Germán Arciniegas, has remarked, at the beginning of the century the city's population was still measured in "souls" but is now measured in "inhabitants." The city, like the rest of the country, is still strongly Catholic—as much so, probably, as any in Latin America; but its spirit has unquestionably become more secular in the past generation.

Comparable to the Bogotá region in degree of isolation, but differing from it greatly in other important respects, is the mid-Cauca region dominated by the now thriving cities of Medellín and Manizales, the capitals of the Departments of Antioquia and Caldas respectively. This region leads the country in the production of coffee (Colombia's principal export commodity) and textile manufactures, and both cities are important commercial centers. At successive stages in its history Medellín became the chief center of the country first in mining, then in coffee, and finally in industry.

Today, it still holds the primacy in all three. In population (about 200,000) and political and cultural leadership, it stands second only to Bogotá.

In view of the natural and other handicaps of Antioquia, this is a remarkable achievement. The choicest area in the department consists of a chain of narrow valleys wedged in between the western and central ranges of the Andes. Until the present century its means of communication with the outside world were primitive, and it has always lacked the political and other advantages that Bogotá enjoyed, from early colonial times, as a principal seat of government. That these handicaps were overcome was due to the fine climate of Antioquia, its great mineral wealth, and the character of its people, who have been likened to the New England Puritans for their thrift, sobriety, and industry, and their combination of individualism with a sense of social responsibility.

Antioquia possesses both geographical and social cohesion in an exceptionally high degree. As Preston James has pointed out, it is one of the few regions in all Latin America, and the only one in Colombia, that has had the same type of frontier expansion that characterized the greater part of the westward movement in the United States—continuous expansion of the settled area without loss of density at the original core.* During this process, the Indian population, relatively small even at the beginning, was either killed off, driven out, or absorbed; very few Negro slaves were imported; and the strong group feeling that the early Spanish settlers brought with them was reinforced by the almost complete isolation in which they continued to live

* According to James, there were three other Latin-American frontier areas of this kind, besides Antioquia, namely, Costa Rica, the Central Valley of Chile, and the three southern states of Brazil. In the rest of Latin America expanding frontiers were "hollow," representing "waves of exploitation moving across a country, followed by abandonment and population decline."

for generations. Whether these early settlers were Jews or Basques is still a fighting question in Antioquia.

This situation goes far to explain the social and political conservatism for which Antioquia has been noted since the founding of the republic. Only in recent years has the situation been greatly changed, for sharp class antagonism has begun to develop under the impact of industrialization and the rise of organized labor.

The neighboring and even more thickly settled department of Caldas is an outgrowth of the expanding frontier of Antioquia and is also one of the country's chief coffee producing areas. Caldas does not approach Antioquia in mineral wealth or industrial production, and therefore relies still more heavily upon the production of coffee for the export market. Most of the coffee is raised by small and nominally independent landowners; but aside from the fact that, as in the case of Antioquia, the local price is largely determined in a foreign market (New York), the small landowners of Caldas seem to have suffered an even greater loss of economic independence through mortgaging their farms than has been the case in Antioquia. For this reason, and also because Manizales is the youngest city in Colombia (it first achieved importance as a source of supply to the contending armies in the civil wars of the second half of the nineteenth century), Caldas is politically somewhat less conservative than Antioquia. Nevertheless, the resemblances are more important than the differences, and on the whole Caldas reinforces the regional pattern of its northern neighbor.

The other two regions, the Caribbean coast and the upper Cauca valley, have two important features in common: both contain large concentrations of the Negro population of Colombia, and neither is dominated by a regional metropolis, the honors being divided in each case between two cities.

The hot, humid Caribbean coast contains three major seaports and is dominated by foreign commerce. By far the least important of the three is Santa Marta, the oldest city in Colombia (1522). Barranquilla, on the Magdalena near its mouth, is the largest and most modern and, together with Puerto Colombia, ten miles farther down at the river's mouth, is much the most important. Cartagena, once the Gibraltar of Spanish America and the greatest seaport in South America, is still an important cultural and political center but has fallen far behind Barranquilla in both airborne and seaborne commerce.

The longest oil pipe line in Colombia, starting in the rich Barrancabermeja field, has its terminal storage for tankers on the Bay of Cartagena, but the city of Cartagena itself represents the old order and has been reduced to piecing out its income by bidding for the tourist trade. In this respect it has much to offer—the natural beauty of its situation on a peninsula jutting out into polychrome waters from which jungle-covered hills rise to the distant Andes; the man-made beauty of fine old colonial houses, churches, and convents; and, dominating all, the still imposing remains of the great network of fortifications whose cost staggered even Philip II, the richest prince in Christendom, and which were never taken by a foreign enemy. The new order is represented by bustling Barranquilla, which handles three-fourths of the nation's export and import trade by way of the Caribbean, and is an important junction for international air traffic between the United States and a large part of South America, and between Panama and Venezuela. It also leads the other two in manufactures.

Negroes are numerous in these coastal cities, and omnipresent in the rural areas behind and between them. Generally speaking, they are the labor force; business, politics, and "society" are still the white man's province; and there are many white families that still boast, as in colonial times, of their racial purity (*limpieza de sangre*). But the color line is not nearly so sharply drawn as in the United States, and racial antagonism is hardly more noticeable than in that utopia of racial reconciliation, Brazil.

A somewhat similar picture is presented by the upper Cauca region above Antioquia and Caldas, where the valley widens out into a basin some fifty miles across. Here, too, Negroes are numerous, and a thriving commercial city, Cali (the fourth largest city in Colombia), is counterbalanced by an important cultural center, aristocratic Popayán. Cali has grown rapidly as a commercial center since its railway link with Buenaventura on the Pacific was completed in 1914; but in the region as a whole, agriculture far outweighs commerce. The altitude ranges from about 3000 to 6000 feet, and a temperate climate, combined with fertile soil and moderate rainfall, have made this one of the garden spots of South America.

The scene of one of the oldest and most famous Latin-American novels, *María*, by Jorge Isaacs, is laid in this region, near Cali. Although the slaveholding society which forms the setting of this novel began to disintegrate a century ago with the abolition of slavery in Colombia (1851), many of its chief characteristics have persisted to the present day. The Negroes have not disappeared, as they did in several other parts of South America after emancipation. They are still there in large numbers, particularly along the first half of the road from Cali to Popayán, where the traveler sees hardly anyone but Negroes, many of them an unsullied black. The color line is sharper here than along the Caribbean coast. So also are caste distinctions based on status. Newer ideas prevail in commercial Cali, but elsewhere the old order is still strong. Though former slaves have long been free, and can and do vote, the gentry are still gentry; they are still sure they know what is best for all, and most of the rest of the people still take them at their own valuation.

Two important exceptions to the regional pattern of

Colombia must be noted. One is far older than Colombia itself; the other is newer than the twentieth century. Both have been unifying forces, though in different ways, and help us understand how it was ever possible to hold together the disparate regions into which nature and man have divided the country.

The first exception is the Magdalena. The basin of this great river, comparable on the Colombian scale to our Mississippi, has never formed a region of settlement remotely resembling our Mississippi valley; but the stream itself has been the principal bond of common interest among three of the country's four principal regions—the highlands of Bogotá east of the upper Magdalena, the Antioquia valley west of its middle course, and the Caribbean coast on both sides of its mouth. The reason is simple: as a place of residence the banks of the Magdalena throughout most of its length have few attractions, and there are many better alternatives in the highlands both east and west; as a transportation route also the river has its drawbacks, but there is no alternative. For all its shortcomings, the Magdalena has served as the principal bond of unity among the regions that constitute the bulk of the country, and the smaller peripheral regions not served by it were held to the main mass by its gravitational pull.

The second exception is provided by the oil fields of Colombia, which is the third largest oil producing country in Latin America. The principal field, Barrancabermeja, may be taken as an example. It lies just east of the Magdalena, about midway between the Caribbean coast and Bogotá. It has its outlet on the Caribbean through the pipe line to Cartagena Bay, which was constructed in 1926; but the headquarters of Tropical Oil Company, which controls the field, are in Bogotá. Though in a different way, Barrancabermeja thus performs the same economic function as the Magdalena in tying various regions of the country together. In a political sense, too, the operations of the oil companies have a unifying effect, for most of them are controlled by foreign capital, mainly British and United States; and xenophobia is one of the pillars of patriotism.

Finally, there are two areas of Colombia which deserve mention, not because they constitute distinct natural regions, for they do not, but because on the contrary they form a part of international regions which link Colombia with its neighbors. One of these is the Cúcuta area in the northeast, which merges almost imperceptibly into the Mérida region of highland Venezuela; the other is the Pasto area of the southern Colombian highlands, which is closely connected with northern Ecuador. In both cases the international region is continuously and fairly densely settled; there is a close similarity between the geographical conditions and the people and their occupations and products on both sides of the international boundary; and intercourse across the line is active. This situation—rare in Latin America, where boundaries generally run through thinly settled or uninhabited regions—helps to give substance to the rather shadowy idea of the unity of the three nations, Venezuela, Colombia, and Ecuador, which once formed Gran Colombia. Trunk highways passing through these regions link Bogotá with the other two capitals, Quito and Caracas.

6. Venezuela: Oil

1. AFTER GÓMEZ

Venezuela, which lies at the northern end of our chain of states, is famous for the long line of dictators it has produced, culminating in Juan Vicente Gómez, "tyrant of the Andes," who ruled the country from 1909 to his death in 1935; but its real dictator in the present generation is oil, and the Venezuelan petroleum industry is controlled by foreigners. It began its reign while Gómez was still in power, and he aided in its rise, which began in 1918, though he had no premonition of the consequences. In fact, so far as the revenues from the new oil industry were not earmarked for his own private pocket, his purpose was to use them as a means of decreasing Venezuela's dependence upon foreign nations. This was to be done partly by diversifying and strengthening the national economy, and partly by paying off the foreign debt that had kept Venezuela in international hot water for years past and in 1902 had even brought down upon it armed intervention by Germany, Great Britain, and Italy.

In some respects Gómez was conspicuously successful. Within ten years after oil production began (1918), Venezuela was second only to the United States in all the world, and far ahead of all Latin-American nations, including Mexico, formerly one of the world's greatest producers of petroleum. The Soviet Union forged ahead of Venezuela in 1932, and has remained there; but the latter still holds third place and supplies about 10 per cent of total world production. The oil fields of Venezuela have now spread out along the whole length of its Caribbean coast. The oldest, largest, and most famous is the one in and around Lake Maracaibo at the country's western extremity; but there are also important fields as much as seven hundred miles eastward, near the port of Barcelona and on the Peninsula of Paria.

With the royalties from oil, Venezuela's foreign debt was paid off, good roads were built, and other improvements were made, including the construction of a big meat-packing plant built at Maracay, which enjoyed a monopoly of the business and was the private property of the dictator.

But the petroleum industry upset Gómez' other calculations. Instead of promoting diversification, it produced an unbalanced, one-commodity economy not matched by any other country in South America, except perhaps Bolivia. By 1940, oil accounted for 90 per cent of the annual exports of Venezuela, and it was an important factor in the shift of population from rural districts to urban centers as well as the oil fields, and in the relative decline of agricultural production. And while it reduced the dependence of Venezuela upon foreign nations in one respect by enabling Gómez to pay off the government's debts to them, it greatly increased this dependence in other respects. For the industry is owned abroad (mainly in Great Britain and the United States), 95 per cent of the product is exported, and the price is, of course, determined in the world market, not in Venezuela. Foreign control is highly centralized. In 1941, 92 per cent of the total production was accounted for by four companies—49 per cent by two subsidiaries of Standard Oil of New Jersey, and 43 per cent by subsidiaries of the Gulf Oil Corporation and Royal Dutch Shell. Their managerial and technical staffs are made up of foreigners, and a large part of the crude petroleum is refined on the Netherlands islands of Aruba and Curaçao, some twenty miles off the

Venezuelan coast near its western end. Moreover, the city-ward drift which has accompanied the rise of the oil industry has led to increasing dependence on imported food-stuffs. This situation is all the more disquieting because, although its proved oil reserves are still among the richest in the world, they will be exhausted sooner or later, and Venezuela is becoming progressively less able to get on without them.

Nevertheless, the oil industry has yielded large royalties to the government of Venezuela and has provided jobs for many of its people—directly for those employed by the oil companies, and indirectly for many more through the increased demand for goods and services. Thus, the population of the city of Maracaibo grew from about 15,000 in 1918 to about 110,000 in 1945, despite the fact that it is the hottest city in South America (82.4°). Its growth was due almost wholly to the development of the surrounding oil fields, which began in 1918. Caracas, too, has felt the stimulus, for in Venezuela, as in Colombia, the oil companies have naturally established their main offices in the national capital.

The new prosperity has not trickled down to the mass of the population, which is still largely agricultural and rural, and the result has been to increase the gap between rich and poor, rather than to raise the general standard of living. The oil companies pay wages above the national level, but the vast majority of Venezuelans are not on their payrolls. The high per capita income of Venezuela—about three times that of Colombia and Peru, and more than six times that of Bolivia and Ecuador—is misleading. The Venezuelan masses are probably little if any better off than those of the other countries.

Venezuela is a preponderantly mestizo nation, and in this respect resembles Mexico and differs from the other Bolivarian countries, especially Ecuador, Peru, and Bolivia. While reliable figures are not available, probably at least two-thirds of the Venezuelan people are mestizos. About 10 per cent are Negroes (including mulattoes and *zambos*, or mixed Indian and Negro) and the pure Indian group is even smaller. The preponderantly white group, too, constitutes only about one-tenth of the population, but it has provided most of the country's leadership.

Four-fifths of Venezuela's population of about 4,000,000 is found in the hills and valleys of the north and west. Venezuela's only overland communication with any other country links this area with Colombia; there is no railroad or highway connection with either Brazil on the south or British Guiana on the east. Venezuela's great back yard, which lies mainly in the Orinoco basin, is thinly settled, and most of its inhabitants live on the *llanos*, or plains, north of the river. The vast area south of it, and in the delta formed by its many mouths, contains 60 per cent of the total area of Venezuela, but only 7 per cent of its population. A large part of this area still remains unexplored.

This hinterland stretches southward to Colombia and Brazil and eastward through a highland area to British Guiana. Since the independence of Venezuela was established, the development of the resources of the region has been carried forward at a few scattered points; for example, near the border of British Guiana in the gold mining area which was a factor in the famous controversy of 1895 between Great Britain and the United States. In the important *llano* area, however, there has been a decline. Agriculture, which had made a modest but promising beginning, disappeared from this area in the latter part of the century, partly because of the abolition of slavery (1854). Cattle raising, a characteristic Venezuelan way of life, flourished here in the late colonial period and produced the tough fighting force of *llaneros*, or plainsmen, who played a leading part in the wars for independence. It was through the back door of the Orinoco and across this country that the Liberator, Bolívar, launched the campaign that at last drove the Spaniards out of Venezuela. After recovering from the setback it suffered during this war, the cattle business continued to grow, with wide fluctuations, until about 1880; but since then, though the fluctuations have continued, the general trend has been downward. The number of cattle in the area at the present time is only about half as large as in 1883, when it reached its all-time high of eight million. The decline has been due in part to political discrimination against the llanos in favor of other areas of the country; but it also reflects the general Venezuelan trend from the rural districts to the towns and cities.

In comparison with the Orinoco basin, the Caribbean coastal zone is thickly settled; but by far the most populous, productive, and closely knit part of this zone—and therefore of the whole country—extends westward from the Federal District past Lake Maracaibo to the Colombian frontier in the Andes. It contains two-thirds of the population of Venezuela, the national capital, the three principal seaports, all the important airports, the richest agricultural region, and the Maracaibo oil fields. Its parts are tied together by the best highways in the country and by most of its railroads, including the only one that has any claim to being called national—there are many other lines, but they are merely local.

This northwestern region contains three distinct areas of settlement: the Maracaibo lowlands in the center, and the two highland areas that flank it to the east and the southwest. The more important of these two, in both population and production, is the one stretching eastward along the Caribbean. Like the Andes on the Pacific side of South America, this upland zone rises quickly from a narrow coastal fringe, is interspersed with valleys roughly parallel to the coast, and is bordered along its inner edge by tropi-

cal lowlands; but it is narrower and much lower than the
Andes. Its maximum width, near its western terminus, is
about 150 miles; the central section, which contains Caracas,
is only about 50 miles wide, but it is the most thickly settled part of the country.

The altitude of Caracas (3400 feet) is high enough to
give it an agreeable climate. The temperature averages 67°
throughout the year, with a variation of only three degrees
from the mean. In 1943 it had an estimated population of
266,000 (about twice that of Maracaibo, the second city)
and was growing rapidly. The censuses of 1936 and 1941
showed an increase of over 30 per cent in these five years.
This was due partly to the rapid growth of industry (textiles, pharmaceuticals, chemicals, cement, tires), which was
centered mainly in the Federal District. Along the Caribbean coast and in Lake Maracaibo fishing is an important
industry. In proportion to population, the Venezuelans
catch and eat more fish than any other people in Latin
America.

South of Caracas, but still within the highland area, lies
an even lower and correspondingly warmer valley, the basin
of Valencia, whose breadth and fertility have made it one
of the principal agricultural areas of the country. It produces sugar, cacao, corn, and other crops, and cattle from
the llanos are fattened here before being sent to the local
slaughterhouse at Maracay or to Puerto Cabello for export.
Standing at the head of this rich valley and possessing a
good outlet to the sea through Puerto Cabello, the provincial city of Valencia enjoys several natural advantages over
Caracas, which is cooped up in a much narrower valley and
was difficult of access even from the near-by sea until, at
enormous expense, tyrant Gómez connected it with the sea-
and airport of La Guaira by a concrete highway winding
around more than four hundred sharp curves and hairpin
turns in the less than twenty miles that it traverses. Though

the advantages of Valencia have been outweighed by the superior climate of Caracas and its political primacy as the capital of Venezuela from early colonial times, the Valencia area has nevertheless been strong enough to maintain a regional identity that has yielded only to a dictator at Caracas.

Most of the people of this first highland area are white, Negro, and mestizo; in the other highland area, the Venezuelan Andes, most of them are white and mestizo, and the feeling of regionalism is even stronger here. The heart of the area is the states of Mérida and Táchira, through which passes the Trans-Andean Highway as it winds up through the mountains on its way from Caracas to Bogotá.

Until the highway was constructed in the 1920's, the means of communication between this area and the rest of Venezuela were rudimentary. On the other hand, as we have already seen, this area has long had close ties with the adjacent Cúcuta area of northeastern Colombia. Dictator Gómez was born in San Cristóbal on the Venezuelan side of the frontier, but spent several years in Cúcuta on the Colombian side. There is a great deal of passing to and fro across this frontier. Coffee, which stands second in Venezuela's list of exports, is the principal crop on both sides of the line where the land rises from about 3000 to 6000 feet above the sea. The Colombian crop is exported through Lake Maracaibo, by a short railroad which is both international and local, since it serves both countries but is not connected with the other railroads of either country. This situation does not lead the people of Andean Venezuela to desire political union with the neighboring region of Colombia, but it does keep alive among them a feeling of localism as a part of Venezuela.

2. BACKGROUND FOR BOLÍVAR

Such facts as these help us to understand Simón Bolívar's political thought, which has left so strong an imprint upon these countries. Born in Caracas, he began his career as liberator of northern South America in Venezuela and the eleven-year struggle for its independence (1810–1821) gave him a firsthand acquaintance with the rural districts and provincial towns as well as the capital. Many of his political ideas were naturally shaped by his observations of man and society in his native country during this formative period. One of these ideas was that the Latin-American peoples would require many years of authoritarian rule before they were ready to bear the responsibilities and enjoy the benefits of democracy. This was necessary, he thought, in order to guard against not only social anarchy among the sharply diversified classes but also the disruption of the new states by the centrifugal force of the regionalism and localism that was rampant in their constituent parts.

Bolívar's diagnosis has been largely justified by the subsequent history of Venezuela, which has been marked by long periods of alternating civil strife and despotism. The twentieth-century Gómez is merely the latest and best-known of a long line of Venezuelan dictators. Probably the most notable of his predecessors is Antonio Guzmán Blanco, a Grand Master of the Masonic order, during whose domination of the country (1872–1888) the Catholic church was stripped of much of its wealth and political power and the first important period of railroad construction occurred. Ever since independence a major source of disturbance has been the conflict between federalism (copied from the United States) and centralization. Federalism has generally prevailed, at least nominally; state's rights have served as a political expression of regionalism, which has tended constantly to broaden them; and dictatorship has been justified as a means of curbing this tendency and maintaining national union.

Venezuela has changed greatly in some respects since Bolívar's time, but it still offers a fair sample of the conditions he had in mind. Though the abyss that separates the Spanish and Indian cultures of Bolivia, Peru, and Ecuador has no counterpart in Venezuela, neither has the latter achieved the degree of social integration of Colombia, and at least as recently as 1945 it offered a striking illustration of the semifeudal land systems characteristic of many Latin-American countries—systems characterized by the concentration of land ownership in the hands of a small fraction of the population, and by starvation wages for the workers. In October 1945 armed revolt brought a left-wing group of reformers to power, with results that will be described in later pages.

In regard to political integration, the contrast with Colombia is still more striking. Though regionalism is even stronger in Colombia, the latter has nevertheless become a much more highly unified nation. Perhaps the explanation lies in the fact that Venezuela has no Magdalena River; its Orinoco, though larger and more easily navigable than the Magdalena, does not flow through the effective national territory. Nor have the operations of the oil companies had the same unifying effect as in Colombia, except in the political sense that the companies have constituted a national problem. Their field of operations has been confined to the coastal fringe and their offices at Caracas are within twenty miles of the Caribbean. Even the extensive road-building program begun by Gómez provided a system that is interurban rather than national, for the new highways connect cities, ports, and oil fields, and are not integrated with the country roads and trails that serve the greater part of the nation.

Throughout the national history of Venezuela, this situation has produced two contrary trends, each held in check by the conditions that have produced the other. One is the trend towards a geographical and social concentration of power, which is restrained by the lack of adequate channels and instruments for making it fully effective. The other is the trend towards a vigorous regionalism which approximates the old states' rights theory and practice in the United States as exemplified in the South Carolina Nullification Ordinance of 1832, but which has to reckon with the sobering fact that the region through which most of the country's only outlet lies—the Caribbean coastal fringe— is usually controlled by the central government.

Partly for these reasons, Venezuela's power position has declined in the present century in relation to that of its better integrated and more populous neighbor Colombia. As a result, some reservations about the idea of collaboration among the Bolivarian states have developed in Bolívar's native country. The general idea is still strongly supported there, but Venezuelans now tend to regard Colombian enthusiasm for it with suspicion, since Colombia would inevitably overshadow Venezuela in any such group of states.

How this situation has affected the relations of Venezuela with the rest of the world, and how it has been modified by recent internal developments, such as increasing urbanization, the growth of a more compact middle class, and the beginnings of an organized labor movement, will be shown in later chapters.

PART II

WARTIME DEVELOPMENTS

7. Political Patterns and Leaders

1. FREEZE AND THAW

While the international role of these five countries since 1939 has been determined partly by circumstances beyond their control, another important factor has been the character of their domestic political regimes. In one important respect—but only one—all of them followed the same general pattern of development during World War II and just after it. First, all the existing regimes were "frozen" in power; then came a thaw, which began with the revolution of December 1943 in Bolivia and which by the autumn of 1946 had profoundly altered the political situation in every one of these five countries. But there was no such close correspondence in the methods employed to bring about these alterations, or in their results. In three cases (Bolivia, Ecuador, and Venezuela), the change was brought about by bullets; in the other two (Peru and Colombia) by ballots. Progressive forces gained ground in Peru and Venezuela, fared less well in Bolivia and Ecuador, and suffered their only clear-cut reverse in Colombia. This was paradoxical, for Colombia has been rightly regarded for many years past as by far the most democratic of the five. The thaw also revealed the growing strength of the middle class in some, and the weakness of communism in all of them.

This diversity is not surprising, for although the political systems of these countries resemble one another closely on paper, they have long differed greatly in practice. On the one hand, all of them have written constitutions and representative governments consisting of an elected president, an elected bicameral congress, and a federal or national judiciary; all their constitutions contain guarantees of certain individual rights, such as freedom of speech and freedom of religion; and all of them also provide that these rights may be suspended by the declaration of a "state of siege" (roughly equivalent to martial law).

On the other hand, from the point of view of actual practice in the generation preceding 1939, the political regimes of these countries fall into three distinct groups. Colombia stands in a class by itself, as the only one of the five in which theory and practice substantially coincided. It was also the only one that had a two-party system of government or indeed any truly national parties at all in the North American sense of the term. Moreover, the labels of the two parties—Liberal and Conservative—meant what they said. After a long period of Conservative rule, the Liberals had come to power in 1930 and seemed more firmly entrenched than ever as a result of their sweeping victory in the election of 1938, which brought President Eduardo Santos into office for a four-year term. Peru and Venezuela had recently emerged from dictatorships (headed by Augusto B. Leguía, 1919–1930, and Juan Vicente Gómez, 1908–1935, respectively), only to pass under oligarchical regimes which maintained themselves in power by fraud or force or both. High army officers were presidents of both countries in 1939 (Marshal Oscar Benavides in Peru, General Eleazar López Contreras in Venezuela).

In Bolivia and Ecuador there was hardly even a pretense of constitutional, representative government, and more or less dictatorial regimes rose and fell with lightning rapidity. In Bolivia the defeat by Paraguay in the Chaco War (1932–1935) was followed by violent changes of regime in 1936, 1937, and 1939. In the last-named case the dictator, Germán

Busch, either committed suicide or was murdered. At the end of 1939 the country was governed by a temporary regime set up by the army chiefs. The election held under its auspices the following year brought to the presidency another general, Enrique Peñaranda, commander of the Bolivian army in the disastrous Chaco War. Turbulent Ecuador had eleven presidents or provisional presidents in the period 1931–1939, plus a president-elect who was declared ineligible. Here, too, a new president, Carlos A. Arroyo del Río, was elected and inaugurated in 1940. Against this background, it may well seem a miracle that Bolivian President Peñaranda remained in office three whole years, and Ecuadorean President Arroyo del Río nearly four. Actually, these cases merely illustrate the general wartime freezing of Latin-American regimes—a process which was encouraged by the United States as a war measure.

The changes of regime that occurred after the thaw set in at the close of 1943 may or may not prove lasting, but at any rate they deserve our attention as case histories in the pathology of politics in our Bolivarian area. They will be discussed in chronological order, not because of any causal connection between them but on the contrary because the adoption of any other order might lead to an unwarranted schematization of what seems to have been a succession of unrelated events. Their only common cause lay in the general Latin-American unrest of which they were a partial expression—an unrest which was apparently due mainly to wartime economic and psychological stresses and to increasing political discontent with the results of the freezing process.

2. BOLIVIA AND ECUADOR

The first overturn in our group of states occurred in Bolivia, always one of the least stable and worst governed countries of Latin America. There, on December 20, 1943, the administration headed by President Enrique Peñaranda was upset by a well-prepared revolt that began after midnight and had triumphed by noon. It was the work of two elements, one military, the other civilian. The military consisted mainly of veterans of the recent Chaco War. At their head stood Major Gualberto Villarroel and other junior officers, who constituted a sort of "majors' clique" resembling and aided by the Argentine "colonels' clique" which had seized control of the government at Buenos Aires six months earlier, in June 1943. The civilians consisted mainly of the quasi-fascist political party M.N.R. (National Revolutionary Movement), organized two years earlier and led by Víctor Paz Estenssoro, a prominent Bolivian intellectual and university professor. The revolution was also supported by a smaller but still influential civilian group, the P.I.R. (Leftist Revolutionary Party). The latter soon broke with the new government and was bitterly persecuted by it.

A revolutionary Junta was set up, with Villarroel as its president and Paz Estenssoro as one of its chief members. In domestic affairs the Junta professed itself the champion of the common man—especially of the tin miners—against exploitation by the "big three" tin mining interests (Patiño, Hochschild, and Aramayo) in league with politicians of the old regime. In a bid for prompt recognition by the other American governments the Junta promised far more zealous fulfillment of inter-American obligations and closer coöperation in the United Nations' war effort than the Peñaranda administration had given, but its sincerity was doubted because of its Argentine and pro-Nazi connections. The Guani Doctrine * was accordingly adopted and applied to Bolivia, with the result that the Junta did not obtain general recogniton until June 1944, after purging itself of Paz Estenssoro and several other of its more objectionable

* See Chap. 9.

members and after taking steps to hold a free and democratic
national election as a basis for the foundation of a constitutional government.

During this six-month probationary period Villarroel conducted his administration with circumspection and a nice
regard for the wishes of the majority of the other American
governments, led by Washington. He had no alternative, for
weak Bolivia was far more vulnerable to threatened economic sanctions than was strong, recalcitrant Argentina.
Argentine beef and wheat were indispensable to the United
Nations; but by 1944 Bolivia's tin, the keystone of that
country's economy, was no longer indispensable to them,
as they had built up large stockpiles of tin ore and had
developed an alternative source of supply in Nigeria.

But once recognition had been accorded, as it was in
June 1944, the Junta threw off the mask. In the "free" election held the following month the M.N.R. and allied groups
won control of the new constituent Congress. Paz Estenssoro and the other recently purged members were brought
back into the administration. A regime of intimidation was
inaugurated. Criticism was suppressed and critics were
beaten and shot. In October a counterrevolution centering
in Oruro was put down with exemplary ferocity, in sharp
contrast to the almost bloodless accession of the Junta to
power the preceding December, when it knew that, until
it obtained recognition, it must steer its course in such a
way as to disarm foreign criticism. And, to cap the climax,
the docile Constituent Assembly elected Villarroel president and took other steps to perpetuate his regime in power.

So matters went until August 1946, when a second successful revolution occurred in an outburst of ferocity that
was worthy of the overthrown Villarroel government itself.
Villarroel was hunted through the government palace by
the mob, caught and hurled to his death from a balcony, and
his body was then strung up on a lamp post in the main

plaza. Several of his associates suffered the same fate, though Paz Estenssoro escaped. The new revolution was attributed by some to the machinations of the tin mine owners. Actually, they only took advantage of the widespread popular hatred of Villarroel's regime. An apparently honest effort had been made by the latter to carry out its promises to the tin miners; but though the miners constituted much the largest labor group in the country, they were only a small fraction of its population. The rest of the people, especially the middle class in the towns and cities, resented the favors shown this minority group, as well as the strong-arm tactics of the government and the corruption that flourished in high places. Paz Estenssoro had made the mistake of basing his political strength too exclusively on a labor group. His failure indicated that in such a backward country as Bolivia, labor could hope to achieve and hold power only by joining forces with the middle class. This lesson emerged even more clearly from some of the other upheavals in our group of countries.

Villarroel was succeeded by a provisional government which held a national election. The election proved to be relatively free and orderly, and the defeated presidential candidate, Fernando Guachalla, immediately offered his support to his successful rival, Enrique Herzog. This was a welcome departure from the familiar pattern of force and fraud; but in view of the troubled history of Bolivia and the grave economic and social problems confronting the country, it seemed more likely to prove the beginning of a brief lull than of a long era of good feelings.

Ecuador was the second country to stage a revolution. This occurred on May 31, 1944, while the Villarroel regime set up in Bolivia five months earlier was still waiting for recognition by most of the other American governments. In this case, too, the overturn was accomplished quickly and almost bloodlessly, for it took the revolution barely twenty-four hours to sweep out the old regime of President Arroyo del Río and install the new regime headed by the exiled former president, Jose María Velasco Ibarra. Also, Velasco showed some sympathy for the Bolivian government by promptly recognizing it (June 17), and he copied its ostensibly democratic procedure by convoking a Constituent Assembly to elect a president as well as revise the constitution. Finally, as in Bolivia, the head of the provisional revolutionary government, Velasco, was elected president (August 10) by the Constituent Assembly.

There, however, the parallel ended. In Ecuador there was no counterpart of either the Majors' clique or the M.N.R. or the tin miners of Bolivia. Unlike Villarroel, Velasco was a civilian. Like Paz Estenssoro he was an intellectual, but he was brought into power not as the head of a single party or class but by a kind of national coalition, and once in office he sought to effect a synthesis of conflicting class interests, declaring that while as an individual he belonged to the left, as a statesman he conceived it to be his duty to stick to the middle of the road.

Velasco's policy of national unification accurately reflected the circumstances that had brought him to power through revolution. Probably the most important factor in this situation was the shock to Ecuadorean national pride caused by the boundary agreement of 1942 with Peru.* That agreement, made in the name of inter-American wartime solidarity less than two months after Pearl Harbor, cost Ecuador most of the territory that she had claimed in the upper Amazon basin—and that at a time when it was widely believed in South America that the exploitation of the resources of the Amazon basin was just about to begin on a large scale. The sense of frustration induced by this

* See below, Chap. 9.

sacrifice, coming on the heels of Ecuador's heavy losses in the undeclared war of 1941 with Peru, created deep resentment throughout the country.

During the next two years resentment grew as the agreement of 1942 was carried into execution, and fuel was added to the flames by the economic dislocations of the war period and by a continuance of the deep-seated regional and class rivalries described in an earlier chapter. Velasco could not hold out any hope of an escape from the consequences of the 1942 settlement, but in domestic affairs his dynamic personality did promise amendment of the sorry state into which Ecuador had fallen under the lackadaisical administration of Arroyo del Río. The very vagueness of Velasco's program of national unification held out to each faction the heartening prospect that in practice it might bend his administration to its particular ends.

The sequel was what might have been expected in a country so completely lacking in political stability and social, ethnic, and geographical homogeneity as Ecuador. The Constituent Assembly adopted a new constitution which made extensive social reform obligatory and provided for functional as well as territorial representation in the national Congress, including four representatives of urban labor and two of rural labor. The Confederation of Ecuadorean Workers was affiliated with the left-wing CTAL (Latin-American Confederation of Workers). A Board of Indian Affairs was established to look after the welfare of the Indians—a measure which did not prevent the outbreak of many strikes among Indian agricultural laborers. In the election of 1945 the conservatives made important gains; the demand for a conservative revision of the new constitution became insistent; and in 1946 new discontents were bred by the post-war readjustment. After two years in office Velasco had made no substantial changes in the political pattern of instability and fragmentation imposed upon Ecuador by the character of its land and people. Though reëlected by the Congress in August 1946, he faced dark prospects in his second term.

3. PERU AND VENEZUELA

By sharp contrast, Peru's peaceful revolution of June 1945 seems to have marked a turning point in the political development of that country. What happened was simply that a liberal coalition won a national election, but this was remarkable for several reasons. First, the election was held under a conservative government, which thus broke one of the strongest and most pernicious rules of Peruvian and Latin-American political life by letting itself be voted out of office. Its magnanimity in doing so was due in large measure to the influence of the outgoing conservative president, Manuel Prado, who subordinated his own interests and those of his party to his conviction that only by the establishment of a truly democratic form of government could Peru be saved from a long period of anarchy and chaos. Second, this election was the freest, most honest, and most popular in Peruvian history. Third, the election brought the Peruvian middle class to power for the first time.

The middle-class character of the new regime became apparent only after it took office. During the campaign its probable character was not at all clear, for the liberal coalition, called Democratic Front, was only partly liberal and partly middle class. Indeed, one of the two main leaders of this coalition was that pillar of the Peruvian oligarchy and one-time scourge of Peruvian liberals, Marshal Oscar Benavides, highest ranking officer in the army, former dictator-president, and former ambassador to the Spain of Franco and the Argentina of Perón. As president of Peru from 1933 to 1939 he had ruthlessly suppressed the Aprista party, with which he was now leagued in the liberal coalition. That he now made common cause with the Apristas in this campaign was apparently due to factional and personal rivalries within the oligarchy. Whether or not he swung many votes, his support was invaluable to the coalition, for his great prestige and his unassailable position in the oligarchy go far to explain why the outgoing conservative administration permitted a free election in which its defeat was a foregone conclusion.

The other outstanding leader of the coalition was Víctor Raúl Haya de la Torre, founder and chief of the Aprista party.* Neither Haya nor his party had hitherto been clearly identified with the middle class. He came of an upper-class provincial family, and ever since its founding a quarter of a century earlier his party had laid heavy stress on its championship of the downtrodden Indian masses. Many other groups, some of them definitely representing middle-class interests, were members of the coalition; but they and their leaders were overshadowed by Benavides the oligarch and Haya the Aprista.

Once in power, however, the new regime rapidly took on a middle-class character. The process was accelerated by the death of Marshal Benavides, which occurred between the election in June 1945 and the inauguration a few weeks later (July 28). His disappearance from the scene undoubtedly contributed to the harmony of the new administration. At first the Apristas took no part in the government. Neither the new president, José Luis Bustamante y Rivero, nor any of his first cabinet ministers were members of that party, which continued the policy it had followed during the campaign of shunning the limelight lest it alarm

* The Aprista party or APRA (*Alianza Popular Revolucionaria Americana*) was officially rebaptized the People's Party (*Partido del Pueblo*) in 1944, but has continued to be generally known by its earlier name.

Peruvian moderates who had long regarded it as the spearhead of revolutionary radicalism. This was not a viable arrangement, however, for the Apristas were far stronger in both houses of Congress than any other group in the Democratic Front, and after two months they had to accept the responsibility of office in a reorganized cabinet. Their middle-class character then became progressively clearer. Their quondam solicitude for the Indian masses slipped into the background and they continued their campaign against the communists, whom the preceding conservative administration had sought to build up as a counterpoise to Aprismo. They pushed labor legislation desired by the labor unions, which claimed a membership of some 300,000 and were their useful but distinctly subordinate allies. The major part of their effort, in regard to price control, education and other matters, was conceived mainly in the interest of the relatively small but intelligent, compact, and powerful groups of persons in moderate circumstances who were the backbone of the party. Its representative man was not so much well-born Haya de la Torre, whose long leadership of it always retained the air of an aristocrat on a lifelong mission of uplift, as Luis Alberto Sánchez, a distinguished intellectual of modest social origins, who was made the party's leader in Congress and Rector of famous old San Marcos University, the capstone of the country's educational system.

A somewhat similar situation developed shortly afterwards in Venezuela, only here the middle class–labor alliance came to power through an armed revolt, which took place in October 1945. By this time General Isaías Medina Angarita had succeeded General Eleazar López Contreras as head of the pseudodemocratic regime of army generals, great landowners, and business men which came into power after the death of dictator Gómez; and there was every indication that, but for the 1945 revolt, President Medina would have procured the reëlection of his predecessor López Contreras. In Venezuela at that time the president was all-powerful; although there was an elected Congress, it was packed with federal officeholders who did the president's will. If the evidence published in 1946 by the revolutionary government can be believed, both López Contreras and Medina had feathered their nests to the tune of several million dollars, besides bestowing lavish favors on their friends, relatives, and political associates.

Apparently with the intention of providing a safety valve for popular discontent, President Medina in 1941 had permitted the exiled socialist leader Rómulo Betancourt to return to the country and, shortly thereafter, to organize an opposition party which called itself Democratic Action. Betancourt, a well-known writer on economic and social problems, provided Venezuela with a politico-intellectual leadership comparable to that of Paz Estenssoro in Bolivia and Luis Alberto Sánchez in Peru. As a socialist he was anticommunist, and the Venezuelan communists opposed him and his party before, during, and after the overthrow of the Medina government. A similar alliance between communist parties and oligarchical regimes existed in both Peru and Brazil at this period. As for organized labor, it was even weaker in Venezuela than in Peru. In 1944 the Confederation of Venezuelan Workers, then only in process of formation, claimed 40,000 members (1 per cent of the total population of the country); the process was suspended as the situation grew more tense during the following year, and the Confederation still existed only in embryonic form at the time of the revolution.

The revolt broke out on October 18, 1945, and triumphed after three days of hard fighting, mainly in Caracas. It was spearheaded by a group of young army officers, but they differed greatly from the Argentine Colonels' clique and the Bolivian Majors' clique of 1943, for the Venezuelan officers' outlook was essentially civilian. As soon as victory was assured, they joined with Betancourt's Democratic Action party in setting up a provisional government under a seven-man Junta, only two members of which were members of the armed forces; the other five, including the provisional president, Betancourt, were civilians. Moreover, the young officers affirmed their own democratic origin and sympathies and their determination to collaborate with Betancourt's party and other civilian groups in establishing a popular, constitutional government at the earliest practicable moment.

Their pledge was made good. No military dictatorship was established, nor yet a dictatorship of the proletariat. For a year the "caretaker" Junta headed by Betancourt gave Venezuela a government which was essentially civilian and middle class. At one extreme it excluded the oligarchy, at the other the communists. Even organized labor was kept in a distinctly subordinate position; strikes were prohibited, arbitration of labor disputes was made compulsory, and the formation of a national confederation of workers remained in suspense.

The watchword was economic, social, and political reform, not revolution. No radical assaults were made on private property or business—not even on big business controlled by foreigners. The giant oil companies were induced to increase their already substantial royalty payments to the government, but their concessions and contracts as determined under the Medina administration in 1943 were confirmed. Aside from emergency measures to reduce the cost of living, supply shortages of food and machinery, and provide more adequate urban and rural housing, the main effort of the Junta was directed towards the development of a better balanced and more self-sustaining national economy, as will be explained more fully in the concluding chapter.

The Junta announced an early election for a Constituent Assembly and promised that it would be free and fair. But the members of the Junta, including Betancourt, campaigned vigorously for the election of delegates who would produce the kind of constitution they wanted. Briefly, they proposed to abandon both the federal system and indirect elections of president and congress, which had played into the hands of the oligarchy and fostered particularism, and to adopt instead a centralized national government based on direct popular elections.

The promised national election was held in October 1946. Like the Peruvian election of June 1945, it was the largest, and apparently the freest and most honest, election in the nation's history, and it resulted in an overwhelming victory for the liberal middle class—that is, for the element best represented by the Junta. The minimum voting age was eighteen, and women as well as men were eligible. Not only was there no literacy test, a great effort was made in the preëlection campaign to bring out the illiterate voters, and the country was plastered with posters addressed to the illiterate urging them to register and vote. About 1,400,000 votes were cast (one for every three inhabitants). Of these, some 13 per cent went to the conservatives, 3½ per cent each to the communists and a splinter republican party, and 76 per cent to the Democratic Action. The latter thus received a far larger majority than was ever won in the United States by Franklin Roosevelt even at the height of his popularity; and, we repeat, the election seems to have been comparatively free and honest—probably as much so as the average national election in the United States. Barring a counterrevolution, the liberal middle class was apparently firmly entrenched for a long time to come.

4. COLOMBIA

Paradoxically, Colombia, though the most genuinely democratic of these five countries, was the only one that definitely swung from left to right in the seven-year period under consideration. The way in which this was accomplished deserves close attention, for Colombia is the largest and politically the most mature of the countries in our group, and the change seems to mark a turning point in its political development.

The Conservative victory in Colombia came at the very end of our period, in 1946, and may have been due in large measure to the fact that the Colombian Liberals had been in power unbrokenly since 1930 and that, to use a phrase that became current in the United States under somewhat similar circumstances in 1946, many Colombians decided that they had "had enough." What cannot be doubted is that the Liberal party's discipline had disintegrated during its long tenure of power.

Since 1934 the Liberal party had been dominated by Alfonso López and Eduardo Santos, who represent respectively the left and right wings of the party. Both are reported to be wealthy; both own newspapers in the national capital, Bogotá (López, *El Liberal*, and Santos, *El Tiempo*); and both have occupied the presidency of the republic since 1934, Santos for one term and López for the better part of two. In his first term, 1934–1938, López gave the country a kind of New Deal administration. Its watchword was "revolution on the march" (*la revolución en marcha*). It was marked by the adoption of an extensive program of social legislation, mainly in the interest of organized labor, whose rapid rise in Colombia dates from that period; by the beginning of a great extension of the educational system, from primary school through teachers' college to national university; and by the negotiation of a reciprocal trade agreement with the United States (1936). Ineligible for immediate reëlection, López was succeeded by the more moderate Santos (1938–1942). Santos did not reverse his predecessor's policies, but neither did he carry the country further along the New Deal line; he was mainly concerned with problems, domestic and international, arising from the outbreak of war in Europe at the end of his first year in office.

The Liberal party was split wide open by the contest over the succession to Santos in 1942. In the face of bitter opposition from the Santos wing, López insisted upon running for a second term. He finally won, but his moral authority was weakened by the notorious electoral frauds that marked his victory, and his political authority was shattered by the rift in his own party, which was skillfully exploited by the Conservative minority. The opposition from these two sources crippled his administration from the moment he took office until he resigned in despair in 1945, a year before the expiration of his term. Some of the sharpest controversies arose over questions of foreign policy, such as the negotiation of a new concordat with the Vatican (December 1942), which gave the government a somewhat larger measure of control over the Catholic church in Colombia, and the transformation of the rupture of relations with the Axis powers decreed by the Colombian government immediately after Pearl Harbor to a state of actual belligerence (November 1943). The case against the López administration was dramatized, however, by several juicy scandals on the home front. In one of these it was accused of complicity in the assassination of one Mamatoco, a pugilist turned politician; in another, the president's own son, Alfonso López Michelsen, was charged with misuse of the funds of a large sequestered German firm of which he had been made administrator.

The seamy side of the López regime was pitilessly exposed by the ultra-Conservative leader Laureano Gómez in his newspaper *El Siglo*, which was the only newspaper in Colombia besides Eduardo Santos' *El Tiempo* that had a nation-wide circulation. A master of the arts of vituperation and backstairs intrigue, Gómez was a dangerous enemy—dangerous not only to López but also to inter-American solidarity and to the United Nations' cause. His strength lay in the fact that he voiced the kind of Hispanicism and Catholicism to which a considerable part of the Colombian people were attached.

Loss of respect for the López administration was matched by mounting unrest over price inflation and other grievances. How serious the situation had become by 1944 was shown by two episodes. Early that year Gómez' attacks on the administration became so inflammatory that he was arrested and jailed; and this led to demonstrations, counterdemonstrations, and widespread street fighting in the national capital, which resulted in numerous casualties before order was restored. In July a military uprising took place at Pasto, in southern Colombia, and President López and some of his cabinet were captured and held prisoner by the rebels for a short time. Though the revolt soon collapsed for lack of support in other parts of the country, the president had been made rather ridiculous and the prestige of his administration remained at low ebb until, in July 1945, he carried out his oft-repeated threat to resign.

To fill out the remaining year of López' term Congress chose Alberto Lleras Camargo, a brilliant young Liberal who had been a member of the left-wing López faction of the party for the past decade, but who now emerged as the leading champion of what was called "National Union" but amounted to a coalition with the Conservative party.

Alberto Lleras Camargo is one of the most interesting figures, and possibly one of the most important, in the recent history of any Latin-American country. Born in 1906, Lleras rose to eminence with meteoric swiftness despite the double handicap of a distinguished family background combined with present poverty. His family background included two presidents of the republic and a minister of foreign affairs; but such family connections are a political liability in Colombia, where it is widely believed that it is unfair for a single family to have more than one member called to serve in public life. To make matters worse for Lleras, his once prosperous family had fallen on hard times, "probably," he writes, "because my father, who owned an *hacienda*, made the mistake of working all his life in the country, a very unprofitable occupation in Colombia." Unable to afford a university education, Lleras started to work for a newspaper at the age of 16.

His exceptional talents as writer and speaker quickly overcame these handicaps and carried Lleras to the top with a rapidity which, by United States standards, was breathtaking. By the age of 25 he was already recognized as one of his country's most promising men of letters. Then, turning to public life, he became a cabinet minister at 29, ambassador to Washington at 37, chief Colombian delegate to the Chapultepec and San Francisco conferences at 38, and President of Colombia at 39. Shortly after the end of his one-year presidential term he was elected Director-General of the Pan American Union—the first Latin American ever to hold that office.

Lleras thus carried on the Latin-American tradition of the man of letters in politics. To be more precise, so far as Colombia was concerned he did not so much continue this tradition as revive it, for in his country it had languished in the period just after World War I. As one Colombian writer expresses it, the rapid rise of business enterprise during this period transformed the "literary republic" into a "financial republic." Lleras not only revived the literary tradition but also gave it the familiar Colombian emphasis on veneration for France. By this time, however, France was deeply divided, and as Lleras was an eclectic the results were at times confusing in so far as his political thought was concerned. On the one hand, he still pointed to the French Revolution as the fountainhead of democracy. On the other hand, his critics charge that he has been strongly influenced by the anti-democratic group in contemporary France represented by Charles Maurras and the Action Française. However that may be, Lleras himself admitted in 1946 that he wavered in his democratic faith during the darkest days of World War II. His defense was that everyone else in Colombia had similar doubts in that crisis: "Let him who is without sin cast the first stone," he said.

At the beginning of his career Lleras Camargo was associated with the Santos wing of the Liberal party, but after 1935 he served under López in various cabinet and diplomatic posts. He was fortunately out of the country during most of López' last six months in office, as head of the Colombian delegations to the Chapultepec and San Francisco conferences, thus escaping the odium that attached to that moribund administration. His distinguished performance at both conferences greatly enhanced his reputation; and the fact that both delegations had been organized on the principle of National Union (that is, bipartisan coöperation) in foreign affairs made Lleras the natural choice for the task of applying the same principle to the domestic political scene.

According to the account given by Lleras in his last message to Congress at the end of his brief term, the situation that faced him at the beginning of it was so extremely serious that there was no alternative to National Union. The impasse reached by the López administration was complete and the country was threatened with political chaos and possible civil war. Accordingly he brought three moderate Conservatives into his cabinet, conciliated their party in every possible way, and promised that the national election which was to be held in May 1946 would be free and honest, without executive interference in either the nominations or the elections. His policy of conciliation met with complete success in its immediate objective. All the important Liberal leaders either supported or acquiesced in it from the start; even the ultra-conservative Laureano Gómez, though at first recalcitrant, came over to it within three months; and public order and confidence were restored. The national election in May 1946 went off without serious incident, and in August 1946 the winner was duly inaugurated. But the winner was a Conservative, Mariano Ospina Pérez, Colombia's first Conservative president since 1930.

The Conservative victory was due to the fact that while Lleras had reunited the nation, he had not reunited his own party. The Liberals, unable to agree on one candidate, had entered the campaign with two, thus enabling the Conservatives to slip in between and win by a comfortable plurality. Generally speaking, the Liberal split followed the now classic line of right wing versus left wing, Jorge Eliécer Gaitán representing the latter and Gabriel Turbay the former, although López, formerly recognized head of the party's left wing, continued to confuse and weaken his party by refusing to commit himself to either candidate.

Thus hopelessly divided, the Liberals marched forward suicidally to certain defeat. The Conservative, Ospina Pérez, won with about 530,000 votes, which was some 200,000 less than the combined votes of the two Liberal candidates. But the latter divided the Liberal support almost equally, Turbay receiving some 370,000 votes and Gaitán 340,000, with the result that Ospina Pérez won by a substantial plurality. The small communist vote was not recorded separately and was split between the Liberal candidates; the bulk of it is believed to have gone to Gaitán, the most vociferous critic of the oligarchy and champion of the common man.

Many foreign governments were represented at the inauguration of President Ospina Pérez on August 7, some by their regular envoys and some by special delegations. Their presence gave rise to political manifestations by various Colombian groups. The delegation from Franco Spain was headed by the aged poet Eduardo Marquina, whom the ultra-Conservatives lionized to such a point that the Liberal *Tiempo* protested publicly lest courtesy to Franco's delegate be mistaken for endorsement of Franco's regime. The more democratic of the Liberals showered attentions on the Peruvian Aprista Luis Alberto Sánchez, though Gaitán's followers reserved their loudest cheers for the ambassador from Argentina.

The Liberals' sixteen-year domination of the national government thus came to a close, but they still had a share in it, for they not only retained a majority in both houses of Congress but were offered, and accepted, half of the ten posts in Conservative President Ospina Pérez' cabinet and half the departmental governorships, which are filled by presidential appointment. In other words, Ospina Pérez continued the recently established system of National Union or coalition government, with the Liberal party as the junior member of the firm. This "collaboration," as it was officially styled, was endorsed by three of the four principal Liberal leaders—Santos, López, and Lleras Camargo; but the fourth, Gaitán, rejected it and continued to fulminate against the exploitation of the Colombian masses by an alliance between the oligarchies of both parties. The peace thus restored after four years of bitter strife therefore appeared to be no more than a truce. How long it would last depended largely upon whether, and how effectively, the administration alleviated the sufferings of the lower classes from the rising cost of living and enabled them to share in the benefits accruing to the upper classes from Colombia's expanding economy.

8. Economic Developments

1. READJUSTMENT BY COÖPERATION

The economies of our five countries were deeply affected by the war, especially after the entry of the United States into it in December 1941. The three major factors which influenced them were first, the loss of markets in Europe and the shortage of shipping, machinery, and other imported manufactures; second, the improvisation of what amounted to a new inter-American economic system, which was supported mainly by the United States; and third, the establishment in each country of "development" corporations, whose purpose was partly to aid the war effort and partly to diversify and strengthen their several national economies in the postwar period. As a result, important changes occurred in the composition and geographical distribution of their foreign trade and in several other aspects of their national economies. Some of these changes were only temporary dislocations; others seemed likely to prove permanent and to have an enduring effect upon their economic policies, domestic and foreign.

Because of the high degree of their dependence upon foreign trade, the Bolivarian countries were very vulnerable to the shock of the war, some of them even more so than during World War I. Thus, the Venezuelan oil industry, which by 1939 accounted for nine-tenths of the country's exports, had grown up wholly since 1918. All five countries depended upon the great industrial nations not only as markets for their principal products but also as sources of supply of the manufactured goods necessary for the maintenance of their domestic economies. Since World War I they had made some progress in industrialization, but this was confined exclusively to light industry, such as textiles and food processing. They still imported all their industrial and farm machinery, machine tools, automobiles, and railroad equipment. Moreover, they felt the impact of the war from its beginning in 1939, since a large share of their trade was with Europe. As the following table shows, the combined shares of the United Kingdom (13 per cent) and Continental Europe (23 per cent) exceeded that of the United States (33 per cent).

Foreign Trade of the Bolivarian Countries, 1936–1938 Average by Principal Geographic Areas

(Value in thousands of U. S. dollars)

	All Countries		United Kingdom		Continental Europe		United States		Other American Republics	
	Value	Per cent	Value	Per cent	Value	Per cent	Value	Per cent	Value	Per cent
Bolivia	61,263	100	27,489	45	15,462	25	8,804	14	7,908	13
Colombia	166,173	100	13,664	8	46,218	27	83,347	50	2,883	2
Ecuador	25,214	100	1,531	6	9,774	39	9,284	37	3,158	13
Peru	140,043	100	24,636	18	41,016	29	38,035	27	19,153	14
Venezuela	269,929	100	17,268	6	39,702	15	78,704	29	2,516	1
	662,622	100	84,588	13	152,172	23	218,174	33	35,618	5

Most of the 49 per cent of Venezuela's foreign trade not accounted for by this table consisted of oil exports to the neighboring Netherlands islands of Aruba and Curaçao. The trade of Continental Europe shown in the table was carried on mainly by Germany, which was cut off from direct contact with these countries from the beginning of the war. Direct trade with the rest of the Continent as well was reduced almost to the vanishing point after the German conquests of 1940. From the outset the economies of the countries in our group suffered from the diversion of shipping, machinery, and other manufactures by the leading maritime and industrial nations. The diversion was begun in 1939 by Great Britain and France, which were followed in the next two years by all the other principal countries, including the United States.

The economic shock of these developments was cushioned by the adoption of what amounted to an inter-American economic system and by the strong support which the system received from the United States. The foundations were laid in 1939 by the First Meeting of American Foreign Ministers, which created the central institution, the Inter-American Financial and Economic Advisory Committee. The structure was completed, and redesigned to aid the war effort, by the Third Meeting of Foreign Ministers, held at Rio de Janeiro in January 1942. These meetings will be discussed in the following chapter, but it should be emphasized here that, from start to finish, this new economic system was planned only as an emergency measure and that it was never conceived in a spirit of "hemispheric isolationism" or closed regionalism. It was intended to lapse with the end of the emergency, and, subject to the requirements of the war, it contemplated the maintenance of the freest possible intercourse between America and other parts of the world even while the war lasted.

The system contemplated inter-American economic cooperation in a broad field, including commerce, transportation, finance, industry, and agriculture. Some of the measures adopted for this purpose were multilateral, applying generally to many or all of the Latin-American states; and other measures were bilateral as between one of the members of our group and one of the other American republics—in most cases, the United States, whose role, it cannot be repeated too often, was decisive in this whole vast network of arrangements. The distinction between multilateral and bilateral, though useful, cannot always be maintained, for in some cases multilateral agreements were carried out by bilateral action, and most of the bilateral agreements were made in accordance with the multilateral policies adopted at Panama and Rio de Janeiro.

Since regimentation became an essential part of this system, it should be noted that the United States still adhered to its Trade Agreements program, launched in 1934, which stood at the opposite pole of economic policy. Such agreements had already been negotiated with Colombia (1936) and Ecuador (1938); others were now concluded with two other members of our group: Venezuela (1939) and Peru (1942). But during the war this program was largely nullified in practice by the emergency system of controls, and the success of the latter stimulated the trend, already strong in Latin America, towards government intervention in the economic life of the country in time of peace as well as of war.

What has been said so far applies to the operation of the system in Latin America at large. Now let us see how it affected the Bolivarian countries in particular.

Two general measures of special significance for them were adopted early in the war on the initiative of the Inter-American Financial and Economic Advisory Committee, which had its seat in Washington and began to function in November 1939. One was the establishment of the Inter-American Development Commission, which was organized in June 1940. The other was the negotiation of the Inter-American Coffee Agreement, which went into force in April 1941, and remained in effect throughout the war. From the practical standpoint, this has proved to be one of the most valuable agreements concluded in recent years and an admirable example of the benefits derived from such a form of inter-American coöperation. Among the Bolivarian countries, Colombia, the second largest coffee-exporting nation in Latin America, was the chief beneficiary under it.*

The Inter-American Development Commission is important because it helped to stimulate the establishment of national agencies in each Latin-American country for the promotion of its economic development on the basis of careful planning, and of the joint participation of government and private enterprise. The Commission's efforts met with a warm response, for national planning had already become the vogue in Latin America in the decade before the outbreak of the war. The name usually given to these agencies was development (*fomento*) corporation or institute. In most cases all functions of this kind were concentrated in a single agency; in some, they were divided on a geographical or economic basis, as in the cases of Peru and Venezuela described below. Though designed primarily to promote long-range development of enterprises which were economically sound, they frequently aided in wartime enterprises, such as the large-scale procurement of rubber and cinchona bark in Ecuador, which had little, if any, hope of standing up against foreign competition in the postwar period.

Such agencies were established in all the countries of our group, beginning with Colombia (1940) and ending with Venezuela (1944). The Industrial Development Institute, organized by the Colombian government in June 1940, with a paid-in capital of about $3 million, promoted the production of forest and mineral products as well as manufacturing and processing enterprises. Within three years it had stimulated a wide variety of undertakings, such as those concerned with the production of iron, steel, coal, tires, woolen goods, glass, river craft, lumber, chlorine, tanning fluid, nitrogen, and dairy products. It also had under consideration plans

---

* Since this agreement was even more important to Brazil than to Colombia, it seems proper to leave the detailed description of it to the volume in this series dealing with Brazil.

for a steel mill and a fabricating plant that would supply about half the estimated postwar steel requirements of Colombia; but, owing to the shortage of equipment, both plants were still in the planning stage at the end of the war.

The Ecuadorean Development Corporation was established in June 1942, with a capital of $10 million, half of which was advanced by the Export-Import Bank at Washington. Though charged broadly with the development of the country's economic resources at large, the Corporation concentrated on the procurement of essential materials for the United States, such as rubber (under a special agreement with the Rubber Reserve Company of the United States), cinchona bark, and balsa wood. Cinchona bark is the source of quinine, which, before the development of atabrine, was extensively used for combating malaria, especially by the United States forces in the South Pacific war zone. Balsa wood, which is exceptionally light and buoyant, was used for a variety of purposes—notably, in the construction of the Mosquito bombers that operated from Britain against Germany. Considerable resentment was aroused in Ecuador by the Corporation's inattention to matters of more direct concern and permanent benefit to that country. Accordingly, in October 1943 the Ecuadorean Congress set up another corporation, the Bank for Provincial Development, which was to occupy itself with strictly national concerns, such as the development of agriculture, industry, and colonization.

Peru's first agency of this kind, the Peruvian Corporation of the Amazon, organized in June 1942, had a broad mandate to develop the economic resources of the country's Amazonian territory; but it was understood from the first that the Corporation would actually concern itself mainly with the production, rationing, and distribution of rubber. In fact, it was created as an agency for carrying out Peru's rubber agreement of April 1942 with the United States. When the domestic rubber requirements had been met, the Corporation was obligated to sell the remainder to the Rubber Development Corporation of Washington, with which it also cooperated in financing the expansion of rubber procurement.

A more truly "developmental" agency was the Peruvian Santa Corporation, a kind of Peruvian counterpart of the Tennessee Valley Authority. Established in June 1942 with a capital of some $16 million provided wholly by the Peruvian government, the Corporation was designed to develop the resources of the Santa River basin on the coast of northern Peru. One of the main projects was a large hydroelectric plant with an eventual capacity of 125,000 horsepower. Others included the construction of a steel mill and a railroad, the exploitation of the anthracite mines of near-by Ancash, and the building and operation of port works at Chimbote, on the Pacific. Some of these projects were delayed by shortages of equipment, but the port of Chimbote was opened to maritime traffic in May 1945.

The Bolivian Development Corporation, organized in September 1942, had an even broader mandate than these Peruvian agencies. It was authorized to develop and exploit the natural resources of the country at large and to construct transportation facilities, public works, and other works of general utility. It started out with the promise of larger financial resources than any other agency of its kind in our group of countries—$10.5 million to be paid by the Bolivian government in three annual installments, and a $15.5 million credit from the Export-Import Bank, making a total of $26 million. During the first two years it did not draw on the latter credit, but received some $5 million from the Bolivian government, with which it financed a considerable number of projects, especially mining, oil, and public works. By 1945 it had shifted its attention largely to agriculture and the potentially important highway from Cochabamba to Santa Cruz.

Venezuela set up a special food production office in 1943, in collaboration with a mission from the United States, but it was far behind the other four countries in establishing a general "development" agency. One was at last created in November 1944. Called the Board for the Development of National Production, it was provided with a fund of $18 million to carry out a program of stimulating agriculture, stock-raising, and industry by granting cheap long-term credits for economically sound projects supported at least in part by private Venezuelan capital. In carrying out this program in 1945 the Board gave preference to industries engaged in processing locally produced animal and vegetable products. It had accomplished little when the revolution of October 1945 brought the Betancourt regime to power. Betancourt announced ambitious plans for reviving and strengthening the nation's "bankrupt" economic system. The Development Board, now renamed Institute, played an important part in his plans. He declared that it would at last become a reality, and that "large sums" would at once be placed at its disposal out of government reserves, so that it might, among other things, promote the mechanization of agriculture, the electrification of the country, and large-scale irrigation projects, in which it was to be aided by a commission of technical experts from the Tennessee Valley Authority in the United States.

These were only a few of the governmental or quasi-governmental agencies set up in our area during the war to shape the course of its economic development. They have been stressed because they are representative, because most of them seemed likely to exert a lasting influence on this development, and because, as the war approached its close, they provided one of the best expressions of the rising tide of economic nationalism in their respective countries.

Through these and other agencies, both old and new, almost the whole range of economic activities was brought under government control in greater or less degree. This was accomplished by a variety of measures, such as the freezing of Axis funds, price controls, rationing, priorities, and export licensing, along the lines recommended by the Rio de Janeiro meeting of 1942. The major purposes of these measures were, on the positive side, to channel all economic activity as far as possible into the war effort, and, on the negative side, to prevent it from benefiting the Axis, whether by the leakage of strategic materials or otherwise.

The former purpose was more fully realized than the latter, for the enforcement of anti-Nazi controls was sometimes lax, and was frequently impeded by inherent difficulties. For example, the considerable leakage of Colombian platinum and Bolivian rubber was due partly in the former case to the fact that the very small bulk of platinum makes smuggling relatively easy, and in the latter case to the impossibility of patrolling effectively the long border between Bolivia and Argentina. Moreover, in Argentina, smuggled rubber commanded a premium price far above the legal price fixed in the agreement by which the Rubber Development Corporation of the United States was given the exclusive right to purchase all Bolivian rubber available for export.

2. U. S. EXPENDITURES

The stimulus given to the national economies of these countries by the United States during the war operated in large part through three channels: (1) The procurement programs of nonmilitary agencies of the United States, particularly by subsidiaries of the Reconstruction Finance Corporation, such as the Rubber Development Corporation and the Metal Reserve Corporation; (2) loans, advances, and financial aid, which were furnished largely by the Export-Import Bank and the Coördinator of Inter-American

Affairs; and (3) military expenditures and supplies, which took the form mainly of lend-lease aid.

The wartime nonmilitary agencies of the United States were organized under legislation approved in June 1940. They immediately began to develop large-scale programs through the negotiation of agreements with the governments or private firms in Latin America, including the countries in our group. The main purpose of the agreements was to obtain supplies of essential and strategic materials—such as rubber, cinchona, wool, copper, tin, and tungsten—for the United States; but in some cases it was stipulated that certain materials might also be made available to other countries of the Western Hemisphere, but to these countries only.

One of the first and most important of these agreements related to Bolivia. Late in 1940 a contract was made for the purchase of 18,000 tons of Bolivian tin annually for five years, and the construction of a smelter in Texas was begun. If this arrangement should become permanent, it would mark a great change in the channels of Bolivia's foreign trade. Hitherto, virtually all the tin exported from that country had gone to Great Britain for smelting; the contract of 1940 diverted to the United States the equivalent of three-fourths of the average annual tin exports of Bolivia to all countries in the three years immediately preceding the outbreak of the war (1936–1938). Whatever its postwar significance might prove to be, the Bolivian tin program was of vital importance to the war effort after Japan's rapid conquest of the Malay States, the Netherlands Indies, and Thailand, which had provided more than half of the total world production of tin before the war. In spite of labor troubles and political instability, the program was carried out with great success. The volume of tin exports rose from an annual average of about 25,000 metric tons just before the war to 39,341 metric tons in 1944 and 43,169 metric tons in 1945.

A similar problem existed with regard to cinchona bark and rubber, which have already been mentioned in connection with the development corporations in Ecuador and other countries. Both commodities were highly essential to the war effort of the United States. Both were indigenous in the Bolivarian area, but the main sources of supply before the war had been in southeastern Asia and were promptly cut off by the Japanese conquest. The countries in our group were now called upon to make up the deficiency.

They were relied upon almost exclusively in the case of cinchona bark, for before the war four of them—Bolivia, Colombia, Ecuador, and Peru—were the only countries in the world outside of the Netherlands Indies and British India that produced this bark in commercial quantities. Bolivia was far ahead of its three neighbors, accounting for about four-fifths of the total production of the group. But this constituted only 8.5 per cent of the world output in the period 1936–1938; nearly 90 per cent of it was provided by the Netherlands Indies. Nevertheless, if money was no object, the prospects were good for greatly increasing production in these four South American countries, where the tree was not only indigenous but widespread. Their prewar output had been held down only because it came principally from wild trees and could not compete in the world market with the more efficiently produced plantation rubber of the East Indies.

Accordingly, cinchona production became one of the major procurement programs of the United States in these four countries. Initiated in 1942, it reached its culmination in the next two years. It was reduced in 1944 because of the development of atabrine and other quinine substitutes, and was liquidated in 1945. On behalf of the United States, it was handled first by the Defense Supplies Corporation and the Board of Economic Warfare, and then by their successors, the U. S. Commercial Company and the Foreign Economic Administration. These coöperated with development corporations and other appropriate agencies in each South American country. The execution of the program involved a wide variety of activities, such as constructing air ports, setting up testing laboratories, and making supply and purchase agreements with local quinine factories. By dint of these measures and a doubling of the price, production was maintained at prewar levels in 1942 and 1943, which was something of an achievement in view of the fact that in Bolivia, the principal producing country, the normal labor shortage was accentuated by the wartime expansion of tin mining. As already noted, the tapering off of the program began in 1944, and in 1945 Bolivian exports of cinchona dropped to 455 tons, which was about half the annual average for 1936–1938.

The rubber program, too, was initiated in 1942, with the Rubber Reserve Company of the United States in charge. Our five countries played a not unimportant part in it, and it had an even more important influence upon them, despite the fact that their share in the world's production of rubber before the war was microscopic, amounting to about .2 per cent in 1936–1938. But rubber, like cinchona, was indigenous and abundant in the wild state in their tropical provinces east of the Andes, and production could be increased if one were willing to pay the price. Since every pound counted in the grave crisis precipitated by Japan's conquest of the main sources of supply in the East Indies, the Rubber Reserve Company contracted in 1942 for the total export rubber production of all the Latin-American countries, including our five, at a price ranging from 33 to 45 cents a pound (as compared with the New York price of 17 cents in August 1939, and 21 cents in December 1940); and, in addition, various United States agencies provided transportation, public health, and other facilities to stimulate production.

The immediate results were much more favorable than in the case of the cinchona program. Rubber exports to the United States from Ecuador, the leading exporter of our group at the outbreak of the war, rose from an annual average of $350,000 in 1936–1940 to a wartime peak of $2.8 million in 1944, an eightfold increase. In the case of Bolivia, the increase was phenomenal: the volume of exports to the United States rose from an average of 343,000 pounds in 1936–1940 to a wartime peak of 8.3 million pounds in 1945, a ratio of increase of 24 to 1.

The long-range results of both programs, however, were of very doubtful benefit to the producing countries. Aside from the fact that there had been considerable suffering and loss of life among the rubber workers sent into the jungle, both projects involved the diversion of energy to enterprises which had virtually no prospect of survival after the war. To the competition of the East Indies had now been added that of the newly developed synthetic substitutes for both quinine and rubber.

The only lasting benefit that our group of countries derived from these programs was the incidental stimulus which they gave to the development of the Amazonian hinterland. They aided in bringing the air age to this area, in building new roads, and in the establishment of agricultural stations around which, by the end of the war, permanent colonization projects were being developed. One of these was at San José, on the Guaviare River, which was an important center of the Rubber Development Corporation's activities in Amazonian Colombia during the war. Another was at Tingo María, in the heart of a rich, undeveloped forest area on the eastern slopes of the Peruvian Andes. Tingo María was one of the most promising of these jungle outposts. It was the seat of one of the largest of the new agricultural experiment stations built to serve the rubber, cinchona, and other projects; the road which already connected it with the settled parts of Peru to the east was extended westward during the war to the port of Pucallpa on the Ucayali River, a tributary of the Amazon; and even before the end of the war the Peruvian government launched a large-scale colonizing project in this area.

Less dramatic than these pioneering projects, but far more extensive and far sounder in the long run, was the aid that the United States gave to the well-established branches of the national economies of our five countries, whether through special procurement agencies or otherwise. The principal beneficiaries were the mining industries, such as tin in Bolivia, which has already been discussed; copper, vanadium, and molybdenum in Peru, which were covered by an over-all agreement with the Metals Reserve Company of the United States (September 1941); and platinum in Colombia. The countries of our group in which the largest expenditures of the procurement agencies were made during the war were Bolivia and Peru, where they amounted to $176 million and $97 million, respectively, for the period from July 1, 1940, to June 30, 1945. What this meant to these countries is indicated by the fact that the expenditures in Bolivia represented five times the total value of that country's exports in 1938 ($35 million); in Peru they exceeded by 20 per cent the total value of all exports in 1938 ($80 million).

Further stimulus was provided by loans, mainly from the Export-Import Bank of Washington, and coöperative projects in a number of fields, such as food supply, public health, and education, in which the Coördinator of Inter-American Affairs took a prominent part. In September 1940, the Bank's lending power was increased from $200 million to $700 million. Of this sum, all but $200 million was earmarked for Latin America, where it was to be used in assisting in "the

development of the resources, the stabilization of the economies, and the orderly marketing of the products" of those
countries. The Bank distributed its funds liberally but not
lavishly, and tried to maintain sound business principles. Its
largest total loans in our group of states were made to Colombia, and amounted on June 30, 1945, to $45 million, of
which $23 million had not been used; of the $22 million
already disbursed, $10 million had been repaid. Of the three
principal credits extended to Colombia, the first (April 3,
1940, $10 million) was to be used for the purchase of indus-
trial and agricultural products in the United States; the
second and third (May 1, 1941, and July 1, 1943, totaling
$30 million), for the development of the economic resources
of Colombia.

The principal aid for coöperative projects went to Peru
($3 million) and Venezuela ($2 million) for health, education, and food-supply programs. For example, all five of our
countries participated in the public health program of the
Institute of Inter-American Affairs, a subsidiary of the
Office of the Coördinator of Inter-American Affairs. This
program was designed immediately to assist in the production of strategic materials by safeguarding the health of the
workers engaged in producing them, and ultimately to
bring about a permanent improvement in public health
services. Among the activities carried out under it were the
construction of hospitals at Quito and Guayaquil, Ecuador,
and Tingo María and Pucallpa, Peru; antimalaria campaigns
in all five countries; the establishment of a course in tropical
medicine in the medical school at Lima; and the establishment of nursing schools, the first of which was opened at
Quito in October 1942. In the long run, this promised to be
one of the most beneficial of all the wartime programs in
the Bolivarian area.

Mainly in connection with these programs, many technicians and experts of various kinds from the United States

were employed in our five countries, and a considerable number of their people came to the United States for training and study. The projects on which the United States experts worked included such diverse matters as the nationalization of German pharmaceutical firms in Colombia, the establishment of tire factories in Colombia, Venezuela, and Peru, a study of the public school system of Bolivia, the building of air ports in the Amazon basin, and the development of vital statistics and meteorological services in several countries. One of the most productive of these missions was the one headed by Merwin L. Bohan, a United States foreign service officer, which spent six months in Bolivia in 1942 studying that country's economic problems. Many of the economic measures adopted in Bolivia during the rest of the war were based largely upon the recommendations contained in the report of this mission.

3. DISLOCATIONS

The wartime changes that occurred in the foreign trade of these countries included a large increase in its value, a major displacement in its geographical distribution, a considerable shift in the relative value of the principal exports and imports, and a sustained excess of exports over imports which led to the accumulation of unprecedented balances of foreign exchange and gold. These changes helped bring about a sharp rise in the cost of living in all five countries.

The total value of the combined imports and exports of the five countries rose from an annual average of $663 million in 1936–1938 to $1240 million in 1945, an increase of 87 per cent. By countries, the approximate rates of increase were 35 per cent for Peru, 80 per cent for Colombia, and 100 per cent for Bolivia, Ecuador, and Venezuela. In both periods Venezuela stood first in combined imports and exports and accounted for nearly half of the total for the whole group; and in both periods Ecuador brought up the rear with less than one-twentieth of the total.

The change in geographical distribution of trade consisted in the virtual elimination of Europe and a corresponding increase in trade with the United States and other Latin-American countries. Trade with Continental Europe approached the vanishing point; Germany, which in 1936–1938 had supplied one-seventh of the imports of Colombia, and one-fifth of those of Peru, disappeared completely from the list after 1940. Even Great Britain, which accounted for 13 per cent of the foreign trade of our five countries in 1936–1938, had dropped to 4 per cent by 1945, and nearly three-fifths of this scanty remainder consisted of its trade with a single country, tin-producing Bolivia. On the other hand, in the same period the share of the United States increased from 33 per cent to 49 per cent, and that of the other Latin-American countries from 5 per cent to 16 per cent. Canada's share fluctuated widely during the war, but was always very small; the Soviet Union's was infinitesimal from start to finish; and the only important branch of trade between any country in our group and the Far East—Peru's cotton exports to Japan—was cut off in December 1941.

The greatest shift in the relative value of export commodities occurred in Peru, Ecuador, and Colombia, whereas in Bolivia and Venezuela tin and oil, which were essential to the war effort, continued to dominate their respective export lists as completely as before the war. In Peru, petroleum dropped from nearly one-third of the total exports in 1936–1938 to barely one-eighth in 1945, while sugar skyrocketed in the same period from 7 per cent to 33 per cent. Cotton, which went mainly to Japan up to the end of 1941, fell from 19 per cent in that year to an average of 9 per cent in the first three years after Japan's entry into the war, but rose to 22 per cent in 1945. All of Ecuador's principal prewar exports—cacao, coffee, and petroleum—which had formerly made up 60 per cent of the total, were cut in half in the three-year period 1942–1944, but all three showed a slight recovery in 1945. On the other hand, Ecuadorian exports of rice, rubber, and balsa wood rose sharply: rice, from 3 per cent of the total in 1936 to 37 per cent in 1944; rubber, from an annual average of 3 per cent in 1937–1940 to 9 per cent in 1942–1945; and balsa wood, from 1 per cent in 1936–1937 to 10 per cent in 1942–1944. In Colombia, petroleum dropped from 31 per cent in 1940–1941 to 8.5 per cent in 1942–1943, and had recovered to only 16 per cent by 1945; and bananas, which made up 6 per cent of the total exports in 1936–1939, disappeared completely in 1942–1944. The difference was made up mainly by a rise in coffee exports from 66 per cent in 1936–1939 to 78 per cent in 1942–1945. The latter figure represented a great recovery from 1940, when it dropped to 59 per cent as a result of the disruption of the European coffee market by the outbreak of war in 1939. The subsequent recovery reflected the operation of the Inter-American Coffee Agreement, from which none of the participating countries derived greater benefit than did Colombia.

There were also some changes in the composition of imports. Most of these countries increased their imports both of foodstuffs and of raw cotton for their rapidly expanding textile production. On the other hand, there was a great reduction in imports of manufactured goods, including machinery and automobiles, as shown by the following table:

Selected Imports
(Millions of current U. S. dollars)

	COLOMBIA			VENEZUELA	PERU
	Steel Mill Products	Industrial Machinery	Automobiles	Metals and Manufactures	Automobiles
1938	10.3	8.0	4.2	19.4	3.7
1940	8.8	8.2	4.4	17.8	2.8
1941	7.3	7.4	6.0	14.4	3.3
1942	2.0	3.3	1.2	9.4	1.4
1943	5.0	3.8	.6	—	.4

The shock was even greater than is indicated by these figures, since they are expressed in current U. S. dollars, and prices rose after 1938. Also, a considerable part of the reduced flow of imported manufactures was channeled not to established enterprises but to new ones directly supporting the war effort. Thus, when machinery for the textile mills of Colombia was unobtainable, a new tire factory at Bogotá was equipped and put into operation with machinery supplied by the B. F. Goodrich Company, of Akron, Ohio. Readjustments of this kind ultimately provided jobs for workers temporarily thrown out of employment; in fact, labor shortages were the rule in all these countries after they recovered from the first shock of the war. But readjustment was not easy for the individual, and many cases of hardship resulted. For example, many Venezuelan oil workers who were thrown out of employment by the depression of the national petroleum industry in 1942–1943 had no recourse but to take up farming on tracts where they were resettled by the joint efforts of the government and the oil companies. Individual hardships might have added up to national disaster but for the fact that a large part of the people in all these countries were already engaged in subsistence agriculture.

As a result of the failure of imports to keep up with exports, most of the countries showed a substantial "favorable" balance of trade throughout the war. Even after the apparent balance had been reduced by allowances for debt service, interest and dividends, and similar charges, it appears that by 1945 our five countries had built up a tidy backlog of some $460 million in gold and foreign exchange, distributed as shown on page 111.

The war period was also marked by large increases in national budgets, in the volume of notes in circulation, and in the cost of living. As shown by the table below, the increase in the national budgets between 1941 and 1946

Country	Gold and Foreign Exchange (Millions of U. S. Dollars)
Bolivia	30
Colombia	175
Ecuador	30
Peru	50
Venezuela	175

ranged from 127 per cent in Peru up to 239 per cent in Venezuela. The per capita rate, however, was still very low. For example, in Colombia, the most prosperous of these five countries, the 1946 budget of about $150 million represented a per capita expenditure of only $16 for the country's population of about 9,300,000. Moreover, these budget increases were offset by the rising cost of living. In the case of Bolivia, living costs mounted even more rapidly than the budget, with the result that, in terms of purchasing power, the budget was actually reduced during this period. The approximate ratios of increase in national budgets and the cost of living in these countries were as follows:

Country	Increase in National Budget, 1941–1946, per cent	Increase in Cost of Living, 1939–1946, per cent
Bolivia	131	229
Colombia	172	76
Ecuador	221	106
Peru	127	101
Venezuela	239	40

Important factors in the rise of living costs were the large accumulation of foreign exchange and gold, the great expansion of the volume of notes in circulation (which increased about 300 per cent in all these countries), and sharp competition for the reduced volume of imported goods, together with the ineffectiveness of price controls and rationing. Real wages declined, and the resulting discontent contributed to the political overturns which were accomplished in all these countries, whether by bullets or ballots, between December 1943 and May 1946.

In all five republics, these wartime dislocations stimulated the trend both towards government intervention in the economic life of the country and towards economic nationalism, which expressed itself mainly in the effort to promote industrialization, by tariff protection and other means. Both trends have been important factors in shaping national economic policy with regard to the new international agencies and agreements in process of formation since 1943, and have also influenced the bilateral relations of these countries with the United States.

9. International Relations

1. THE INTER-AMERICAN SYSTEM, 1939

When war broke out in Europe in 1939, our five republics faced the crisis as members of the inter-American system, which had only recently adopted comprehensive measures with a view to just such an eventuality. These measures, which took shape mainly at the inter-American conferences of Buenos Aires (1936) and Lima (1938), were based upon principles of hemispheric peace, solidarity, and freedom. Like the other countries of Latin America, our five were deeply devoted to hemispheric peace in the sense of non-involvement in the European war, and to continental solidarity in support of a neutral policy; but as for peace in the abstract and freedom in the sense of political democracy, two of them (Peru and Ecuador) were engaged in a boundary dispute which in 1941 led to undeclared but very real war between them, and only one of the five (Colombia) had a government that rested on a broad base of popular consent. Moreover, each of these countries responded to the stimuli of the war period in a different way, according to its own peculiar character. Yet all of them, by one route or another, ultimately arrived at the same terminus of direct participation in the war and membership in the United Nations.

From 1939 to 1945 the American republics participated in five important international gatherings of a political character. Three of these were inter-American consultative

Meetings of Foreign Ministers, a new type of meeting, which will be explained below; they were held at Panama in 1939, Havana in 1940, and Rio de Janeiro in 1942. The other two were conferences held in 1945—the Inter-American Conference on Problems of War and Peace, at Mexico City, and the United Nations Conference, at San Francisco. All the members of our Bolivarian group took an active part in the five gatherings, but Venezuela distinguished itself particularly in the three Meetings of Foreign Ministers, and Colombia in the two conferences of 1945. All became charter members of the United Nations and figured in several other noteworthy international developments of this period, such as the revival of the idea of Grancolombian or Bolivarian unity, the settlement of long-standing boundary disputes between Venezuela and Colombia, and between Ecuador and Peru, and the adoption of the new inter-American doctrine of recognition known as the Guani Doctrine, which was the result of a revolution in Bolivia in 1943.

In 1939 the inter-American system was still a loose-jointed aggregation of states rather than a true regional system, but it had gained considerably in coherence and strength in the past six years. The change was due mainly to the Good-Neighbor policy of the Roosevelt administration, the decline of the League of Nations, and the increasing threat of aggression by the Axis nations. The growing sense of regional solidarity was more important than the specific measures adopted in this period. Two of these measures did, however, prove of great value when war finally came. One, adopted in 1936 by the special Inter-American Conference for the Maintenance of Peace, at Buenos Aires, established the principles of continental solidarity in case of an attack on any American republic by a non-American power, and of inter-American consultation to meet such an emergency. The other measure, adopted in 1938 by the Eighth Conference of American States at Lima, provided the machinery for such consultation. This was to consist of meetings of the American Ministers of Foreign Affairs, which could be called at any time by any member state. The first consultative meeting of this kind was the one that began at Panama in September 1939, less than nine months after the adjournment of the Lima Conference and three weeks after the outbreak of hostilities in Europe.

For our purpose it is important to note that Colombia took the lead in the effort to strengthen the inter-American organization during this prewar period. At the Buenos Aires Conference of 1936 Colombia proposed the establishment of an Association of American Nations. The proposal was referred to the Lima Conference of 1938, at which Colombia advanced it again after combining it with a similar plan for an American League of Nations sponsored by the Dominican Republic. The new project provided for a Pan-American Congress, meeting annually; a Permanent Secretariat; procedures for the peaceful settlement of disputes; the renunciation of neutrality in all wars of aggression; a definition of the aggressor; specific sanctions to be enforced against an aggressor (these included diplomatic and economic sanctions, but not armed force); and collaboration, as a regional organization, with the League of Nations at Geneva. This was reminiscent of projects for an American league proposed by President Wilson in 1916 and by President Baltasar Brum of Uruguay in 1920. Like them, the Colombian proposal was not adopted, but it is of great interest to us, first, because it vividly illustrates the new enthusiasm for American regionalism developed in Colombia after the advent of the Liberal party to power in 1930, and, second, because it expresses ideas that were to play an important part in the subsequent discussion of projected postwar international organization, particularly at the Mexico City (Chapultepec) Conference in 1945.

2. NEUTRALITY AND DISSENSION

When war broke out in Europe in September 1939, Colombia again took the lead in advocating inter-American solidarity. Its President, Eduardo Santos, immediately initiated a telegraphic consultation regarding the crisis with the presidents of the other American republics. It was decided to make prompt use of the new inter-American agency of consultation, and the first Meeting of American Foreign Ministers accordingly assembled at Panama (September 23–October 2, 1939).

Two of the principal measures adopted by the Panama Meeting were initiated by members of our group: the establishment of the Inter-American Neutrality Committee, by Venezuela; and the authorization of regional economic conferences, by Bolivia. The significance of these measures will be made clearer by a brief sketch of the general character of the Panama meeting.

The two main purposes of this meeting were to affirm and defend the neutrality of the American republics, and to cushion them against the economic shock of the war. On the subject of neutrality there was no dissent. Each of the twenty-one governments had adopted it as a national policy and all were determined to maintain it. What they did at Panama was to make neutrality a Pan-American policy and reinforce it by a striking innovation in international law: the establishment of a Neutrality Zone, or "chastity belt," stretching 300 miles or more out into the Atlantic and the Pacific, far beyond the limit of territorial waters recognized by international law. This innovation complicated the already difficult problem of neutrality.

It was to meet the need created by this situation that Venezuela proposed, and the Meeting approved, the establishment of the Inter-American Juridical Committee. The functions of this Committee were to coördinate the enforcement of the neutrality system and suggest needed amendments. The committee sat at Rio de Janeiro and consisted of seven members. Each member was named by a designated American government, but nominally represented not that government alone but all the twenty-one governments. Venezuela was the only one of our five republics which was given the right to name a member of it.

In the economic field the most important measures adopted by the Panama meeting were the agreement to coöperate on a broad inter-American scale, and the establishment of another wartime agency, the Inter-American Financial and Economic Advisory Committee, to sit at Washington. Since this Committee consisted of twenty-one members, one for each of the American governments, all of our five republics were represented on it.

This action was supplemented by the Bolivian project for regional conferences of small groups of American states on economic problems of special interest to them. The Bolivian government had three such conferences in mind: one for the River Plate area, one for Amazonia, and one for the west coast of South America. Though Bolivia's proposal was approved by the Panama meeting, only one of the conferences was actually held. This was the River Plate Conference of 1941 at Montevideo. An Amazonian conference was strongly urged in 1940 by President Vargas of Brazil, who named four countries of our group (Bolivia, Colombia, Ecuador, and Peru), along with his own country, as the proper participants in it; but the rising tension between Ecuador and Peru over their conflicting territorial claims in the Amazonian basin created the danger that, though the conference might be called for economic purposes, it would be wrecked by this explosive political question. An alternative solution—bilateral agreements between the United States and each of these countries—grew out of the wartime quest for strategic materials obtainable in Amazonia. Similarly, the projected West Coast economic conference was blocked by political complications, for Chile feared that Bolivia, perhaps aided by Peru, might take this occasion to reopen the Tacna-Arica Question.

Again at the Second Meeting of Foreign Ministers, held at Havana July 21–30, 1940, just after the fall of France and the Low Countries, Venezuela proposed one of the most important measures adopted by the American republics, the "Declaration of Reciprocal Assistance and Coöperation." The Declaration gave substance to the principle of continental solidarity by stipulating that an attack by a non-American state on any American state would be considered "an act of aggression against all the states which sign this declaration" and by authorizing enforcement measures. It was not a treaty of alliance, it created no machinery for truly inter-American enforcement action, and it imposed no specific obligation upon the signatories except that of consulting among themselves, in case of such an aggression, "in order to agree upon the measures it may be advisable to take." Yet even so the Declaration went far beyond the vague generalizations of previous inter-American agreements. In fact, it provided the principal basis for the decisive measures adopted by the next meeting, at Rio de Janeiro in 1942.

Venezuela also had a special interest in the resolution of the Havana Meeting prohibiting the transfer of any European colony in America to a non-American power. In effect, the resolution Pan-Americanized the "no transfer" principle of the Monroe Doctrine. Its purpose was to prevent Germany from acquiring Dutch Aruba, Curaçao, and Guiana, French Guiana and Martinique, and (in case Britain, too, should fall) British Honduras, Jamaica, Trinidad, and Guiana. The reasons for Venezuela's great interest in this matter are obvious. It has a common frontier with British Guiana; Aruba, Curaçao, and Trinidad lie just off its coast; and a large part of its oil was shipped to them for refining.

The Pan-American neutrality system adopted at Panama was not altered by the Havana Meeting; but from now on the United States moved steadily forward along the path of aid to the Allies. The bulk of the Latin Americans, on the other hand, favored strict adherence to the Panama system and resented what they regarded as the unilateral sabotaging of it by the United States. This was an important factor in producing the atmosphere of tension that marked inter-American relations during the year and a half between the Havana meeting and the Japanese attack on Pearl Harbor. Combined with other factors, it created a particularly dangerous situation in the three southernmost countries of our group, Bolivia, Peru, and Ecuador.

In Bolivia, which had not yet recovered from its demoralizing defeat by Paraguay in the Chaco War, there were evidences of growing Axis influence in 1941. A clear-cut case, in which the Bolivian military attaché in Berlin, Major Elías Belmonte, and the German minister at La Paz, Ernst Wendler, were central figures, was the conspiracy to bring about a Nazi coup in Bolivia in July of that year. This affair doubtless reflected the influence of earlier German military missions to Bolivia. One of the latter included no less a person than Ernst Roehm, who later became an outstanding leader in the Nazi regime and was the most conspicuous victim of Hitler's "purge" of 1934. Another evidence was the rise of a new political party in Bolivia, the M.N.R. (National Revolutionary Movement), which, while not openly affiliated with the Axis regimes, spoke their language and played their game.

Professing solicitude only for the Bolivian common man (who certainly needed solicitude), the M.N.R. was totalitarian and anti-Semitic; it denounced the Allied cause as an essay in economic imperialism; and it opposed Bolivia's participation in the inter-American defense system, which it branded as a tool of the plutodemocracy of the United States. The two latter points expressed the widespread Bolivian resentment against the control of the tin mines and other parts of the national economy by British and United States capital. The anti-Semitism of the M.N.R. was an effort to capitalize on the widespread popular dislike of the thousands of Jewish refugees who in the past few years had been admitted to Bolivia as agricultural immigrants, but who settled not on farms but in the cities, where they competed with native shopkeepers and artisans. The improper issuance of Bolivian visas to such refugees had become an international scandal. Some easy-going Bolivian diplomats were said to have made a fortune from accepting bribes for such visas, and this scandal ultimately played a part in the overthrow of the Bolivian government in December 1943.

The chaotic state of world affairs and the confused state of inter-American relations in the year following the fall of France probably goes far to explain why an undeclared war broke out between Ecuador and Peru in 1941. The points at issue between the two countries were not new; they involved rival territorial claims reaching back into colonial times. The dispute related to a small area on the Pacific coast and a much larger one in the upper Amazon basin, whose great potential resources had recently begun to excite world-wide interest. Hitler, for example, was believed to have ambitious plans for the development of Amazonia after his definitive victory. This may help to explain why, unlike the boundary disputes between Colombia and Venezuela, and between Costa Rica and Panama, which were peaceably settled at this time, the one between Peru and Ecuador resisted all efforts at accommodation. Negotiations begun at Washington in 1936 dragged on fruitlessly for years and were broken off in 1939. Border brushes became frequent in 1940, and full-fledged hostilities broke out in July of the following year, though neither side made a formal declaration of war, either at this time or subsequently.

The recrimination that followed was directed against the Axis powers and the United States as well as against the two principals. Ecuadorean spokesmen compared Peru's action to Hitler's aggression against Czechoslovakia and Poland, and charged the Peruvian government with receiving direct military aid from Japan and with seeking to aid Hitler in his attack on Russia, which had just begun, by diverting the attention and energy of the United States to South America and thus reducing the efficiency of its aid to Britain and Russia.

Peruvians, on the other hand, not only accused Ecuador of provoking the conflict—as was to be expected—but also went on to accuse the United States of instigating Ecuador's aggression. The two motives most commonly assigned to the former were, first, that the United States wanted to involve weak Ecuador in a hopeless conflict and then, as the price of rescuing it, extort the cession of Ecuador's Galápagos Islands, which were to be converted into a major American base for the defense of the Panama Canal; and, second, that Ecuador was being used as a cat's-paw to obtain oil concessions in the disputed Amazonian territory for private interests in the United States, including one of the highest officials in the State Department. These were not the irresponsible yawpings of yellow journalists. The latter charge was made orally to the present writer in September 1941 by a high official of the Peruvian Ministry of Foreign Affairs; the former charge was contained in a book, published in November 1941, by the Peruvian ambassador to Argentina, Felipe Barreda Laos.

Barreda's book went far beyond this particular allegation. In fact, it was an all-out assault on the whole Latin-American policy of the United States. It still stands today as the most notable expression of Latin-American discontent over the United States' desertion of the Pan-American neutrality policy which it had helped to set up at Panama in 1939. The United States, Barreda charged, was wrecking the Pan-American system, first by unduly extending its functions; then by exploiting these for its own unilateral purposes in utter disregard of the spirit of reciprocity and mutual regard that ought to characterize the system; and finally by sowing discord among the Latin-American states (as, for example, between Peru and Ecuador) in order to divide them and thus rule them the more easily. Barreda's conclusion was that Latin America's only salvation lay in adhering to its own true policy of neutrality and in abandoning Pan-Americanism in favor of Pan Latin-Americanism.

Many Peruvians, including the popular Aprista party,* dissented strongly from the views expressed by Barreda. For example, the Aprista leader Víctor Raúl Haya de la Torre reversed his earlier anti-Pan-Americanism, conquered his deep-rooted Yankeephobia, and pleaded strongly for vigorous Latin-American coöperation with the United States against the Axis. This was not surprising, for the Apristas were the most genuinely democratic party in Peru. But at this time the party was proscribed, its chief was in hiding, and among the ruling classes there was strong support for Barreda's views. This was offset mainly by the strong economic ties existing between Peru and the United States, and by the realization that in view of the world situation, Peru's freedom of action was narrowly restricted. This situation did not, however, make for better feeling on the part of Peruvians towards Washington.

In such an atmosphere it was not easy for the United

* For the Aprista party, see above, Chap. 7.

States, Argentina, Brazil, and Chile to succeed in their effort, begun immediately after the outbreak of hostilities in July 1941, to bring about a peaceful settlement of the conflict between Ecuador and Peru. An armistice was arranged on October 2, and negotiations looking towards a settlement were begun. But two weeks later Peruvian opinion was shocked by the news that the United States War Department had seized eighteen bombing planes which the Peruvian Government had purchased in Canada and was about to ship from New York to Peru. The War Department explained that these planes had been commandeered to meet urgent military needs, and Peru was promised (and ultimately received) compensation. At Lima, however, the seizure of the planes was regarded as another proof that the United States was supporting Ecuador against Peru. The negotiations for a peaceful settlement languished, and were still hanging fire on December 7.

In sharp contrast to the bloody conflict between Peru and Ecuador was the peaceful settlement at the very same time of a similar dispute between Colombia and Venezuela. Here too the dispute was of long standing and involved a considerable area at more than one point on the common frontier. Yet on April 5, 1941, the two governments reached a global settlement of the various points at issue, and despite sharp opposition in Venezuela the treaty was duly ratified and executed. The difference was doubtless due in part to the fact that the territory in question was less extensive and less valuable than the territory in dispute between Ecuador and Peru. Most of the latter lay in Amazonia, whose great potential wealth was being widely publicized at that time. But other factors too must be taken into account. Though Colombia had more than twice as many inhabitants as Venezuela, there was no such disparity in military strength between these two as between Peru and Ecuador. Moreover, Colombia was then governed by the essentially civilian and pacific administration of President Eduardo Santos, who was much more concerned with the development of the effective national territory of Colombia than with projects of expansion on its periphery, and who was also deeply impressed with the need for unity among the American states in the face of the now imminent danger of their involvement in the war. Finally, by great good fortune the foreign ministers of both countries at this time were exceptionally intelligent, talented, and courageous men—Esteban Gil Borges, of Venezuela, and Luis López de Mesa, of Colombia. By mutual concessions they brought about a prompt and sensible settlement of an ancient controversy, and thus paved the way for that revival of the Grancolombian idea which was to become one of the major international developments in northern South America during the war years.

Despite the uneasy state of its relations with the United States in 1940–41, Peru as well as three other countries in our group—Bolivia, Colombia, and Ecuador—coöperated with Washington in its policy of eliminating Axis nationals from the control and operation of air lines in Latin America. As a result, German lines in these four countries were either nationalized or liquidated: Lufthansa in Peru, Scadta in Colombia, Sedta in Ecuador, and Lloyd Aéreo Boliviano in Bolivia. There was no German line in Venezuela.

Scadta presented a problem which was particularly difficult because of the firm hold it had won in Colombia, and highly important because of Colombia's close proximity to the Panama Canal. Established in 1920 by German and Austrian aviators with the aid of Colombian capital, it was the oldest commercial air line in America. In the intervening twenty years its pilots had acquired a unique knowledge of flying conditions in Colombia, which were exceptionally difficult because of the country's rugged terrain; and they continued to operate its planes even after control of the company passed into the hands of Pan American Airways in 1938. The completion of the purge in 1940 required the coöperation of the Colombian government. A large part of the credit for the wholeheartedness with which it gave its coöperation belongs to the United States Ambassador to Colombia at that time, Spruille Braden. As Sumner Welles, then Undersecretary of State, has said, Mr. Braden's "personal activity [was] in no small part responsible for Colombia's realization of the danger to her internal safety and even more to the security of the Panama Canal from the German aviation interests operating in that country." As a result of the purge, Scadta was supplanted by Avianca, a national line affiliated with Pan American Airways.

3. WAR AND SOLIDARITY

The Japanese attack on the United States on December 7, 1941, and the declarations of war on the United States by Germany and Italy four days later, called into play the existing agreements regarding continental solidarity and defense, and made it necessary for the Latin-American governments to define their attitude toward this new phase of the war. Their various responses may be considered under two distinct though related aspects—first, their individual action on such matters as the declaration of war on the Axis powers, or mere severance of relations with them; and, second, their joint action as members of the inter-American system. The latter was taken at a Meeting of American Foreign Ministers held at Rio de Janeiro in January 1942.

Before the Rio meeting opened, all twenty Latin-American states had in one way or another signified their intention to honor their inter-American obligations. The most decisive action was taken by nine small states of the Caribbean area which by December 12 had issued declarations of war. The five states in our South American group acted with equal promptness but less decisively. By the same date all of them had adopted such measures as the freezing of Axis funds or the suppression of Axis propaganda. Only two of them, however, had severed relations with the Axis when the Rio meeting opened, and none of them had declared war. Colombia again led the way, severing relations with Japan on December 8 and with Germany and Italy on December 19, 1941. Venezuela followed by breaking with all three on December 31.

The third meeting of American foreign ministers (Rio de Janeiro, January 15–28, 1942) was held at one of the gloomiest periods of the war for the Allies. Yet every one of the twenty-one American republics was represented at this meeting, and it unanimously adopted declarations in support of the Allied cause and measures designed to promote their collaboration in the war effort, economic and political as well as military. Thus the neutrality system adopted at Panama in 1939 was abandoned. The change of policy was symbolized by the transformation of the Inter-American Neutrality Committee into the Inter-American Juridical Committee. Its composition and place of residence remained the same, but henceforth its principal function was the planning of postwar inter-American organization.

In addition, two new inter-American wartime agencies were created: the Inter-American Defense Board, consisting of twenty-one members (one for each government) and sitting at Washington; and the Inter-American Committee for Political Defense, consisting (like the Neutrality Committee set up at Panama in 1939) of seven members and sitting at Montevideo. Both agencies were merely advisory; neither possessed executive functions or coercive authority. The main purpose of the Montevideo committee was to combat subversive activities by Axis agents and sympathizers by advising the several governments regarding the best means of intensifying and coördinating their efforts. None of our group of five states was chosen to designate a member of this Committee.

In only one respect did the Rio meeting fail to come up to expectations. A resolution making it obligatory for all member states to break with the Axis was introduced and almost adopted, but under pressure from Argentina the obligation was watered down to a recommendation. This resolution was proposed by two members of our group, Colombia and Venezuela, together with Mexico. No such commitment in favor of declarations of war was even attempted, and the United States did not suggest such a commitment.

Except that the boundary dispute between Peru and Ecuador was placed in the way of settlement during this meeting, though not formally as a part of it, our group of five states played a minor role at Rio. The spotlight was held by the larger states and their delegates. Foremost among the latter were Sumner Welles of the United States, Oswaldo Aranha of Brazil, and Ezequiel Padilla of Mexico, who voiced the strongly pro-allied sentiments of the majority, and Enrique Ruiz Guiñazú of Argentina, who expressed somewhat uncertainly the neutrality policy of his government, which was to be a major cause of contention among the American governments during the next three years.

The day before the meeting opened, Ecuador threatened to walk out of it unless its dispute with Peru were put on the agenda. Though this was not done, the dispute was made the subject of parallel action and an agreement to settle was announced on the closing day of the meeting. There was nothing in the terms of the agreement to make Ecuador happy that it had forced the issue at this time, for when the settlement was finally completed in 1945, Peru had been awarded the bulk of the disputed territory east of the Andes and as a result Ecuador had been virtually eliminated as an

Amazonian power. This result was foreshadowed in the agreement of 1942, and many Ecuadoreans were embittered both against the other American governments for imposing the sacrifice upon their country in the name of continental solidarity in the war and against their own government for consenting to it.

This affair had far-reaching consequences. It weakened the regime in Ecuador and contributed to its overthrow in 1944. It also tended to draw Chile and triumphant Peru closer together by establishing a community of interest between them, for Chile had cut Bolivia off from the Pacific as Peru now cut Ecuador off from the Amazon. In both cases the losers had been granted transit rights through the lost territory, but neither country was satisfied with this consolation prize, and it seemed not unlikely that they would revive their claims when a suitable opportunity offered.

The Rio meeting virtually completed the framework within which the participation of our five republics in the war was carried on until the close of hostilities three and a half years later. In addition to providing for inter-American coöperation in the war, the Rio settlement also contemplated inter-American coöperation in the making of peace and the shaping of postwar international organization. The remainder of the present chapter will be devoted to a brief survey of the primarily political developments within this framework which were of special concern to our five countries.

A legal problem of considerable practical importance to all five countries arose at the time of the Rio meeting and remained unanswered, so far as three of them were concerned, until early in 1945. This involved the definition of their status in relation to the war under the classical concepts of international law regarding neutrality, belligerency, and alliances. For a long time after the Rio meeting, none of these concepts fitted their status. By February 1942 they had abandoned neutrality by severing relations with the Axis and adopting anti-Axis declarations and enforcement measures. Yet they did not become belligerents and allies until they first declared war and then signed the United Nations Declaration, which was opened for signature at Washington on January 1, 1942.

The first of our group to take such action was Bolivia, which issued a declaration of belligerency in April 1943.* The others followed suit at long intervals—Colombia in November 1943, and Ecuador, Peru, and Venezuela in February 1945. Their tardiness did not necessarily argue lack of enthusiasm for the United Nations cause. There were many other reasons, one of the most important of which was stated by a Venezuelan writer who said that these little countries would only make themselves ridiculous by declaring war, since it was out of the question for them to take any effective part in military operations and the Axis powers might not even deign to notice their declarations.

As a matter of fact, their formal entry into the war did possess practical significance in two important respects, first, in facilitating political and economic warfare against pro-Axis elements in each country, and second, in qualifying these governments to participate in the United Nations Conference at San Francisco. The latter consideration was apparently decisive with Ecuador, Peru, and Venezuela, for their declarations of war were made only about two months before the opening of that conference, and followed hard on the heels of a warning from the principal Allies that no nation which had not taken such action would be admitted to it.

---

* Since the Bolivian Congress was not in session at that time and there was consequently some doubt about the legality of this declaration, it was repeated with Congressional approval early in December of the same year.

4. THE WAR EFFORT

Aside from their important contribution to the war effort through the production of strategic and essential materials and the elimination of Axis air lines, which have already been discussed in Chapter 8, our five countries also aided it by coöperating with the United States in military defense measures and economic and political warfare on pro-Axis elements in their respective territories.

The military role of our group of states was most important in the dark period from the fall of France in June 1940 to the Allied invasion of North Africa in November 1942. Even during this period the danger of invasion was remote, except for a short time after the United States Navy was crippled by the Pearl Harbor attack. At that time it was feared that the Japanese might seize the Galápagos Islands and occupy the coast of Ecuador, which was the most vulnerable point in the area comprised in these five countries and which would provide not only a base for attacking the Panama Canal but also the shortest approach to the strategically important Amazon basin. By 1943 the crisis had passed and henceforth the countries in this area possessed only minor importance from a military point of view. Until the end of hostilities in 1945, however, it was found necessary to continue the antisubmarine campaign, which was vitally important in protecting the flow of oil from Venezuela and of other strategic materials from the rest of the group.

Their military coöperation was directed mainly towards defense against invasion, protection of the Panama Canal and the approaches thereto, and the antisubmarine campaign. This military coöperation was based upon staff agreements between each country and the United States which were initiated in June 1940. It included the use and improvement of existing naval and air bases, installations and other facilities, the establishment of new bases, and participation in the antisubmarine patrol by sea and air. Important bases were those in Ecuador, both in the Galápagos Islands and at Salinas on the mainland coast north of Guayaquil, and at Talara, Peru. Besides facilitating the use of such bases, the United States, Colombia, and Peru shared in the antisubmarine patrol of the Southeast Pacific, while Ecuador, Colombia, and Venezuela patrolled their own territorial waters. As Secretary of the Navy Frank Knox wrote in December 1943, they thus rendered "great assistance" to the United States, which was thereby enabled to reduce the number of its own patrol vessels assigned to this duty.

The expense was borne largely by the United States, which paid out about $50 million on this account from July 1, 1940, to June 30, 1945. This was about one-seventh of its total military expenditures in Latin America, one-half of which were accounted for by Brazil alone. In addition, lend-lease aid was extended to all five of our countries. Bolivia was the only member of the group with which a lend-lease agreement was concluded before Pearl Harbor.

Country	Lend-Lease Aid, 1941–1945 *
Bolivia	$4,392,000
Colombia	5,285,000
Ecuador	4,847,000
Peru	13,996,000
Venezuela	2,715,000
Total	$31,235,000

* The Treasury Department's latest report on lend-lease, cumulative through March 31, 1947, shows a total of $489,298,000 for all Latin America, of which $48,433,000 (about 10 per cent) went to the Bolivarian countries, as follows:

Country	Lend-Lease Aid, 1941–1947
Bolivia	$ 9,149,000
Colombia	8,257,000
Eucador	7,791,000
Peru	18,725,000
Venezuela	4,511,000

From March 1941 to July 1945 lend-lease aid to the whole group amounted to $31.2 million, which was 11.5 per cent of the total for all Latin America. Brazil again led the list with $154 million, or nearly 60 per cent of the total, and was followed by Mexico and Guatemala, each of which received about $21 million, or 8 per cent. The distribution by countries for our group is shown in the table on the preceding page.

Economic warfare in our five countries was conducted for the same purpose, and in much the same way, as in the rest of Latin America, but the results differed widely from one country to another. The purpose was to shut off all trade between the Axis countries and this area and to destroy the political and economic influence of Axis nationals and sympathizers in it. The effort to accomplish this took many forms, mainly that of the elimination of Axis-dominated firms. The attack on the latter was carried on through various instrumentalities. The first to be adopted was the United States' "Proclaimed List of Certain Blocked Nationals," popularly known as the black list of pro-Axis firms and individuals. First proclaimed by President Roosevelt in July 1940, the list included a large number of firms and individuals in Latin America, and many more were added after Pearl Harbor. Latin Americans objected strongly to it, just as they had to a similar list proclaimed by the United States in World War I, partly on the ground that no such list was proclaimed by the United States for certain other countries, such as Great Britain and Canada.

To meet this objection, the United States ultimately agreed to reduce the Proclaimed List in proportion as the Latin-American countries increased the efficiency of another instrumentality for eliminating Axis-dominated firms, namely, their own national enforcement measures. These were based upon Resolution V of the inter-American meeting at Rio de Janeiro in January 1942, which recommended the elimination of Axis-controlled firms and which was in turn a concrete application of the general principle of continental defense adopted at the Havana meeting in July 1940. Enforcement measures included the blocking of funds, "intervention" (the appointment of an interventor, a kind of alien property custodian, to supervise the operations of a designated firm), forced sales, and expropriation. In framing and applying these measures each country was aided by the United States, which provided expert advice through the office of the Alien Property Custodian, through economic specialists on the embassy staffs, and otherwise, and by Great Britain, whose secret service was able to supply important information about defects in enforcement.

Quite aside from technical difficulties, enforcement presented delicate problems, political, economic, and legal. Great Britain and, still more, the United States had to gauge their support of it with nice precision, since any overzealousness on their part was sure to be interpreted by many Latin Americans as proof that these two great capitalist powers were using economic warfare on the Axis as a device for riveting their own economic domination on Latin America. Similarly, the economic consequences were certain to be deplorable if enforcement action were too drastic, for Axis firms occupied key positions, and sometimes enjoyed monopolies, in important sectors of Latin-American economic life. Thus, German firms dominated pharmaceuticals, dyes and chemicals, and the construction, electrical, and engineering fields. In our group of states these included such companies as Anilinas Alemanas of Colombia and its Peruvian counterpart, General de Anilinas, S. A., and Bayer subsidiaries in all five countries, Bayer itself being a branch of one of the colossal firms in Germany. In some cases, thanks to international cartels in which British and United States firms participated before the war, control reached the point of monopoly, with the result that the German firms could not be replaced immediately. In such cases the Axis spearhead was not destroyed but passed into other hands through expropriation or forced sale. So far as possible, provision was made for permanent national-ization of the business, and where local technological skill was not adequate for the purpose the United States dis-patched special missions to aid in the process. For example, an important mission of this kind was sent to Colombia in the autumn of 1943, and one of its results was the formation in 1944 of a new pharmaceutical company by private inter-ests in Colombia and the United States which took over the business of German Schering.

Yet another obstacle was presented by legal impediments, which were, of course, greatest in those countries that had not declared war. As already noted, the five in our group did not take this step until long after their military impor-tance had been reduced to very minor proportions by the rising tide of Allied fortunes. Consequently, during the greater part of the war, Axis nationals in these countries were not legally enemy nationals, and therefore "the con-stitutional authority of the administration to proceed with an elimination program was open to serious question," as was pointed out in a review of this whole problem by Wil-liam L. Clayton, then Assistant Secretary of State, in June 1945. "In many cases," Clayton continued, "the worst of the Axis firms were incorporated under local law and well able to claim the protection of the law." Legal impediments of this kind were most formidable precisely in those coun-tries, such as Colombia, where the people were most strongly attached to the traditional democratic principle that it is a primary function of government to protect the individual in his right to life, liberty, and property under the law.

The achievements and failures of the attack on Axis spear-heads in our five states before any of them had declared war are illuminated by two reports of June 30 and July 1, 1943, written by the Bayer subsidiary in Argentina to Farbenindustrie in Germany and intercepted by the British at Gibraltar. Reporting by countries, these letters stated:

"*Colombia*. The sister firm in this country has been directly under control of a governmental interventor since the beginning of 1942 and can openly carry on normal business in a relatively unhindered manner. . . . We still keep in touch with Colombia and believe that your products will remain in the market for some time. Only recently, we shipped additional supplies to them."

"*Venezuela*. The last word we received directly from Caracas was that the situation there was about the same as in Colombia . . ."

"*Ecuador*. In this country the United States got the general controls in their hands immediately after the declaration of war and have effectively hindered the further shipment of goods to the company there."

"*Peru*. In Peru also the enemy have the controls fast in their hands. . . . Although all gentlemen known to you have been deported, your Peruvian agency remains in good hands. . . . The last time we sent them goods was in February 1943. . . . We understand that after this delivery the market is provided for until about the end of the current year."

"*Bolivia*. In Bolivia the situation was about normal until a short time ago. We hope that even after our representative there was placed under the control of a government interventor we will be able to deliver goods (against payment) at least for some time."

How enforcement fared during the balance of the war is indicated by the report made by Assistant Secretary Clayton in its closing days. The halfway measure of "intervention" had, he said, "proved a pretty feeble effort to control." The results of the thoroughgoing method of elimination of Axis spearheads in our five countries were summarized as follows (Argentina and Brazil, representing opposite extremes, are included here for purposes of comparison):

Country	Spearheads completely eliminated	Spearheads in process of elimination	Spearheads in which no action or nonelimination action has been taken to date
Argentina	0	4	104
Brazil	48	70	0
Bolivia	6	12	
Colombia	22	23	10
Ecuador	10	0	1
Peru	10	11	4
Venezuela	13	2	5

That these results were less satisfactory, at least to the United States government, than they might appear to the superficial observer is indicated by facts regarding the United States black list brought out by Assistant Secretary Clayton at the same time. As noted above, it was the policy of Washington to reduce the list for each Latin-American country as it increased the efficiency of its own enforcement measures. Consequently, the reduction of the list for any country was an index of the effectiveness of its local controls. Judged by this standard, Ecuador was the only country in our group which showed any marked improvement between 1941 and 1945. In that country the number of names on the list reached its peak of about 400 early in 1943 and remained at that level until May 1944, but was then cut to less than 200 by January 1945, a reduction of more than 50 per cent. In none of the other four did the reduction approach that ratio. They ranged from Colombia, which came next with about 15 per cent (a reduction from about 1150 names at the peak in 1943 and 1944 to about 1000 early in 1945), down to Bolivia, in which the reduction from the 1943 peak of about 400 was negligible.

In carrying on political warfare the governments of our five countries coöperated with the Inter-American Committee for Political Defense at Montevideo and with the Committee's members who were sent on consultative visits to each country. In this way effective curbs were imposed on espionage, sabotage, and propaganda by enemy nationals and agents. Their own disaffected nationals, however, presented a problem which some of them never solved. For example, in Colombia ultra-conservative Laureano Gómez' newspaper *El Siglo*, which was very sympathetic towards the Falange of Franco Spain, was openly hostile to the United States before Pearl Harbor, going so far as to assert that, from Colombia's point of view, the Panama Canal might as well be controlled by Japan or Germany as by the United States. Even after Pearl Harbor *El Siglo's* language was only slightly less provocative. It bitterly assailed the liberal administration's declaration of Colombian belligerency in November 1943 and continued to snipe at the United States, the Pan-American system, and the United Nations through most of the war. Only when victory was assured did it cease its attempts to cripple Colombia's participation in the war effort.

5. BOLIVARIAN PROBLEMS

As shown in the preceding section, the Bolivarian countries made important contributions to the war effort from the beginning of the United States' participation in the war; and they did so at the risk, which for a time seemed considerable, of Axis reprisals of every kind, both internal and external. Nevertheless, the fact remains that, from the strictly legal point of view, all five of these countries remained in the twilight zone of quasi-belligerence for nearly two years after Pearl Harbor. This fact reflects no discredit upon them, and their statesmen and publicists did not feel called upon to apologize for it at the time and have not done so since. On the contrary, with typical Latin zeal for exact legal definition, they addressed themselves with evident zest to the task of clarifying their peculiar status under international law, and made this problem the subject of intergovernmental consultations.

This situation created a community of interest amongst them which probably contributed to the revival of the Grancolombian or Bolivarian idea. We have already discussed the meaning of these terms and have seen that "Bolivarian" embraced all five countries and Panama as well, whereas "Grancolombian" included only Colombia, Ecuador, Venezuela, and Panama; but the terms were sometimes used interchangeably, and in both cases the idea had its main roots in Colombia and Venezuela.

A new chapter in its long history was written during the war. From November 1942 to January 1943, three Grancolombian diplomatic consultations were held with a view to agreement among the governments of Colombia, Venezuela, and Ecuador on a common course of action on specific international problems. Colombia took the initiative in the first case (the severance of relations with the Vichy Government), and Venezuela in the other two (the refusal to recognize the legality of property transfers in countries occupied by the Axis powers, and the recognition of the Czech government-in-exile). In all three cases an accord was reached and was announced simultaneously in Caracas, Bogotá, and Quito. Further development of the idea along this particular line was arrested when Colombia declared its belligerency in November 1943, thereby destroying the identity of status of the three countries. It was not restored until the other two countries of the group also became belligerents in the closing months of the war.

In the summer of 1943 Venezuela broadened the movement geographically to include all the Bolivarian countries, and no less a personage than the president himself, Isaías Medina Angarita, made a five weeks' tour of their capitals in support of it. Ecuador, feeling the need of support against Peru, showed great enthusiasm for the narrower Grancolombian movement, especially after the overthrow in 1944 of the administration which had made the Rio de Janeiro "surrender" to Peru. The new president of Ecuador, José María Velasco Ibarra, featured this movement time and again in his public pronouncements and gave his support to one of its principal concrete results, namely, the formation in April 1946 of the Grancolombian Merchant Fleet (*Flota Grancolombiana*). Colombia took the initiative in this matter and supplied 60 per cent of the initial capital of $20 million, the remainder being provided by Venezuela and Ecuador. It is interesting to note that almost immediately the enterprise encountered opposition in some quarters in Venezuela, where it was criticized as an expression of Colombian "imperialism."

Whether in the Grancolombian or the broader Bolivarian form, this movement might have been regarded as an essay in balance-of-power politics and as a threat to continental solidarity; but both implications were vigorously denied by its supporters. There was to be no military alliance among these countries, their spokesmen said, much less a fusion of their sovereignties. The purpose was merely to furnish an example of the application of Pan-American principles by the promotion of diplomatic coöperation and cultural and commercial interchange among a group of neighboring countries bound together by many common traditions and other ties; and there was to be nothing exclusive about these arrangements. The latter point was borne out by the conduct of the several governments during the war. Thus, Venezuela negotiated commercial and cultural agreements with Brazil and Chile as well as with Bolivia, Peru, and Colombia; and when in 1943 the last-named initiated a consultation regarding the juridical status of countries which were neither neutral nor belligerent, it addressed itself not only to the other Bolivarian countries but also to Chile and Paraguay.

Bolivia, whose external interests were concentrated mainly on improving its outlets to the Atlantic and the Pacific, played a very minor role in the Bolivarian movement, which had its headquarters in the countries fronting on the Caribbean. But Bolivia provided the occasion for another noteworthy international development of this period, namely, the adoption of the Guani Doctrine by a large majority of the American republics.

The event that touched off action was the Bolivian revolution of December 20, 1943, which brought the Villarroel regime to power in that country.* Since there were strong indications that the revolution was, in part at least, the work of pro-Axis elements operating mainly in Argentina and with support from members of the Argentine military government, the Inter-American Committee for Political Defense recommended to the American governments on December 24 that, for the duration of the war, they should agree not to recognize any new American regime established by force without first exchanging information and consulting with one another regarding the circumstances of the revolution and the probable attitude of the new regime towards the war effort. The Committee's recommendation was approved by almost all the governments and became known as the Guani Doctrine because the chairman of the Committee was Alberto Guani, of Uruguay. The new doctrine was applied first to the current case of Bolivia, whose new regime consequently did not obtain general

* See above, Chap. 7.

recognition until after a six months' probationary period had elapsed, and subsequently to other revolutionary regimes, including the one set up in Ecuador in May 1944.

A discussion of the merits of this wartime innovation in inter-American policy has no place in the present volume, but it should be pointed out that the application of the Guani Doctrine produced no lasting benefits in the case of Bolivia and broke down in the case of Ecuador, and that the latter government promptly showed its disesteem for the Doctrine by recognizing the Villarroel government of Bolivia without waiting for the majority of the American governments to make up their minds. In fact, dissension over the use of recognition as a diplomatic sanction was one of the chief sources of the serious discord which developed among the members of the Pan-American family in 1944. For it was used in such a way as to strengthen the growing feeling in Latin America that the United States was taking advantage of nominally inter-American procedures to impose its unilateral policies on the other American governments. By autumn it was evident that in two leading cases —the related cases of Bolivia and Argentina—those policies did not even have the merit of success.

6. CHAPULTEPEC, SAN FRANCISCO, AND AFTER

Another source of Latin-American discontent was the failure of the United States to consult with the other American republics regarding the proposed general international organization until after the adoption of the Dumbarton Oaks Proposals by the Big Four in August and September 1944. Indeed, Washington showed an invincible reluctance to hold a consultative meeting with them on any subject. In October Argentina took advantage of the widespread resentment aroused by this attitude to make a well-timed formal request through the proper channel, the Pan

American Union, for an inter-American consultative meeting to consider the "international aspects" of "the Argentine question."

The emphatic endorsement which the Argentine request immediately received in several Latin-American countries was a warning to Washington that it must change its course. This situation probably helps to explain why the United States at last came out in favor of holding the long-delayed inter-American meeting, though other factors certainly weighed heavily in the decision. At any rate, the meeting was scheduled for February 1945, which was the earliest possible date and was two months in advance of the date fixed for the United Nations meeting in San Francisco.

Members of our group of states took an active and important part in this series of events. The three Grancolombian countries were among the first to support Argentina's request for an inter-American meeting. Venezuela presented the State Department with one of the first and most outspoken critiques of the Dumbarton Oaks Proposals. Delegates from all five countries distinguished themselves at the two international conferences of 1945. One of them, the brilliant young Colombian Alberto Lleras Camargo, won a position in the front rank of the delegates from all the countries represented at both conferences.

At the Inter-American Conference on Problems of War and Peace, which met in Chapultepec Castle, Mexico City, from February 21 to March 8, 1945, our five states enjoyed a prominence and influence out of all proportion to their numbers. It fell to the Venezuelan Foreign Minister, Caracciolo Parra-Pérez, to speak for the conference in replying to the address of welcome by the President Avila Camacho of Mexico. At a later stage he rendered an important service in helping to curb the tendency towards excessive regionalism and to keep the American system subordinate to the world organization. Three of the seven commission chairmanships were occupied by delegates in our group, all three of whom were Ministers of Foreign Affairs of their respective governments: Alberto Lleras Camargo, of Colombia (Commission on the Inter-American System); Camilo Ponce Enríquez, of Ecuador (Commission on Coördination); and Manuel C. Gallagher, of Peru (Commission on Economic Problems of the War and the Transition Period). More important, these and other delegates from our group did a great deal to shape the decisions of the conference on leading questions. Víctor Paz Estenssoro, of Bolivia, made a strong impression as reporter for the Committee on Postwar Social and Economic Problems. Carlos Lleras Restrepo, of Colombia, led the bloc of Latin-American protectionists which forced the modification of commitments, championed by the United States, in favor of a lowering of barriers to international trade. Above all, Alberto Lleras Camargo took the lead in the adoption of the Act of Chapultepec, which gave the American republics their first system of security against internal as well as external aggression. He also fathered other important changes in internal organization, including the Pan American Union, and was reputedly a member of the triumvirate (the other members of which were Ezequiel Padilla, of Mexico, and Nelson Rockefeller, of the United States) which designed the settlement of the thorny Argentine problem.

The Act of Chapultepec was apparently not only adopted under Colombian leadership but originated in that country. According to an article by former president Eduardo Santos published in Bogotá in the spring of 1947, he himself was the father of the Act; he proposed the plan of such an act to President Roosevelt in a conference at the White House in January 1945; and Roosevelt was won over to it, thus assuring it of the indispensable support of the United States delegation at the Chapultepec Conference. This story appears to be true; and in any case the Act was certainly a long step in the direction of Colombia's proposals of 1936 and 1938 for an American League of Nations and reproduced almost verbatim their enumeration of the successive degrees of sanctions to be employed against an aggressor.

In this, as in all other matters, the conference subordinated its regional instruments and agencies to the overriding authority of the incipient world organization. Nevertheless, when the charter of this larger organization was framed at the San Francisco Conference of the United Nations from April to June 1945, the American republics had to fight long and hard to preserve the Act of Chapultepec from having all its teeth drawn by globalists bent upon concentrating all enforcement authority in the United Nations. Again, Lleras Camargo of Colombia led the fight. In the end he and his many able associates from his own and other American countries succeeded in retaining for regional organizations the right to take defensive (though not preventive) enforcement measures in the absence of action by the United Nations. The latter stipulation was closely connected with the introduction of the Great Power veto by the Yalta agreement of January of this year. A strong effort to curb the veto power was made by several of the smaller states, including Colombia; but when the curb came to a vote, Colombia alone of the five Bolivarian states supported it. Bolivia, Peru, and, Venezuela abstained, and Ecuador was absent.

Delegates from other countries in our group took a noteworthy though less conspicuous part in the work of the conference—for example, Caracciolo Parra-Pérez as chairman of the Committee on Juridical Organization, and Manuel C. Gallagher of Peru as Chairman of the Committee which drafted the statute of the world court. Several of the delegates aided in liberalizing the original Dumbarton Oaks draft, through the introductory statement of principles and otherwise. Finally, Bolivia created a brief flurry by attempting to revive the old issue of its outlet to the Pacific, despite the fact that territorial questions were excluded from the agenda of the conference.

When the San Francisco Conference had completed its work of drafting the United Nations Charter, the Bolivarian countries promptly ratified the Charter * and joined in carrying its provisions into effect. In the short period of its operation covered by this volume (that is, to the beginning of 1947), the member of the group to which the most important posts were awarded was Colombia. The chairman of the Preparatory Commission of the first United Nations meeting in London early in 1946 was Eduardo Zuleta Angel, a prominent member of the Colombian delegation at San Francisco. At the end of that year Colombia also gained one of the coveted seats on the Security Council upon the expiration of the short term of Mexico, an original member of the Council. To fill this seat the Colombian government named Alfonso López, former president and veteran leader of the Liberal party. Among the other countries of the group, Peru won special distinction through the work of its delegate to the Economic and Social Council, Manuel Seoane.

On the other hand, the financial contributions of the Bolivarian countries to the United Nations are very small, as shown by the following table drawn from the contributions scale of the United Nations for 1947. For purposes of comparison, several other countries are included; among these are Argentina and Brazil, the largest Latin-American contributors.

The microscopic contributions of the Bolivarian states reflect, not a lack of enthusiasm for the United Nations,

* Ecuador was, however, the last of the Latin-American countries to deposit its ratification (December 21, 1945). The dates of deposit by the other Bolivarian countries were: Peru, October 31; Colombia, November 5; Bolivia, November 14; and Venezuela, November 15.

United Nations Contribution Scale, 1947: Selected Countries

Country	Per Cent
Bolivia	.08
Colombia	.37
Ecuador	.05
Peru	.20
Venezuela	.27
Bolivarian group	.97
Argentina	1.85
Brazil	1.85
Canada	3.20
Norway	.50
United States	39.89
Yugoslavia	.33
All countries	100.00

but their relative poverty, for the scale is based upon national income. It will be noted that while their aggregate population is nearly twice as large as that of Argentina, their aggregate contribution is only a trifle more than half as large; and that Argentina in turn contributes considerably less than Canada, although Argentina's population is one-fourth as large again as Canada's. Latin America in general is relatively poor, and the Bolivarian countries are no exception to the rule. The above figures tell us more about internal conditions in these countries than about the value of their contributions to the world organization, for the most important of these cannot be measured in money.

In the field of inter-American affairs, the period after the close of the San Francisco Conference was marked by the failure to follow up the strong regional trend forecast by the Mexico City conference. One of the main reasons was the recurrence of "the Argentine question" in an acute form. Nominally an inter-American question, this took on more and more the aspect of a controversy between Washington and Buenos Aires. The small countries in our group remained discreetly on the side lines, but it was increasingly evident that they disliked what they took to be Washington's thinly disguised reversion to unilateral intervention—a practice absolutely prohibited by an inter-American agreement adopted at the Buenos Aires Conference of 1936 and duly ratified by the United States in 1937. An Uruguayan proposal of joint intervention, made late in 1945 and obviously aimed at the Perón regime in Argentina, was warmly endorsed by Secretary of State Byrnes; but its reception in our group of states was lukewarm at best. Even the new popular government of Venezuela, which was least critical of the proposal, stated that in its opinion joint intervention should not go beyond diplomatic sanctions and should not extend to interference in the domestic affairs of any country. When Juan Domingo Perón was elected president of Argentina in a free and honest election in February 1946, the Colombian Liberal government still maintained a discreet silence; but the country's leading Liberal newspaper, *El Tiempo* of Bogotá, came out with an editorial sharply criticizing the State Department's effort to prevent Perón's election and declaring roundly that, whether they liked Perón and his regime or not, the other American governments must accept the decision of the Argentine people as expressed in their choice of him. "Nonintervention," said *El Tiempo*, "is the cornerstone of international coöperation."

That expressed the views of all the members of our group on this important question. They were devoted to the principle of international coöperation, but they understood this to mean coöperation among nations. After the war, nationalism was even stronger among them than before and they emerged from it determined not to let their national independence be undermined either in the economic field by a lowering of trade barriers or in the political field by the revival of intervention.

PART III
RETROSPECT

10. Relations with the United States to 1939: Historical Highlights

1. GENERAL

From the beginning of their independence early in the nineteenth century the five countries founded by the internationalist Bolívar have played an important role in the development of the Latin-American policy of the United States, sometimes as its collaborator, sometimes as its antagonist. The degree of its political and economic interest in these five countries has generally varied in direct proportion to their distance from it and was in fact negligible in the case of the most distant of them, Bolivia, until after World War I. But other members of the group have been prominently associated with some of the most important acts of the United States in regard to Latin America from the beginning of its formal relations with the new states in 1822 to the present day.

Though these countries have never fully realized the ideal of acting as a Bolivarian bloc, their individual political relations with the United States have tended to run along roughly parallel lines. This has been particularly true since the close of the nineteenth century, when the United States began to emerge as a great power.

From that decade to the present the status of the United States as a great power has been the dominant factor in its relations with these five very small powers. This has overshadowed all other factors, including the policy pursued by Washington at any given time. It therefore provides a thread of continuity since the 1890's which has not been broken even by such major policy shifts as the abandonment of the Big Stick in favor of the Good Neighbor. We shall accordingly run very lightly over the earlier period and concentrate our attention on the political and economic developments of the half century ending in 1939, for these are much more relevant to the problems that confront us today. Developments during World War II have already been discussed in earlier chapters.

Cultural relations will not be discussed, for they have not been of first-rate importance to either side. There have been some interesting exceptions to this rule which we should like to discuss if space permitted. To give only two random examples, the University of Pennsylvania Museum took the lead in the 1890's in the modern, scientific study of the rich archaeological remains of the Inca Empire and earlier civilizations in Peru; and more recently many students from the Bolivarian area have come to the United States for training in medicine, dentistry, engineering, and architecture. But generally speaking the cultural orientation of the whole Bolivarian area has been very definitely towards Europe, whose influence has far exceeded that of the United States. This point is illustrated by the history of the penal systems of the area, where, despite the fact that the plan of the Eastern Penitentiary of Pennsylvania has been widely followed for a long time past in the construction of prison buildings, the guiding ideas of all those systems have always come from Europe.

2. RELATIONS TO 1889

The short-lived state of Gran Colombia played a foremost part in Latin-American relations with the United

States before it broke up in 1830 into Venezuela, New Granada (now Colombia), and Ecuador. It was the first of all the Latin-American states to gain recognition of its independence by the United States (1822); the first to call for an official interpretation of the Monroe Doctrine (which it did in 1824 by proposing an alliance with the United States as a means of implementing the Doctrine), and the first to conclude a commercial treaty with the United States (1824).

Some Colombian historians have claimed that the Monroe Doctrine itself was inspired by their country's first minister to the United States, Manuel Torres; but the claim is not well founded. What Torres urged Monroe to adopt was (to use a modern term) a Pan-American policy; what Monroe actually issued was a unilateral declaration of the national policy of the United States, and he made no effort to obtain the coöperation of Latin America against the Holy Alliance. Though implications of Pan-Americanism can be found in the Doctrine, they were not developed by the United States until near the end of the century. Monroe himself rebuffed all Latin-American efforts to develop them. One of these efforts was Gran Colombia's proposal of an alliance in 1824.

Partly for this reason and partly because he set more store by the aid and friendship of Great Britain, Bolívar did not plan to invite the United States to the international Congress of 1826 at Panama, which, it will be recalled, was a part of Colombia at that time and remained a part of it until 1903. An invitation was finally extended and accepted; but the United States was so slow in appointing its delegates that they were unable to take part in the Congress. It had a delegation ready to attend the adjourned session which was to have met in Mexico in 1827, but this was never held.

The real or apparent indifference of the United States towards inter-American coöperation gave rise to resentment which was particularly keen in Gran Colombia and Peru, the leading exponents of the idea. One result was the growing popularity of preferential tariff treaties among the Latin-American states, to the exclusion of the United States as well as non-American powers. One such treaty was concluded between Colombia and Mexico in 1826. Another result was the strengthening of the element opposed to including the United States in international meetings initiated in Latin America. Three such meetings of a political character were held between the Panama Congress of 1826 and the Washington Conference of 1889–1890. Two of them took place at Lima, in 1847 and 1864.

The United States was invited to the last named meeting because of the revival of the European menace—for example, the French intervention in Mexico was going on at this time, and Spain was threatening Peru. The invitation came in the midst of our own Civil War, however, and was declined by Secretary of State Seward. The United States government was not indifferent to the plight of Peru; it merely preferred independent, unilateral action. This took the form of strong representations to Spain in the language of the Monroe Doctrine, which may have sped the Spanish withdrawal, although the defeat inflicted on Spain's fleet by Peru and its neighbors would probably have been enough by itself to bring this about.

Although the long and troubled history of the Panama question is discussed in detail in another volume of this series, the question overshadowed all other aspects of relations between the United States and the Bolivarian countries so completely that the principal stages of its development must be recapitulated here.

In the period ending in 1889, the United States gained a preferential position for itself in Panama by the Bidlack-Mallorino Treaty of 1846 with Colombia (then New Granada), by which the United States guaranteed the neutrality of the Isthmus and Colombia's sovereignty over it. The development of this preferential position was soon hampered by the conclusion of the Clayton-Bulwer Treaty of 1850 between the United States and Great Britain, which stipulated, among other things, that any interoceanic canal must be jointly built and owned by the two powers. Despite this handicap and the opposition of Colombia, the United States met with some success in the next few decades in asserting its claim to a special status in Panama. More important, the idea that it was entitled to such a status took firm root in the United States. Already by 1856 this country was pressing for a protectorate over a twenty-mile zone across the Isthmus, and while the Colombian government resisted this pretension successfully, it was obliged on several occasions before the close of the century to permit or even request American intervention to restore order in turbulent Panama. Colombia's main reliance for protection against the United States was the Clayton-Bulwer Treaty.

The driving force behind the diplomacy of Washington in this matter was generated partly by the desire of North American economic interests for a shorter route to Asia and the west coast of South America, but mainly by the expansion of the United States to the Pacific coast through the settlement of the Oregon boundary dispute with Great Britain in 1846 and the acquisition of California from Mexico in 1848. For political and military as well as economic reasons it was essential to improve communications between the new territories and the rest of the country. The difficulty and danger of overland travel made the sea voyage, with a land portage at Panama, one of the most popular routes for this purpose until the first transcontinental railroad was completed in 1869. By that time the feeling that the United States had a national interest in Panama had taken firm enough root to stand alone. Moreover, it was soon strengthened by the first stirrings of the expansionism that was to find full expression at the turn of the century. When the Panama canal company headed by the Frenchman Ferdinand de Lesseps, launched its project in 1879, President Hayes declared in a message to Congress that such a canal would be "virtually a part of the coast line of the United States" and that "the policy of this country is a canal under American control."

The other diplomatic highlight of this period was the War of the Pacific (1879–1883) between Chile on the one hand and Bolivia and Peru on the other. In the course of this war the United States lost prestige and gained enmity in both Chile and Peru by the "meddling and muddling" of Washington and by a bitter controversy that arose between its own ministers to Lima and Santiago, each of whom espoused the cause of the government to which he was accredited. Peruvians complained that the United States first encouraged them to resist and then let them down in the negotiations. Chileans charged that the American Secretary of State in 1881–1882, James G. Blaine, had an improper interest in Peruvian nitrate and guano beds, and the charge (though never proved) was repeated by Blaine's political enemies in the United States. By the Treaty of Ancón (1884) which ended the war, Chile made territorial acquisitions that cut Bolivia off from the Pacific and deprived Peru of its two southern provinces of Tacna and Arica. But the settlement was not definitive and in the 1920's the Tacna-Arica question provided the occasion for more meddling and muddling in Washington.

United States investments in the Bolivarian area amounted to only a trickle before 1900, but from the beginning of its independence American citizens played an important part in its foreign trade and in revolutionizing its means of transportation and communications by the introduction of steamship, railroad, telegraph, and cable. Although the process was slow and uneven, enough had been accomplished by the end of our first period (1889) to prepare all five countries for the much greater wave of foreign enterprise that has swept into them since then.

Pioneer contributions from the United States included the introduction of the river steamboat (on the Magdalena River in 1824, Lake Maracaibo in 1826, the Orinoco in 1849, and the Guayas River, Ecuador, in 1858); the telegraph (in Colombia, 1865, and in Bolivia and Ecuador two decades later); and the cable (on the Pacific coast north of Lima, in 1882). This cable, running from Chorrillos, just south of Lima, to Galveston, Texas, was backed by J. P. Morgan. British capital controlled the first two ocean steamship lines to this area (1840), one on the Caribbean coast, the other on the Pacific coast, but the latter was organized by William Wheelwright of Massachusetts.

Citizens of the United States also took a prominent part in the construction of the first railroads in the Bolivarian countries. Foremost among them was the up-state New Yorker Henry Meiggs, whose achievements in Peru are among the most remarkable in the annals of railroading in any part of the world. His greatest achievement was the building of the line from Lima up over the towering western range of the Andes to Oroya on the way to some of the richest agricultural and mining areas of Peru. Rising sharply to an altitude of nearly 16,000 feet through rugged and extremely difficult terrain, this is still the highest standard-gauge, direct-traction railroad in the world. It was a triumph of Yankee enterprise and engineering skill; but some years later it was acquired (and is still owned, along with most of the other railroads of Peru) by a British firm, the giant Peruvian Corporation.

3. BIG STICK OVER THE CARIBBEAN

The beginning of a new era in the relations of the United States with the Bolivarian countries and the rest of Latin America was marked by the First International Conference of American States, held at Washington in 1889–1890. For one thing, this conference ushered in the modern Pan-American movement and produced the inter-American system, whose multilateral agreements have been a conditioning factor of increasing importance in the United States' relations with the individual states of Latin America. More immediately important, however, was the fact that this conference also marked the emergence of a more ambitious and dynamic foreign policy in the United States, which was to attain full development a few years later under the leadership of such men as Theodore Roosevelt, Henry Cabot Lodge, Alfred Thayer Mahan, and Albert Shaw. The new policy was the product of many diverse factors, both domestic and foreign, such as the rise of the United States to great industrial power, the accumulation of surplus goods and capital for export, and the growth of the new imperialism of the great powers of Europe, one of whose most dramatic results was the partition of Africa at this time. In the United States the response to this latest wave of European expansion was partly defensive and partly imitative. On the one hand, Lodge was moved to write to Roosevelt in 1895, "We must not permit South America to become another Africa"; on the other, both of these men and many others besides thought the time had come for the United States to help Europe "carry the white man's burden" and to discharge the other obligations of its new status as a world power.

The "large policy" which developed under these circumstances contained two conflicting tendencies, one towards a more dynamic national policy, usually called imperialism; the other, towards international coöperation. A three-cornered conflict, involving these two new and divergent policies and the older stay-at-home isolationism, has run through the history of United States foreign policy ever since the decade of the 1890's.

Until World War I, dynamic nationalism was in the ascendant, and some of its most significant developments related to members of our Bolivarian group of states. The two members principally concerned were Colombia and Venezuela. This is not surprising, since both of them are major Caribbean states and this period was marked by the emergence of a distinct Caribbean or Panama policy at Washington. For it was now that substance was given to President Hayes's assertion of 1879 that Panama forms a part of the coast line of the United States.

To begin with, Venezuela furnished bold Cleveland with the occasion for his ringing reassertion of the Monroe Doctrine in 1895–1896. Though the United States was not a party to the long-standing dispute over the boundary between Venezuela and British Guiana, Cleveland intervened in it and insisted that Britain accept arbitration. His interposition was based squarely upon the Monroe Doctrine. The British Foreign Minister, Lord Salisbury, replied in effect that while the Monroe Doctrine might be all very well as a national policy of the United States, it had no standing in international law, and that therefore this dispute was no affair of the United States. Cleveland thereupon submitted the matter to Congress in a message that was widely regarded as a threat of war. In the face of this threat, and of simultaneous threats from France, Germany, and Russia in various parts of the globe, Britain yielded, agreed to arbitration, and in effect recognized the Monroe Doctrine.

This was one of the great turning points of modern history, for it marked the beginning of a reversal of the United States' relations with Britain and Russia, and of a power revolution in the Caribbean area. The Anglo-American rivalry of the past century and a quarter was henceforth supplanted by a kind of entente between the two powers. Partly for this reason, the traditional friendship between the United States and Russia, which had rested in large measure on common antagonism to Britain, gave way to mutual suspicion and a conflict of interest which was focused in eastern Asia. In the Caribbean, Britain's surrender of 1896 proved to be only the beginning of a process which within a decade converted that hitherto British-dominated sea into a primary defense zone of the United States.

Cleveland had won one of the greatest diplomatic victories in the history of the United States; but it was a victory for the United States and the Monroe Doctrine, not for Venezuela and Pan-Americanism. The fact that the arbitration resulted in the award of most of the disputed territory to Britain did not in the least diminish the luster of Cleveland's triumph, for he had made it unmistakably clear from the start that his purpose was not to get any particular territory for Venezuela but to force Britain to accept arbitration and recognize the Monroe Doctrine. In fact, his insistence on this point, together with the result of the arbitration, left the Venezuelan people with a feeling of resentment rather than gratitude towards the United States for its part in the affair. Moreover, the assertion in one of Secretary Olney's notes to Lord Salisbury that "the United States is practically sovereign on this continent, and its fiat is law" caused resentment and alarm in Venezuela and Latin America at large, for it was regarded as proof that the United States regarded its southern neighbors as inferiors, not as equals. Read in its context, the passage actually gave little ground for alarm, since, like the original Monroe Doctrine, the note was intended as a warning to Europe, not as a claim to hegemony over Latin America. Yet the fact remained that throughout this affair the United States acted alone, as sole guardian of the Hemisphere, and made no effort to obtain the coöperation or counsel of the other American states, although it had recently taken a leading part in initiating the modern Pan-American movement.

Colombia was the country mainly affected in the next few years by the advance of the United States and the retreat of Britain in the Caribbean. It was from this point of view that Colombians judged the Spanish-American War and its aftermath. To them, the fact that the United States had aided Cuba in winning its independence from Spain was less significant than that the United States had annexed Puerto Rico, acquired a naval base at Guantánamo Bay in Cuba, and established a protectorate over the Cuban republic by the Platt Amendment. While these advances into the Caribbean were taking place, the United States in 1899 reached out on the other side of Colombia for Ecuador's Galápagos Islands in the Pacific, but was rebuffed by the government at Quito. In 1902, however, the United States took another forward step that was highly distasteful to Colombia, for in February of that year it concluded with Great Britain the Hay-Pauncefote Treaty by which the latter surrendered its right under the Clayton-Bulwer Treaty of 1850 to share in the building and control of the projected Isthmian Canal. The treaty of 1850 had been Colombia's main reliance for the protection of its interests in Panama, and uneasiness over its abrogation was all the greater because of the insistence of the United States in the course of the negotiation that Britain recognize this country's right to acquire sovereignty over the canal site and to fortify and defend it. This was done by clear implication in the treaty of 1902.

Once the British obstacle was removed, the government at Washington, now headed by Theodore Roosevelt, pushed vigorously for the conclusion of a canal treaty with Colombia. The painful sequel—the high-handed "taking of Panama" late in 1903 when Colombia did not move fast enough to suit the Rough Rider in the White House—is described in detail in another volume of this series. It was an intricate story of high finance and *haute politique*, complicated by a bitter contest in the United States between the adherents of the Panama route and the rival Nicaragua route, and by a civil war in Colombia which lasted until June 1903. The break came when the Colombian Congress refused to ratify a canal treaty that its representative had signed after a long negotiation in Washington. A rebellion broke out in Panama and the United States first assured its success by preventing Colombia from sending troops to the area by sea (they could not reach it by land) and then hastily recognized the new Republic of Panama and concluded a canal treaty with it.

While the United States was guilty of a shocking abuse of power and Colombia was not entirely blameless, both governments probably acted as they did not so much from ill will as from ignorance. Indeed, this episode deserves to be remembered as a striking instance of the disastrous consequences of ignorance in the conduct of foreign affairs. On the one hand, misinformation or lack of information about the state of opinion in the United States and Panama betrayed many of the men in authority at Bogotá into grossly underestimating the gravity of the situation. As a result, members of both the administration and the opposition made the fatal mistake of faulty timing. Both acted as if they were dealing with a normal situation, not with an emergency. Hence the slowness of the administration in negotiating the treaty, which profoundly irritated both the United States and Panama; hence also the irresponsible sniping of the Colombian opposition at its own government, which contributed to the rejection of the treaty and thus precipitated the revolution in Panama. Legally, both the government and the opposition in Colombia were well within their rights at every stage of this affair; but the ill-advised uses which they made of their rights added up to obstructionism. Their misinformation in turn was a function of the remoteness of Bogotá and its inadequate communications with the outside world; it was then one of the most inaccessible capitals in the Western Hemisphere.

Similarly, while Washington was in close and constant contact with many parts of the world, Colombia was a blind spot to the three American statesmen who had this matter in hand at the most critical stage—President Roosevelt, Secretary of State Hay, and State Department Counselor John Bassett Moore. President Roosevelt, who was personally responsible for his government's course and later boasted publicly that it was he who took Panama, was crassly ignorant of the people with whom he was dealing. The authorities at Bogotá, among whom were men who at least equaled him in culture and integrity, were described by him as a gang of bandits, and he lumped them together with all other Latin Americans under the designation of "ridiculous little Dagoes." If he had more than a rudimentary knowledge of the geography, government, or history of Colombia, he never gave any evidence of the fact. His Anglophile Secretary of State, John Hay, was no help to him in this matter, and his legalistic counselor in the State Department, John Bassett Moore, was worse than useless. His Secretary of War (and, from 1905 to 1909, Secretary of State), Elihu Root, might have helped, for Root was one of the principal precursors of those who developed the Good-Neighbor policy; but he was not consulted at the most critical stage of the affair. In any case, even Root never succeeded in making a dent in the racial prepossessions of his chief, who was a firm believer in Anglo-Saxon superiority over all other races, particularly the "decadent" Latins and "mongrel breeds" south of the Rio Grande.

The aftermath of the Panama affair of 1903, in so far as the Bolivarian states are concerned, may be considered under two aspects. In the first place, the building of the canal (which was opened to traffic in 1914) led to a great increase in the economic or military importance, or both, of all five countries to the United States. A great impulse was given to its commerce with the west coast of South America, and investments were built up along with trade. As a result, the United States became for the first time an important economic factor not only in Ecuador, Peru, and Bolivia, but also in southwestern Colombia, whose rich upper Cauca Valley, almost inaccessible from the Caribbean before the air age, has its main outlet at Buenaventura on the Pacific. Venezuela was less directly affected by the opening of the Canal, but its long coast line along the eastern sea approaches to Panama now acquired great military importance for the United States. More recently the development of military aviation has brought Venezuela, Colombia, and Ecuador within the primary defense zone of the Canal.

In the second place, while the taking of Panama naturally embittered the Colombian people against the United States, the diplomatic settlement of the controversy finally arrived at in 1921 actually led to a further extension of the economic influence of the United States in Colombia. The first important effort to reach a settlement was made under Woodrow Wilson, who sought eagerly but not very successfully to reverse the rising tide of Yankeephobia in Latin America. Realizing that one of the first and most essential steps for this purpose was to right the wrong done to Colombia in 1903, Wilson promptly (1914) negotiated a treaty with the government of that country in which the United States expressed its "sincere regret" for its course in 1903 and agreed to pay $25 million damages to Colombia, and the latter obligated itself to recognize the independence of Panama. Violently opposed by former President Roosevelt and his Senatorial friend, Henry Cabot Lodge, the treaty failed of ratification.

After the Republican return to power, Secretary of State

Hughes renewed the effort to promote better relations with Latin America; the key importance for this purpose of a settlement with Colombia was again recognized; and the treaty of 1914 was fished out of the files, revised by the deletion of the "sincere regrets" clause, and duly ratified by both governments (1921). This happy consummation followed the acquisition of extensive oil concessions in Colombia by Standard Oil of New Jersey and other United States interests in 1916, and was in turn followed by more sympathetic treatment of these interests by the Colombian government. In 1925 Gulf Refining, a Mellon company, bought into this field. "Dollar Diplomacy," which is popularly identified with the Taft administration (1909–1913), actually reached its apogee under the Harding and Coolidge administrations in the 1920's; and the settlement of the Panama question with Colombia in 1921 provided one of the first and most conspicuous illustrations of its workings.

Another of the Bolivarian countries, Venezuela, had already played a leading part in the development of another expression of Yankee imperialism—the Roosevelt Corollary to the Monroe Doctrine (1904–1905), which claimed for the United States an "international police power" in the Western Hemisphere and the right to intervene unilaterally and at its own discretion in the Latin-American countries. The United States publicly disavowed the Corollary in 1930, surrendered the right of intervention on any ground in 1936, and did not at any time in this period exercise the right in any of the Bolivarian countries. We shall therefore confine our attention to its origins in the crisis of 1902–1904 in the foreign relations of Venezuela.

In 1902 Cipriano Castro, prodigal and unscrupulous dictator of Venezuela, provoked Germany, Great Britain, and Italy to intervention in his country by his long course of defaults and denial of justice to their nationals in the courts of Venezuela. Remembering Cleveland's strong stand only a few years earlier in this same country's dispute with Britain, the European governments first obtained Roosevelt's assent.

This was given in view of the fact that intervention in such a case was sanctioned by international law, though Roosevelt stipulated that there must be no permanent occupation of Venezuelan territory. But the intervention led to violence and bloodshed, highlighted by the bombardment of Puerto Cabello, Venezuela, by British and German warships, which called forth indignant protests in the United States and Latin America. Roosevelt then swung his support to a request from Castro for arbitration, which was finally agreed to. The question whether the intervening powers should be granted priority over Venezuela's other creditors was referred to the new Hague Tribunal.

The most notable of the Latin-American protests against this intervention was contained in a note from the Argentine Foreign Minister, Luis F. Drago, setting forth what came to be known as the Drago Doctrine. Proposed as an economic corollary to the Monroe Doctrine, the Drago Doctrine was designed to prevent further intervention in America by European powers in support of pecuniary claims. Using Venezuela as an example, Drago pointed out the growing danger that such interventions would serve as a screen behind which the new economic imperialism of Europe would undermine the independence of the American states. His note received only a noncommittal acknowledgment in Washington. In 1904, however, the Hague Tribunal aggravated the danger by deciding the question of priority of claims against Venezuela in favor of the intervening powers. In effect, the Tribunal's decision not only endorsed armed intervention but put a premium on prompt resort to it. Roosevelt and Elihu Root, then Secretary of State, thereupon came around to Drago's view that a new policy must be adopted to meet this new type of European threat; but they still did not adopt his formula of barring all intervention.

Instead, they adopted a formula already suggested by Britain, which barred intervention in America by European powers, but claimed a general right of intervention in America for the United States. This was the Roosevelt Corollary, which was first stated in 1904 and amplified in 1905. At the outset the Corollary was a purely protective measure, designed to protect America against Europe; and the European power against which it was principally aimed was Germany, concerning whose designs in America Roosevelt had become suspicious since the beginning of the Venezuelan crisis in 1902. These designs gained added importance from the fact that by 1904 the United States had begun construction of the Panama Canal.

A highly modified version of the Drago Doctrine was embodied in a Convention adopted by the Hague Conference of 1907, in which most of the Latin-American governments took part. Only six of them ratified the convention, however, for it still left the door open to intervention in cases of denial of justice. Not a single member of our Bolivarian group was among the ratifying states.

Only two other events prior to the outbreak of World War I require notice here. One was the circulation of the Pérez Triana Memorandum; the other, the meeting of a Bolivarian Congress at Caracas. Both occurred in 1912 and both illustrate the defensive reaction of the Bolivarian countries against the expanding power of the United States. The Pérez Triana Memorandum, named for its author, the Colombian Minister in London, and addressed to all the American governments, proposed the extension of the principle of the Monroe Doctrine to inter-American relations by the proscription of territorial conquest by any American state. A score of years later the United States was to take the lead in establishing this rule not only for America but for the world at large; but under the circumstances of 1912 its anti-Yankee bias seemed so obvious that the diplomatic representatives of the United States in Latin America were instructed to "belittle" the proposal if it should be brought up by the governments to which they were accredited.

4. HISPANICISM AND WILSONISM

The Bolivarian Congress held at Caracas, Bolívar's native city, in 1912, had a similar bias, though it was less obvious and less dominant. Attended by the representatives of Venezuela, Colombia, Peru, and Ecuador, the Congress was in a sense merely a revival of the nineteenth-century tradition of solidarity among these countries. One of the main reasons for its revival at this time, however, was their growing uneasiness over the rapid strides the United States was making towards preponderance in the Caribbean area and northern South America, the simultaneous withering away of the British counterpoise, and the lack of any prospect that a new check on the ambition of the Colossus of the North would be supplied from any other source. The Congress confined itself largely to the celebration of the centenary of independence and to adopting resolutions in favor of closer cultural and commercial relations among the Bolivarian countries. Bolivia was not represented. Its ties with the northern members of the group were very tenuous. For example, the first Minister from Colombia was not sent to La Paz until 1911.

The Caracas Congress was essentially an expression of the native Bolivarian tradition, but this in turn was now being modified and stimulated by the Pan-Hispanic movement, which had its fountainhead in Spain. Originating in the 1880's and led since about 1900 by the talented Spanish historian and jurist Rafael Altamira, this movement had by 1912 produced an appreciable effect upon various Latin-American countries, including those in the Bolivarian group. Mainly cultural and commercial in its avowed purposes, the movement was aimed at the reconciliation of the mother country and her estranged children, the former colonies, and at the spiritual reintegration of the Spanish "race" in all parts of the world. Political motives were not often avowed, but the movement nevertheless had considerable political significance, particularly for the United States. Sometimes Pan-Hispanic leaders sought to advance their own cause by feeding Latin-American fear of the Colossus of the North, not merely as a land-grabber and economic exploiter but also as a materialistic Caliban threatening to destroy the more spiritual culture of the Hispanic Ariel. The emphasis which they laid upon the Spanish, rather than the more broadly European, origin of Latin-American culture tended to build up a feeling of antagonism towards the "Anglo-Saxon" United States.

Ideas of this kind were propagated not only by books, magazines, and occasional visiting lecturers from Spain and by individual sympathizers in America, but also by permanent institutions such as the *Academias de la Lengua* (Academies of the Spanish Language) which were set up in all the Spanish-American countries, beginning in the 1880's, as branches of the *Academia de la Lengua* in Madrid. Some of these American branches, notably the one in Lima, played an important role in the cultural life of their respective countries. Even when the movement did not create better feeling towards Spain, it fostered a sense of the unity of Spanish America and of its difference from Anglo-Saxon America. This climate of opinion stimulated international coöperation among the Spanish-American nations. Ideally, this should have included all of them; actually, for practical reasons, it was confined largely to small groups of neighboring states. A good example of the latter phase is the Bolivarian Congress held at Caracas in 1912.

Viewed in this light, the Bolivarian movement presents us with a paradox. The movement had originated in the wars of independence against Spain, yet it now owed much of its strength to propaganda proceeding from Spain itself. And the United States, which a century earlier had seemed to many people in the Bolivarian area a natural ally of their embryonic states, was now the principal nation against whom they felt it necessary to unite in defense of their culture and perhaps of their independence as well. The feeling was strongest in those members of the group—Colombia and Venezuela—that were closest to the Colossus.

Between Woodrow Wilson's first inauguration in 1913 and the entry of the United States into World War I, his efforts to improve the relations of the United States with Latin America were unproductive so far as the Bolivarian countries were concerned. As already noted, his principal effort, the treaty of 1914 with Colombia, failed for lack of approval by the United States Senate. Another effort—his acceptance of the mediation of Argentina, Brazil, and Chile in the Vera Cruz incident with Mexico—gave offense to Peru, which was jealous of the ABC powers; and Bolivia was the only Bolivarian country included in the Latin-American group that advised the United States regarding the recognition of the Carranza regime in Mexico. It was again to the ABC powers alone that Wilson turned for advice in drafting his projected Pan-American Pact of 1916. Not one of the Bolivarian countries was consulted about it, and one of the main reasons why it failed of adoption was the existence of an old and thorny dispute to which one of these countries was a party—the Tacna-Arica controversy between Peru and Chile. About all Wilson had to show for his efforts in our group down to 1917 was the conclusion of Secretary Bryan's "cooling off" treaties with Bolivia, Ecuador, and Peru; Colombia did not sign, and Venezuela signed but did not ratify.

The only favorable development of lasting importance in this period was due not to anything said or done at Washington, but to developments in South American power politics. Offended at its exclusion from the ABC group and fearing that Chile might be actively supported by the other members of the group in the Tacna-Arica controversy, the government of Peru decided to protect itself by cultivating friendly relations with the United States. It adhered to this policy for many years—to the advantage of the United States during World War I, but not to its own advantage either then or later on.

5. WORLD WAR I AND THE LEAGUE

Throughout this war the Bolivarian countries remained neutral, though all of them in varying degrees adopted a benevolent attitude towards the Allies. The degree was greatest in the three that had been least affected by the new dynamic policy of the United States since the turn of the century—that is to say, in Ecuador, Peru, and Bolivia. After the United States entered the war, the governments of these three countries severed relations with the Central Powers and gave some aid (though it was far short of war) to the Allies. Thus in 1918 Peru seized ten German merchant vessels in her waters and leased them to the Emergency Fleet Corporation of the United States. Even Colombia and Venezuela, though they never broke with the Central Powers, permitted armed merchantmen under the United States flag to trade freely in their ports, as did also Ecuador, Peru, and other Latin-American countries. Also, Colombia and Venezuela, alone of all the Latin-American states, did not accept the Argentine government's invitation to attend a conference of neutrals in the spring of 1917, a conference which—naturally, under the circumstances—was viewed with disfavor in Washington.

Though circumstances varied with each country, in every case benevolence towards the Allied cause seems to have been due to sympathy not so much for the United States as for the European Allies, Britain, Belgium, Italy, and, above all, France. And where sympathy was lacking, its place was supplied by economic pressure exerted through the control of the high seas which was maintained throughout the war by the Allies, with the aid of the United States after 1917. The two major weapons of economic warfare employed by the United States were bunker control and the black list. Bunkers of coal and ships' supplies were used as a means of forcing neutral as well as allied ships to operate under the regulations prescribed by the War Trade Board of the United States. Important bunker controls in our area were set up at Curaçao, three Venezuelan ports (La Guaira, Puerto Cabello, and Maracaibo), and the Panama Canal Zone. This system proved highly effective; for example, as Thomas A. Bailey has pointed out, it gave United States authorities "complete control over certain Chilean and Peruvian lines that had been operating in the service of a German-owned sugar plantation in Peru."

Three comprehensive black lists (enemy trading lists) were issued by the United States in 1917–18. The first list related only to Latin America, which also bulked large in the second and third lists. This weapon was used much more sparingly then than in World War II, for the lists were much shorter and included only enemy firms, or firms directly aiding the enemy. For example, even newspapers that openly favored the German cause were not to be included unless they received support from Germany. In the light of these facts it appears that the Central Powers were well represented in our group of states in proportion to their population. Thus, in the first list, Bolivia and Venezuela stood fifth and sixth, respectively, among the twenty Latin-American states; and in the final list, all five Bolivarian countries were in the upper half, Bolivia still ranking fifth, Peru sixth, Venezuela and Ecuador in a tie for seventh place, and

Colombia tenth. This partly explains why the United States' cable censorship was applied with special rigor to South America. The black list was disliked in all the Latin-American countries, but friction over it was reduced by the practice, begun early in 1918, of consulting the governments concerned regarding additions to the list and deletions from it. None of the Latin-American governments registered an official protest at Washington against its basic principles.

Though on a far smaller scale than in World War II, a United States propaganda service was set up in Latin America in 1917–18 by the Committee on Public Information, commonly called the Creel Committee, for its chairman, journalist George Creel. The efforts of this committee in Latin America, which have been described by James R. Mock, were concentrated mainly on Mexico and the ABC countries, but it also engaged in some interesting activities in the Bolivarian group, particularly Colombia and Peru. In the latter country, the Committee employed a propagandist formerly in the service of the local British Patriotic League. For the soberer journals he provided pictures showing the industrial power of the United States (not battle scenes, with which the British and French had already surfeited the Peruvian public), and a daily 200-word cable dispatch from Washington or New York, which was translated into Spanish in the American Legation at Lima. For the popular periodicals he supplied photographs of glamour girls of stage and screen, hoping that these would "act as a sugar-plum in securing the publication of more substantial and informative material." The Committee's agent in Colombia, confronted at the outset by a "cold and neutral" metropolitan press in the national capital, was able to thaw it out by applying a technique formerly used with great success in South Carolina by Senator "Pitchfork Ben" Tillman. As Tillman had systematically started waves of support in the rural districts to overcome resistance in Charleston, the Committee's agent now made it a practice to feed his information service first to the provincial press of Colombia. Since the service was free, extensive use was made of it, with the result that the Bogotá editors soon saw what they took to be a tidal wave of anti-German sentiment sweeping over the country. Some of them, wrote the agent, "thereupon promptly came out on our side, and have been with us ever since."

During the long armistice from the Treaty of Versailles in 1919 to the outbreak of war in Europe in 1939, relations between the United States and the Bolivarian countries were marked by two opposite trends: in the economic field, towards a great strengthening of the relations of each of them with the United States on a bilateral basis; in the political field, towards the increasing use of multilateral procedures and agencies. Some of the more significant details of the economic story will be told below; here we need only note that this period saw a great expansion of United States trade and investment in the Bolivarian area and that little success attended the efforts of the United States to check the rising world tide of nationalism in foreign trade, as represented by British and German policy—the Ottawa system of imperial preference, the Roca-Runciman agreement between Britain and Argentina, and the numerous barter arrangements made by Germany with various countries, including some in our group. In 1930 the United States itself contributed notably to the rise of this tide by the Hawley-Smoot Tariff. In 1934 it reversed its economic foreign policy and adopted the Trade Agreement system. Up to the outbreak of war in 1939, however, this system had done little to correct the situation in the Bolivarian group. Colombia (1936) and Ecuador (1938) were the only members of the group with which Trade Agreements had been concluded by that time.

The increasing resort of the United States to multilateral action in political matters was in part the result of a change in the world climate of opinion which even the so-called "isolationist" administrations of Harding and Coolidge could not have ignored if they had wanted to. More particularly, in our area it resulted from the establishment of the League of Nations, which won enthusiastic support in Latin America and offered the United States a new kind of competition there. The competition was not direct, for far from challenging the United States or its inter-American system, the League showed a meticulous consideration for the susceptibilities of Washington. But the League did provide a forum for the international discussion of political questions, whereas hitherto—thanks mainly to Washington—such questions had been banned in inter-American conferences. The League not only discussed; in the first fifteen years of its life it also acted. And some of the most important posts in it were held by Latin Americans. Moreover, the League was widely regarded in Latin America as a welcome escape from the Pan-American system and, because of its guarantee of the independence and territorial integrity of its members, as a possible protection against Yankee imperialism.

As a result, while membership and interest fluctuated from year to year, all the Latin-American states were members of the League at some time between 1920 and the beginning of its disintegration after the Ethiopian fiasco of 1935, and nearly all of them were members of it at any given time. Except for Ecuador, which was late in joining, the Bolivarian states maintained their membership throughout this period; though Peru and Bolivia were inactive for several years after they were disappointed in their effort to have the Tacna-Arica question reopened by the League. The group was well rewarded for its fidelity. Three of the countries—Venezuela, Colombia, and Peru—were elected to seats on the League Council (first a six-man, then a nine-man body), and a Colombian, Francisco José Urrutia, was chosen president of the League Assembly for a term.

While the League thus set the pace for the United States, there were also changes in this country itself. For one thing, its expansionist urge had achieved the desired goals in the Caribbean, and the main thing now was to develop the ground gained, rather than to push further on. Above all, what Washington wanted in the 1920's was to smooth the path for investments and business enterprise, and it had learned by experience that, in Latin America as elsewhere, honey catches more flies than vinegar. Also, in the United States itself as well as in Latin America, there was growing opposition to the whole pattern of conduct—a unilateral pattern—traced by the Big Stick of the first Roosevelt, Taft's Dollar Diplomacy, and the well-intentioned but misguided interventionism of Wilson. Already in 1928 Franklin Roosevelt, still five years away from his first term in the White House, was saying that "single-handed intervention by us in the internal affairs of other nations must end" and that the United States must learn to "associate itself with other American Republics" in joint study of common problems—and in joint action.

6. THREE BOLIVARIAN DISPUTES

This new view did not reach its full development until Roosevelt himself was in the White House, but it had already begun to give a new orientation to policy in the preceding administration. The change was expressed to a large extent in a more energetic cultivation of the inter-American system, with the result that the history of an important part of the relations of the United States with the Bolivarian countries in the long armistice belongs to the general history of the regional system in that period. That is a story which cannot be told here, for our concern is with problems of more direct and special interest to the Bolivarian states. Three such problems in the political field require our attention:

the Tacna-Arica question, involving Peru, Bolivia, and Chile; the Chaco War between Bolivia and Paraguay; and the Leticia controversy between Colombia and Peru.

First, let us glance briefly at some important changes in the bilateral relations of the United States with the members of the Bolivarian group, for these relations were still of great importance despite the increasing trend towards multilateral action. The most conspicuous changes were a great improvement in relations between the United States and aggrieved Colombia, the consequent decline in the enthusiasm of the Peruvian government for coöperation with Washington, and the rapid spread of American business enterprise in all five countries.

The improvement of relations with Colombia was one of the main objectives of United States policy after World War I. The most important reasons were strategic and economic. Something has already been said about the economic reasons, particularly with reference to oil. It need only be added that Colombia's proximity and rich natural resources made it attractive to other American business interests as well in the decade of great overseas expansion that followed this war. Strategically, too, Colombia had become even more important than before 1914 in relation to the defense of the Panama Canal, for the war had made it clear that air power would play a leading role in the next conflict.

Accordingly, the newly restored Republican administration in Washington took two important steps. One was the conclusion of the Treaty of 1921 which, as already noted, wrote the diplomatic finis to the Panama question. The other step was the support that Washington gave Bogotá in reaching a satisfactory solution of its long-standing boundary dispute with Peru in the Amazon basin. This dispute was settled by the Salomón-Lozano Treaty between those two countries, which was signed in 1922, but which encountered such strong opposition in Peru that it was not finally ratified and executed until 1928. The opposition was due mainly to the fact that the treaty gave Colombia title to a wide corridor stretching southward from the Putumayo River to the Amazon and forming a salient in Peruvian territory. According to the view held strongly and almost universally in Peru, Colombia had no just claim whatever to any territory on the Amazon.

Why, then, did the Peruvian government sign this treaty and, though tardily, carry it out? The answer to this question explains why Lima began to eye Washington askance at this time. As Lima saw it, Uncle Sam was the villain of the piece. The leading Peruvian authority on the subject, Alberto Ulloa, maintains that Washington sacrificed its too obliging Peruvian friends in order to forward its reconciliation with Colombia, compensating the latter for the loss of Panama by helping it to a slice of Peruvian territory in Amazonia; and that Peru consented to the sacrifice because it was governed by a dictator, Augusto B. Leguía, who depended upon United States loans to carry out his ambitious plans for the development of Peru, and who was therefore highly responsive to pressure from Washington. This pressure, says our authority, also explains why Brazil, which at first protested against the treaty as prejudicial to its own rights in Amazonia, later came to terms with Colombia and withdrew its protest, thus depriving Peru of its only important foreign support and making the completion of the sacrifice unavoidable. The agreement between Brazil and Colombia was signed on March 4, 1925.

Worse still, on the very same day President Coolidge, as arbitrator of the Tacna-Arica controversy, handed down an award which Peruvians regarded (and still regard) as flagrantly unjust. To them, its most offensive feature was the stipulation that the question should be settled by a plebiscite, as provided in the Treaty of Ancón (1884), though the territory had been under Chilean administration through all these forty-odd years and it was therefore almost a foregone conclusion that Chile would win the plebiscite. The news of the award provoked violent demonstrations against the United States in Lima, and the Peruvian government filed a formal protest against the award. Unmoved by the protest, President Coolidge sent a plebiscite commission to the area. Its authority, however, was flouted by the Chileans in control, and it soon withdrew (1926). This fiasco gave a further blow to the prestige of the United States in Peru and elsewhere.

Ultimately, after many solutions had been proposed and rejected, the question was settled in June 1929 by direct negotiation between Chile and Peru, the former keeping Arica and the latter recovering Tacna, together with the free use of the port of Arica. This formula had been suggested by President-elect Hoover on his South American tour early in 1929, and he is therefore often given the credit for settling this dangerous dispute. Actually, the very same formula had been proposed before, only to be rejected by Peru; and the latter now accepted it because of fear arising from the conduct of the United States on two recent occasions. The first occasion was the failure of the United States to react positively against Chilean disrespect for its plebiscite commission. This convinced the Peruvians that there was no basis for their long-standing hope that a third power could somehow be induced to intervene in their favor. The second occasion was Secretary of State Kellogg's proposal (November 1926) that the dispute be settled by giving both Tacna and Arica to Bolivia—a proposal which was accepted unconditionally by Bolivia and in principle by Chile. This was a warning to Peru that further insistence upon recovering both provinces might only result in failure to get any part of either of them.

Peru was therefore in a mood for compromise and welcomed the resumption of diplomatic relations with Chile,

which took place in October 1928, after an interruption lasting seventeen years. The natural sequel was the accord
reached by the two countries in June 1929. Under the circumstances, it is hardly surprising that Peruvians feel little
gratitude to President Hoover or his government for their
part in this long-drawn-out affair.

The definitive settlement of the Tacna-Arica question
closed the door to Peruvian and Bolivian aspirations on the
Pacific. Both countries thereupon started a *drang nach Osten*
which embroiled them in fresh conflicts with their neighbors, Peru with Colombia and Ecuador in the upper Amazon
basin, and Bolivia with Paraguay in the upper Plata basin.
Again the United States was drawn into the efforts to find a
peaceful solution. By this time, however, Washington had
learned that while multilateral peacemaking diffuses the glory
of success, it also cuts the liabilities in case of failure.

In 1930 a revolution in Peru overthrew President Leguía,
whom his fellow countrymen held personally responsible for
the hated treaty of 1922 with Colombia. On September 1,
1932, a group of Peruvians seized Leticia, on the Amazon,
the only town of any size in the territory gained by Colombia through that treaty. This barefaced aggression was apparently the act not of the government at Lima but of an unruly
band of "frontiersmen" in the remote Amazonian province
of Loreto, bordering on Leticia. Nevertheless, the new Peruvian president, General Sánchez Cerro, created the impression that their aggression had been inspired by him. He not
only refused to dislodge the Peruvian filibusters, but demanded that the question of the 1922 settlement be reopened,
and backed up his demand by sending warships and other
reinforcements to the upper Amazon by way of the Panama
Canal. As a matter of equity, Peru had some ground for
complaint, for Leticia, perched on the southernmost fringe
of the almost uninhabited Colombian territory of Amazonas
(2200 inhabitants in 48,000 square miles), served mainly as

a means of harassing Peruvian commerce on the Amazon and of carrying on contraband trade with the much more populous Peruvian province of Loreto across and up the Amazon (population 150,000 in 119,000 square miles). But legally Peru's case was untenable, and one of its warmest latter-day apologists could find little to say in its defense except that it was not as bad as Hitler's seizure of the Sudetenland.

The United States won further unpopularity at Lima by openly condemning Peru's course in this affair and by refusing to provide supplies for the Peruvian expeditionary force as it passed through the Panama Canal. But Washington was far from making any effort to settle the controversy alone or even to keep the settlement of it within the Hemisphere. Secretary of State Stimson encouraged the League of Nations to handle the case, and, when it did so, the United States agreed to join with Brazil and Spain in administering the territory pending final settlement.

The situation was eased when the bellicose Sánchez Cerro was assassinated (by one of his fellow countrymen), and the way for a peaceful settlement was paved by a dramatic peace gesture made by Alfonso López of Colombia. Heir apparent to the presidency of that country, he flew to Lima to talk things over with the new Peruvian president, Oscar Benavides, with whom he had formed a friendship in London when the two were there on diplomatic missions. This set the stage for a successful though tedious negotiation which took place in Rio de Janeiro and was concluded in 1934. Peru expressed regrets and Colombia kept Leticia.

Balked in this direction too, Peru next undertook a vigorous prosecution of its claims in the area in dispute with Ecuador. The sequel—border conflicts leading to the undeclared war of 1941 and the diplomatic victory of Peru at Rio de Janeiro in 1942—has already been described in an earlier chapter.

The new trend in United States policy after World War I

was also illustrated by the history of the Chaco conflict, in which three of the Bolivarian states were directly concerned, one—Bolivia—as belligerent, and two—Peru and Colombia—as would-be peacemakers. The story of the international efforts to find a peaceful solution is long and intricate, extending from 1929 to 1938 and involving several American agencies and the League of Nations as well, and only a sketch of those aspects of it which are germane to the subject of the present volume can be given here.

Like most other boundary disputes in Latin America, the Chaco controversy between Bolivia and Paraguay dated back to the colonial period; but it developed into a major crisis only after the Pacific door was shut in Bolivia's face by the resumption of diplomatic relations between Peru and Chile in 1928 and the final settlement of the Tacna-Arica question by their treaty of 1929. Bolivia still had the free use of the port of Arica, and of the railroad from La Paz to Arica, under its treaty of 1904 with Chile, but Bolivian pride and interest demanded a direct outlet through national territory. Such an outlet could be obtained by pushing to the limit Bolivia's claims in the Chaco, which, although very sparsely settled, lay along the navigable Pilcomayo River, a branch of the great Plata system, and was believed to be rich in oil. If the assertion of its claim should lead to war, Bolivia could reasonably hope to win. Its population (3 million in 1930) was three times as large as that of Paraguay, and since 1920 its army had been trained by German officers, among them General Kundt and the subsequently notorious Nazi leader Ernst Roehm. Paraguay was no less bellicose than Bolivia. Border incidents multiplied after 1929, and from 1932 to 1935 these two little countries fought one of the bloodiest wars in the history of Latin America.

The efforts at international pacification began in 1929 at the Inter-American Conference on Conciliation and Arbitration, then in session at Washington, and the United States,

Colombia, and Peru took an important part in them. The conference appointed a Commission of Neutrals to settle the dispute; two of its five members were the United States and Colombia. Its principal achievement was the initiation of the declaration of August 3, 1932, adopted by nineteen American states (all except Bolivia and Paraguay), which embodied the "Stimson Doctrine" of nonrecognition of territorial conquests and applied it specifically to the Chaco conflict. This was done at the request of Secretary Stimson himself; before making it, he had consulted four Latin-American governments, one of which was Peru.

Meanwhile, Argentina had organized a rival commission of four neutrals, and Peru was again distinguished by inclusion in the group. When neither American commission made any headway, the dispute was taken to the League of Nations. At first, the United States discouraged the League's intervention, but this stand was reversed by Secretary Stimson shortly before he went out of office in 1933. The League's efforts also failed, however, and the war raged on until both belligerents were bled white. Bolivia suffered even more than Paraguay, partly because its soldiers, accustomed to life in the high, cold Andes, were unable to endure the humid heat of the low-lying Chaco.

In 1935 an armistice was at last arranged by still another commission of American neutrals, headed by Argentina and including, among others, the United States and Peru. These two countries also shared in arranging the final peace settlement and fixing the boundary line (1938). Spruille Braden, representing the United States, took an important part in these negotiations. He did his work well, but naturally Bolivia, the loser, was not pleased.

Pronounced anti-United States feeling developed in that country and was partly responsible for its government's expropriation in 1937 of the properties of the Standard Oil Company, which had been accused of fomenting the war with Paraguay. The Bolivian government's action, which was taken under circumstances that seem to justify Samuel Flagg Bemis' description of it as "particularly heinous," came after Standard Oil had "invested $17,000,000 in developing a concession for which it had contracted in good faith" in 1922. This expropriation preceded by one year the much better known expropriation of foreign oil properties by the Mexican government.

By 1939 the political relations of the United States with the Bolivarian countries had thus become enmeshed with two international organizations, the League of Nations and the inter-American system. But because of the loose-jointed structure of the latter and the decline of the former after 1935, these relations still rested mainly on a bilateral basis and consequently varied considerably from country to country. Although in 1939 more or less resentment still lingered in Colombia, Peru, and Bolivia because of the conduct of the United States in relation to Panama, Leticia, and the Chaco, no major issues were outstanding with any of the five countries at this time.

Since 1933 the Good-Neighbor policy had improved relations with all of the countries in our group except possibly Ecuador, where the political situation in the 1920's and 1930's was so utterly chaotic that no generalization about its foreign policy is possible. Even Bolivia's expropriation of Standard Oil did not create a major issue, for under the Good-Neighbor policy the United States gave little support to the pecuniary claims of its citizens in Latin America. In this case, so far as the records show, it did not even request arbitration.

The greatest improvement had taken place in the cases of Venezuela and Colombia. With a flood tide of royalties pouring into the national treasury from oil companies largely controlled by United States capital, Venezuela seemed very well disposed. The reconciliation with Colombia, begun in the 1920's, was strengthened in the following decade by the political affinity between the New Deal administration in the United States and the Liberal party in Colombia, which gained control of the government of that country in 1930 and kept it uninterruptedly until 1946.

7. U. S. ECONOMIC EXPANSION

Among the major potential sources of discord in 1939 were the spread of European totalitarian doctrines and the brand of Hispanicism promoted by the Franco regime in Spain, of which we have already spoken. Another major source was the dichotomy that sometimes existed between the policy of the United States government and the conduct of American business interests in the Bolivarian countries.

The half century ending in 1939 was characterized by the rapid growth of these business interests and by the increasing concentration of control over them in the hands of a few large firms. Their range was broad but not all-inclusive, and it was somewhat narrowed, especially after 1929, by the adoption of national planning and the extension of government control in the Bolivarian area. They were concerned mainly with mineral production (including oil), agriculture, commerce, shipping, and airways. They included to a much smaller degree manufacturing, which was frequently financed by local capital; railroads, which (as of 1939) were largely owned either by British stockholders or the several governments; and public utilities, which also were passing under public ownership.

The activities of United States citizens in the field of transportation and communications were important long before 1890, as already noted, but it was not until after that date that they became leaders in maritime shipping. The United Fruit Company (Colombia and Central America) and W. R. Grace and Company (Venezuela, Colombia, and the West Coast of South America) rose to the front rank in this field, and both engaged in other activities as well. United Fruit owned and operated banana plantations, and Grace built up a veritable economic empire. In Venezuela, Colombia, and Ecuador the pioneer telephone systems installed by American citizens about 1885 later passed under British control, but in 1930 the International Telephone and Telegraph Corporation, backed by J. P. Morgan, acquired a dominant position in Peru.

Mineral production was a favorite field of American enterprise in this period and produced some of the largest industrial giants of the Bolivarian area. Notable among these are the Cerro de Pasco Copper Corporation, organized in Peru in 1906, and three oil companies, organized since World War I: the Creole Petroleum Corporation, Venezuela; the Tropical Oil Company, Colombia; and the International Petroleum Corporation, Peru. The Cerro de Pasco Corporation produced copper in an area that up to 1898 had produced only silver, and has long dominated Peruvian production of copper, which constitutes one of the country's principal export items. International Petroleum (owned partly in Canada) has won a similar position in Peruvian oil production, which until 1901 exceeded that of any other Latin-American country and was then divided among many small companies. Tropical Oil, organized in 1919 and controlled by the Standard Oil Company of New Jersey, was one of the firms benefited by the reconciliation of Colombia and the United States in the 1920's. It shares the Colombian oil business with other American firms, one of which was for a time controlled by the Mellon interests; but it is much the largest of the group. Creole of Venezuela is also a Standard subsidiary and, together with another of its subsidiaries, accounts for half the oil production of Venezuela, which in turn accounts for about 90 per cent of the country's total exports. It should be noted, however, that despite this quasi-monopoly, the terms under which these companies operate are exceptionally favorable to the Venezuelan government—at any rate, they are regarded by many people in other Latin-American countries (notably Colombia) as a model for their own governments to follow.

A good deal of American capital and technical skill also went into agriculture. One example—the United Fruit Company's banana plantations in Colombia—has already been mentioned. Others are furnished by Grace and Company, which accounts for a large share of Peru's sugar production, and by the Eder family, which from the close of the nineteenth century contributed notably to the development of sugar and coffee production in Colombia's rich Cauca Valley.

Germans and Austrians established the first commercial air services in Colombia (1920), Bolivia (1925), and Ecuador (1928), but Americans led the way in Peru (1920) and Venezuela (1929). Keen competition was offered by European countries, especially by France and the Netherlands in Venezuela, and by Germany in Colombia, Bolivia, and, for a short time after 1938, in Peru. Nevertheless, United States lines forged ahead in the 1930's with the aid of government airmail contracts and diplomatic support, such as their European competitors were receiving from their own governments. The chosen instruments for this purpose were Pan American Airways and its West Coast affiliate Panagra (Pan American Airways–Grace). Yet it was not until after 1939, when the world crisis enabled the United States to enlist the political aid of the Bolivarian governments, that the politically dangerous German lines were eliminated. Even then, control of local air services within these countries passed not to the United States lines, but to national lines.

The economic position that the United States had gained in the Bolivarian states by 1939 is indicated by its share in their foreign trade and investments. Commercially as well as geographically they occupied an intermediate position between the Middle America–West Indies group, which carried on the bulk of its trade with the United States, and the southern South American group, which carried on the bulk of its trade with Europe. Venezuela received slightly more than half of its imports from the United States but sent back only one-fourth of its exports in return. Colombia reversed the order by sending nearly two-thirds of its exports (mainly coffee) to the United States and taking somewhat less than half its imports from this country. In Ecuador and Peru, the United States accounted for about one-third of the aggregate foreign trade; and in Bolivia, for one-fourth of the imports but (since all of Bolivia's tin went to Britain) for less than 10 per cent of the exports.

The period of greatest expansion of United States investments in these countries was the decade immediately following World War I. The growth of portfolio investments from 1914 to 1929 is shown by the following table:

All Securities
(Millions of dollars)

Country	1914	1919	1929
Bolivia	8.2	9.5	62.1
Colombia	——	.6	167.4
Peru	2.0	——	76.8
Venezuela	——	——	10.0
Total	10.2	10.1	316.3

During and after the world-wide depression that began in 1929 the default record of all of these countries except Venezuela was very bad,* but investigations brought about

* Venezuela had no foreign debt. The default record of the other four countries at the end of the period discussed in this chapter is indicated by the following table showing the status of interest service on dollar bonds (including national, state, municipal and government-

by the defaults showed that the record of some of the lending institutions in the United States was also bad, in point of both prudence and integrity. The highlight of the latter record was the revelation that the Chase National Bank had paid a $415,000 commission to the son of President Leguía of Peru in order to facilitate the completion of a loan to that government. Two wrongs did not make a right, but they discouraged the development of belligerent self-righteousness on either side and contributed to preventing this economic shambles from producing the political tension that might have arisen under other circumstances. Moreover, under the Good-Neighbor policy, reinforced at this point by the Buenos Aires Nonintervention Protocol of 1936, the United States government refused to intervene on behalf of the creditors. At least no justification was given for raising the cry of Big Stick again. The defaults in question involved only government bonds; direct investments fared much better—in fact, they fared well even in comparison with similar investments in the United States. Nevertheless, the investment of United States capital in the Bolivarian countries, as in the rest of Latin America, was reduced to a trickle in the decade after 1929.

A well-known authority on Latin-American affairs, J. Fred Rippy, has observed that "capital and technology under corporate control have been and will continue to be a very fundamental factor in Pan American relationships." This is quite true and it is particularly apposite to the relations of the United States with the Bolivarian countries in

---

guaranteed corporate issues) as of December 31, 1940. The table is taken from Samuel Flagg Bemis, *The Latin American Policy of the United States*, p. 341:

Country	Outstanding	In Default as to Interest
Bolivia	$60,852,927	$59,422,000
Colombia	137,556,953	134,602,500
Ecuador	12,262,700	12,262,700
Peru	85,656,500	85,656,500

the half century ending in 1939, when American enterprise
was making itself increasingly felt in those countries and
when this enterprise was coming increasingly under concentrated corporate control. It is not easy to assess the conduct
of the key enterprises; but whether that be judged good or
bad, their influence on inter-American relations was clearly
deleterious. Intentionally or not, they tended to become
identified with local elements opposed to the rising tide of
liberalism and radicalism in those countries and thus brought
down upon themselves the charge that they were aiding
and abetting the "feudal order" and the "oligarchies." An
excellent illustration of this point is the running fire kept
up for years against the "economic imperialism" of the
United States by Víctor Raúl Haya de la Torre, leader of
the popular APRA party of Peru.

Moreover, these American enterprises were disliked
partly because they were big, rich, and powerful (a sentiment which people in the United States should understand,
since it parallels our own long campaign against "Wall
Street" and "economic royalists"), and partly because they
were foreign (a sentiment which also has not been unknown
or without political consequences in this country). Illustrations of this point are the Colombian attack on the United
Fruit Company, which was precipitated by the massacre
of Colombian banana workers in 1928 but was rooted in
earlier grievances as well, and the Bolivian government's
expropriation of Standard Oil in 1937. Political relations
with these countries were good at the end of this period, but
trouble was brewing on the economic front, and, if one
may hazard a guess, only the diversion of attention to other
issues by the outbreak of war in Europe kept the pot from
boiling over.

PART IV

PROSPECT

11. Problems of Today and Tomorrow

1. GENERAL

Like the Near East, which was the subject of a recent volume in this series, northwestern South America is the seat of an ancient civilization, contains some of the world's greatest known oil reserves, and consists of several small, weak states which play an important but subordinate part in world affairs. It is also a world crossroads, for its position in relation to the Panama Canal is somewhat the same as that of the Near East to the Suez Canal, and it is a corridor for international air lines linking southern South America with Middle America and the United States. Unlike the Near East, however, it is not—and, in the visible future, is not likely to become—a focus of rivalry among the three great world powers. The reason is simple. Neither of the other two great powers has the means to rival the United States, whose preponderance here is overwhelming. The withering away of the British counterpoise, which began a half century ago, was carried to virtual completion during World War II. As for the Soviet Union, it has never had any important point of support in or near this area. Soviet trade and cultural relations with it are negligible; and the political support which Moscow receives from the weak, divided communist parties of the area has at most a nuisance value. Iran and Palestine have no counterpart here.

This situation is a factor of prime importance in the problems that face the five Bolivarian countries of northwestern South America. On the one hand, they know that there is now only one great power, the United States, which can effectively either aid or injure them. This limits their freedom of choice among foreign policies by making it impossible for them to engage in the dangerous game of playing off one great power against another. On the other hand, as a result of the United States' commitment to the rule of nonintervention and its observance of the rule on most occasions, they retain a considerable degree of freedom of action within this framework. Ordinarily, therefore, the solutions of their problems will be of their own choosing, though prudence may be expected to counsel the avoidance of extremes that might forfeit that indispensable aid from the United States without which these poor, weak, and backward countries cannot hope to maintain themselves in this hard postwar world, much less better their condition.

The importance of this situation lies, first, in the fact that it is understood and, however reluctantly, accepted by most people in these five countries, and, second, that it seems likely to remain substantially unchanged for a considerable time to come. Indeed, it is difficult to see how the situation can be greatly altered in the next generation unless the United States' position as a great power is gravely impaired either by a deep and prolonged economic depression or by defeat in war. Only in such an eventuality does it seem conceivable that the communist ideology or any foreign power except the United States might become a factor of first-rate importance in the Bolivarian countries in what we sometimes fondly call the predictable future.

Local conditions, and therefore both domestic and foreign policy, differ considerably from one country to another in this group. Yet all of them have certain features in common. All are small powers, all are economically colonial, all have a very low standard of living and a high degree of illiteracy, and none of them, not even Colombia, has yet succeeded in maintaining a stable democratic government over a considerable period of time. These conditions, common to all the members of the group, lie at the base of most of the chief problems that face each of them individually. Their domestic and foreign problems are inextricably intertwined, but in the interest of clarity it is better to discuss these separately; and since their foreign policies are designed mainly to aid in the solution of domestic problems, let us begin with the latter.

2. POLITICAL PROBLEMS

The number one political problem of all the Bolivarian countries is that of maintaining stable governments based upon the democratic processes which have long been their professed ideal. The problem arises not so much from the survival of the old dictatorship habit, though that is still strong in Ecuador and Bolivia, or from the new vogue of communism, which has recently been the occasion for much nervous twittering in the United States, as from what has been called "creole fascism."

A keen analysis of this problem, attributed to ex-President Alfonso López, was published in the newspaper *El Liberal* of Bogotá in July 1946. His views were briefly as follows. Under the impact of the titanic competition between the United States and the Soviet Union, and of the rise of the middle class in several Latin-American countries, former political lines are breaking down and new ones are taking shape. These middle classes, caught in the squeeze of inflation and determined to use their growing political power in self-defense, are unwilling to follow the pattern of either of the two greatest powers. They are opposed to communism because they are Catholics, and to democracy because its chief exponent is the United States and they equate the latter with the imperialistic plutodemocracy which they regard as the main source of their present economic hardships. They therefore turn to the alternative of a "creole," or Spanish-American, version of the Falangist system of Franco Spain—as they have already done in the Argentina of Perón and, to a less extent, in the Venezuela of Betancourt, where labor unions have been suppressed in the interest of this middle class.

A very different conclusion was reached in a series of articles on communism in Latin America, written by W. H. Lawrence of the *New York Times* after an extensive field study and published in the *Times* in December 1946 and January 1947. So far as the countries in our group are concerned, the results were reported as follows (Bolivia was not included): In Venezuela the communists polled 50,000 votes in the 1946 election; they were then weakened by a three-way split but have since been united, and the threat which they constitute "should not be underestimated." In Peru they have grown from not more than 2000 members in 1942 to between 35,000 and 40,000 at present and are gaining ground at the expense of the Apristas, the largest party. In Colombia they have a voting strength of 25,000, are at the moment split and declining, and are "not so secure" in their control of the Colombian Confederation of Labor as they were a few months ago. In Ecuador they have only about 2500 members but control about half of the top jobs in the Confederation of Ecuadorean Workers.

These figures are not impressive, but the *Times* reporter nevertheless reached the conclusion that the communist threat was serious in these countries as well as in the rest of Latin America. His opinion was apparently based not so much upon the demonstrated strength of the communists themselves as upon the assumed weakness of the best defense against them—the middle class. Indeed, he asserted flatly that there is no middle class in any of the countries except Chile and Argentina—a statement which might have been true a quarter of a century ago, but is certainly not true today. Again, as five or ten years ago, we seem to be in danger of misunderstanding the nature of the political problems of our southern neighbors by overestimating their responsiveness to whichever of the great powers happens to be our chief rival at the moment. Then it was Germany, and so we saw pro-German Latins behind every bush and under every bed; now it is Moscow, and the threat has been transformed almost overnight from nazism to communism.

The problem is much better stated by the writer in *El Liberal* of Bogotá. The middle class not only exists but is in control in Colombia, Peru, and Venezuela, and the danger is not that it will fail to check the rise of communism but that, in the hope of protecting itself against economic ruin, it will aid in riveting "creole fascism" on these countries. For this purpose it might find allies in one or more of several quarters—in the conservative classes, which have been sympathetic to Spanish Falangism for a decade past; in the army, with which the Betancourt regime in Venezuela is already closely linked; in the new labor movement, which is apparently overwhelmingly non-communist; or in the new industrial classes, who are seeking support for increased protection of domestic manufacturing.

How serious the political situation is in the states of our group can be judged from the case of Colombia, the soundest of them all. As already described in Chapter 7, even Colombia, which has had a much more stable and democratic government than any of the other four in the past forty years, has exhibited some alarming symptoms since 1934. First, for several years one of the two national parties, the Conservative minority, followed an intransigent policy of nonparticipation; then, after a brief period of reconciliation under the moderate Liberal administration of President Santos, the revival of Conservative intransigence, combined with internal dissension among the Liberals, plunged the country into a long series of grave crises which in 1944 and 1945 brought it to the brink of political chaos, with the threat of civil war and dictatorship not far off.

Though disaster was momentarily averted by the establishment of a coalition government under President Lleras Camargo, the crisis still continues. Indeed, the cure may prove to have been worse than the disease, for the cure—coalition—has been made permanent through adoption by the Conservative administration of President Ospina Pérez, who took office in August 1946. As a result, Colombia no longer has responsible party government, which is an essential feature of democracy. In this respect that country has lost ground since the 1930's, and its once great Liberal party has failed to produce the courageous young leaders so urgently needed to supplant the faltering older leaders and reunite the party in support of a genuinely liberal program. Instead, most of the Liberal leaders have given their support to a coalition dominated by the Conservative party, in which they are junior partners and which stands to the right of center. Some of the best of the older Liberal talent is represented in it, but the coalition does not represent the more popular, progressive forces in Colombian life. Rather, it makes it more difficult for them to express themselves effectively.

The worst of it is that coalition has been accepted as a permanent arrangement by some of the most influential Liberals. Conspicuous among these is young Alberto Lleras Camargo, president of the republic in 1945–46, a man of exceptional talent and probity, who for a time gave promise of providing that courageous, progressive leadership so badly needed by his party and by the country at large.

Instead, he accepted coalition, first in 1945 as an emergency measure to avert national chaos, and then in 1946 as a permanent system. This issue is so important for Colombia's political future, and Colombia plays so important a role as political bellwether of the Bolivarian states, that it will repay us to examine the reasons he gave for what amounted to an abdication of political leadership. These were stated in his last presidential message to Congress, and they were couched in such carefully considered terms that the message seems to have been intended as a political creed for the guidance of Colombia for many years to come.

In this message Lleras formally recanted his lifelong faith in what he called the "classic" party system—that is, government by the majority party, with the minority party constituting a loyal opposition. His argument may be summarized as follows: Admitting the theoretical superiority of the classic system, experience has demonstrated the doctrinaire folly of trying to make it work in Colombia. There are two main reasons for its failure in this country. The first is the political, social, economic, and psychological backwardness of the Colombian people. Most of them not only lack the economic and social independence necessary to make such a system work; they are also still shackled by ignorance and prejudice. "Only a few miles away from the national capital itself," he said, "the people are living back in 1897; in remoter rural regions, they are living in the colonial period." In the second place, Colombia has chosen a form of government—combining the presidential system with a high degree of national centralization—that is incompatible with the classic party system. The arbitrary use of power is checked in Great Britain by the parliamentary system, and in the United States by the federal system. In Colombia no such check exists, and the president possesses so great a concentration of power over the whole nation that he ought not to be the mere head of one party. Though fortunately no recent president has abused this power except in isolated cases, the ever-present danger that he may do so hangs like a sword of Damocles over the minority and explains why in Colombia the opposition has always been so intransigent and political life has had the character of bloodless civil war.

As an explanation of the failure of party government in Colombia, Lleras' statement is persuasive, and for that very reason profoundly disturbing to any well-wisher to democracy in Colombia and its even less advanced neighbors. He did not propose any specific remedy, whether by constitutional amendment or otherwise. Indeed, he did not seem to feel that a remedy was needed, for he denied that coalition meant the abandonment of the two-party system for the one-party system. Rather, he compared coalition government to a joint stock company.

Another feature of Lleras' discussion of this and other national problems in his last message was the stress that he laid on political manifestations, to the neglect of the grave economic and social problems mentioned above. The net result of the message was to leave the impression that nothing much could be done about them. "Where in this country," he asked, "is there any mechanism for the oppression of the proletariat? And where in our Congress are there any agents of capitalism and industry, of the banks and business? . . . Certainly, there is poverty and injustice and suffering, and above all an immense mass of Colombians who have neither property nor ambition; but this situation exists, not because any class is trying to keep them down, but in spite of the constant efforts of the government, the taxpayers, the politicians, and even, in exceptional cases, the employers, to improve their lot—a thing which no one fears, no one combats. We may say without boasting that, within the limits imposed by our general poverty, there are few countries in the world where President Roosevelt's four freedoms can be enjoyed in greater tranquillity than in Colombia."

The significance of this optimistic view in relation to the political problems of Colombia lies in the fact that it is strongly held by many of the people of that country, and as strongly combated by others. It is in fact becoming the touchstone of politics. According to the veteran political observer Luis López de Mesa, of whom we have already spoken, the issue in the presidential campaign of May 1946 which made the deepest impression on the Colombian electorate was that of the oligarchy. The bitterest attacks on the oligarchy were made by one of the Liberal candidates, Jorge Eliécer Gaitán. A skillful rabble-rouser, who used simple language that the masses could understand, and who drove his points home by a tireless repetition that earned him the cognomen "the man of a single speech," Gaitán was compared by some of his opponents to Hitler, by others to Perón of Argentina. His earlier career gave added point to the comparison, for, educated in the Italy of Mussolini, he had established a short-lived organization of the fascist type after his arrival in Colombia. He had also proved himself adept in the art of combining proletarian appeal with ultranationalism on the occasion of his attack on the United Fruit Company for its alleged complicity in the banana-zone massacres of 1928.

For these and other reasons he seems more likely than any other leader on the Colombian political horizon of 1947 to capitalize on the widespread social discontent of the postwar period. It is for this reason that conservatives and moderates regarded him with alarm despite the fact that he received the smallest vote of the three presidential candidates in 1946. His following includes a sprinkling of upper-class ultranationalists and intellectuals, but its main strength seems to lie in the lower middle class, which is suffering most from the rising cost of living. Much will depend upon the attitude of organized labor, which already has some 400,000 members and is growing steadily, but is still standing politically at the crossroads, dissatisfied with the old-line Liberal leadership and yet uncertain what alternative to choose.

If the political outlook is clouded in Colombia, it is still more heavily overcast in the other four countries. Though the middle classes are at present in control in both Venezuela and Peru, their numbers are small and their strength is confined mainly to the cities. Moreover, they are subjected to constant sniping by extremists of both the right and the left, who seem bent upon provoking a revolution, each apparently convinced that it could come out on top in case of an overturn. In Peru the middle-of-the-road Bustamante regime is under fire for making concessions to the "economic imperialism" of the United States (specifically, to the International Petroleum Company, a Standard of New Jersey subsidiary, and to the holders of some $83 million worth of Peruvian bonds in default since 1932) and for not undertaking an anticlerical campaign. In Venezuela the Betancourt regime is threatened on the one hand with a counterrevolution by the "oligarchy" that it ousted in 1945, and on the other with serious trouble from labor groups, whose organization and development it has checked on the plea that for the moment the Venezuelan people must subordinate everything else to maximum production. In both countries important factors are discontent over the rising cost of living and the contagion of world-wide unrest.

In so unstable a situation no prudent person would venture to make a firm forecast of the turn that the political situation will take. Nevertheless, there does seem some ground for the prediction of *El Liberal* of Bogotá that Peru and Venezuela will be among the Latin-American countries in which creole fascism will flourish in the years just ahead, with the middle class as its core. In both countries this class, though small, is compact; it has a trained leadership that the infant labor movement cannot yet supply; and it has tasted power and has developed a long-range program which it regards as essential to national salvation. If the present experience should show that the atomized society of these countries cannot be brought to support any such programs, the middle classes might exchange democracy for authoritarianism as the only way out. In neither country would they lack national precedents for doing so.

In Bolivia and Ecuador, each of which saw about a dozen changes of regime in the decade before World War II, there is no present prospect that the kaleidoscopic age is nearing its close. The Velasco Ibarra government has held on at Quito since the summer of 1944 by dint of a shift from slightly left of center to right which has excited violent protests on the left. There have been strikes among the once supine agricultural laborers of the mountain zone; and at a higher social and economic level the regional rift represented by Quito and Guayaquil still persists. The rise and fall of the Villarroel government (1943–1946) seems only to have deepened the confusion of Bolivian politics by driving a wedge between the tin miners and most of the other elements formerly allied with them.

In none of these countries is organized labor yet strong enough to play an important role in politics. While accurate figures are unobtainable for most Latin-American unions, the estimated strength of the principal unions in these five countries at the end of 1944 was as follows:

Bolivia (Syndical Confederation of Bolivian Workers)   25,000
Colombia (Confederation of Colombian Workers)   200,000
Ecuador (Confederation of Ecuadorian Workers)   150,000
Peru (Confederation of Peruvian Workers)   300,000
Venezuela (Confederation of Venezuelan Workers)   80,000
      (in process of formation)

Though numerically strongest in Peru, labor is over-shadowed politically there by the APRA party, and no Peruvian labor leader can compare in political influence with Haya de la Torre, supreme chief of the Apristas. In Colombia the labor movement took firm root under the Liberal administration in the 1930's, and in 1944 Colombia played host to the left-wing international Latin American Confederation of Workers (CTAL), headed by Vicente Lombardo Toledano, which held its annual congress at Cali. But the Colombian labor organizations are closely supervised by the government, and in President Lleras Camargo's term a law was passed prohibiting the formation of labor unions of either a political or a religious character. Moreover, the movement suffered a serious setback when the National Labor Congress held at Medellín in August 1946 resulted in a split between the communists and the anti-communists. A similar split has recently occurred in Ecuador. The national labor movement has never got well under way in Venezuela; and in Bolivia it is still suffering from the general public reaction against what was regarded as the excessive partiality of the Villarroel government towards the tin miners.

Aside from the oligarchy, which is by no means done for yet, the army, which is usually closely meshed with it at the top, is the only other secular group which is likely to take the lead in the political developments of the near future. Colombia is an exception, for here the army has never in recent times taken any part in politics; and the fiasco of the coup attempted by a handful of army officers in 1944 has strengthened this tradition, which dates back to one of the founding fathers, Bolívar's contemporary and rival, Francisco de Paula Santander. In the other countries the political role of the army has been much more impor-tant—decisive, for long periods up to our own time. But its importance seems to be diminishing, partly because of inner conflicts such as the one between junior and senior officers, which was probably inspired by the example of the Argentine "Colonels' Clique" of 1943, but which also reflects social changes that have been taking place in these countries. The decline is indicated by the recent reverses suffered by military regimes in Venezuela and Bolivia, and by the political alliance of 1944 between Marshal Benavides and his quondam victims, the Peruvian Apristas. At any rate, while military men will doubtless continue to appear on the political stage in all these countries except Colombia —the habit of a national lifetime is not easily broken—there is no reason to expect that they will continue to monopolize all the best parts.

In this connection it may be remarked that in these countries events have belied the prediction, made with great confidence not many years ago, that the increasing mechanization of warfare would strengthen the already powerful hold of the military on the governments of Latin America. The prediction was repeated during the late war when lend-lease military equipment was sent to those countries. It might have been fulfilled if the armies had possessed monolithic unity; but they did not, and as a result modern arms, including lend-lease arms, have been used by one army group to turn another army group out—sometimes to the advantage of civilians, as in the case of the Venezuelan revolution of 1945.

In conclusion, while we should not exaggerate the strength of the middle classes, the evidence supports the contention of the writer in *El Liberal* of Bogotá that they occupy a key position in the political systems of the three principal countries of our area—Colombia, Peru, and Venezuela. The main question before them is whether they can obtain enough coöperation from other elements to carry their reforms through by democratic processes. If not, they are less likely to abandon the programs than to try the alternative of what is vaguely called creole fascism. Since the heart of their reform programs is economic, let us turn next to the economic problems that face these countries.

3. ECONOMIC PROBLEMS

Whatever their shade of political complexion, all the governments of our area are now primarily concerned with economic problems. And despite differences in method and emphasis, one dominant theme runs through all their programs: diversification of the national economy in order to strengthen and stabilize it, raise the standard of living, and free the nation from the bondage of economic colonialism. There is even a large measure of agreement on one principal method of achieving this end, namely, industrialization, and on the wisdom of government intervention, through tariff protection and otherwise, to promote the development of industry.

Obviously, such programs involve important political as well as economic issues and the political issues are potential sources of serious discord both within each of these countries and in their relations with other countries. On the home front the proposal to reorient the national economy arouses opposition from those who are satisfied with the status quo and from taxpayers who believe that they will have to foot the bill while others collect the profits. For example, in all these countries the proposal to grant tariff protection to industry encounters the familiar opposition of agrarian interests whose major source of income is the export trade. In order to appease such domestic discontents, the national welfare motive is played up for all it is worth, with the result that economic nationalism is highly developed in all these countries, especially in those that have—or think they have—a good prospect of large-scale industrialization in the near future.

Yet this in turn at once threatens complications on the foreign front, particularly with the United States. For this country is not only committed to the contrary policy of a general lowering of barriers to international trade, but is also the only source from which the Bolivarian countries can hope to obtain the large credits that are indispensable for the execution of their ambitious plans of economic diversification and development.

Beset by these political perils at home and abroad, the Bolivarian governments are following a conciliatory course which is obviously designed to realize as much of their program as possible with a minimum of friction. If they cannot avoid it on both fronts simultaneously, they naturally choose to tilt against the foreign adversary, and particularly against Yankee imperialism, for that is a sure-fire vote-getter in those countries. As between loans and votes, the latter must obviously come first; but they greatly prefer to remain on good terms with rich Uncle Sam if this can be done without giving too much offense to the folks at home.

The transforming effect of this motive is illustrated in Peru under the present Bustamante administration. Though it is dominated by the Apristas, once fierce critics of the economic imperialism of the United States, this administration is endeavoring to win national support for the payment (after scaling down, to be sure) of the long-defaulted Peruvian government bonds held in the United States, thereby paving the way for an Export-Import Bank loan of about $100 million to aid the administration's national economic development program. What is more, its recent concessions to the International Petroleum Company have in effect reversed the policy decision of 1943 in favor of nationalizing new developments in this field. Both measures have aroused sharp opposition, and the outcome is still in doubt at the present writing. But whatever the immediate decision may be, the basic problem of reconciling economic

nationalism with the imperative need for foreign aid in
financing national developmental programs will continue to
haunt the governments of Peru and the other countries in
our group for a long time to come.

The spirit of moderation which characterizes the domestic as well as the foreign economic policy of the rising
middle class in this area is strikingly illustrated by the program announced by the new Betancourt regime in Venezuela in late 1945 and 1946. On the foreign front, Betancourt not only confirmed the contracts made with the oil
companies in 1943 by the Medina administration which he
overthrew in 1945, but also invited new foreign investments and fervently promised them security and fair treatment. On the home front he gave business strong representation in an economic council which was set up to study
the country's economic problems and adopt a plan for
dealing with them. And while he recognized the urgency
of the agrarian problem centering in the *latifundia*—large
estates worked by semiservile labor—he made it clear that
his government had no intention of following the revolutionary and often doctrinaire methods of expropriation and
the breaking up of private estates which the Mexican Revolution had employed in attacking this problem in the 1920's
and 1930's. Land for the landless would be provided by
granting small parcels to farmers when this seemed economically desirable. But private property would be re-
spected, and such grants would have to come either from
lands already in public possession or from private estates
whose owners voluntarily entered into a contract with the
government for this purpose. Moreover, warned Betancourt, when it seemed desirable to preserve the economies
of large-scale operation, even public lands would not be
parceled out among small farmers, but would continue to be
operated as a unit under government management. The
emphasis was not so much on individual rights as on in-

creased production in the interest of the general welfare, which was to be obtained not only by diversifying the national economy but also by increasing the efficiency of each type of production. In agriculture, this meant, among other things, mechanization and electrification—Betancourt talked about setting up a TVA in Venezuela—and such a program could be carried out much more successfully on a collective than on an individual basis.

Programs of economic diversification in the other countries of the group as well give great weight to agriculture. They also stress the improvement of transportation facilities, particularly within national borders, in order to create a wider and genuinely national market for domestic products of all kinds and thus obtain the economies of large-scale production and distribution.

Industrialization, however, is the watchword of the new day, especially in Colombia, Peru, and Venezuela, where greater progress has been made than in Ecuador and Bolivia, and where it is believed that the prospect for further progress in the near future is much better. This is likely to continue to be a favorite public policy in these three countries for a long time to come. Since it is taken for granted that industrial expansion will require government protection, through the tariff and otherwise, the international significance of this issue is obvious.

The reasoning behind the demand for industrialization through protection is clear. To the patriot mind it is persuasive despite its doubtful economic validity, for it is regarded as offering an escape from "economic colonialism." One of the commonest complaints in all the Latin-American countries is that, though they won their political independence a century and a quarter ago, in an economic sense they are more colonial today than they were under the Spanish domination, since their economies are more unbalanced and more dependent upon foreign markets for the sale of their products and upon foreign factories for finished goods, and the means of production and distribution are owned to a greater extent by foreigners. They think that the best way to correct this situation is by industrialization, and the only way to industrialize is through protection. The adoption of protectionism is thus a declaration of national economic independence; but it is not motivated merely by patriotic pride. It is also designed to increase the national income and thus facilitate the solution of many domestic problems by providing the means for better education, housing, and health.

The protectionist principle has been accepted for a good many years past in the Bolivarian countries and is implemented by them through tariffs and in a number of other ways. The history of their tariff policies follows a pattern similar to our own, though with a lag of a half century or more. First they were for revenue only and were the main source of revenue; then they were converted piecemeal to the protection of selected commodities locally produced, agricultural as well as industrial; and full-fledged protectionism arrived in the 1920's, the loss of customs revenues being made up from new sources, such as taxes on incomes and property. Tariff levels vary widely. In recent years Venezuela has stood at the top of our group and Colombia at the bottom, with an average of about 70 per cent and 20 per cent, respectively, on all dutiable goods.

Several other protectionist devices are widely used. Indirect protection is afforded by exemption of new industries from taxation, by import quotas (that is, by guaranteeing a certain percentage of the domestic market to home industry), and by export duties on raw materials. Exchange restrictions and the depreciation of currencies have also been used as indirect aids. Direct assistance likewise has taken many forms, such as subsidies, guarantees of fixed return on capital investments, loans at low rates of interest, and outright grants of government funds. Protectionism has become enmeshed with other public policies, fiscal and monetary, and governments join with private interests in propagating the idea that protection is essential to national welfare and progress.

Small wonder, then, that political leaders in our area are opposing the wholesale lowering of trade barriers by international action. Led by Colombia, they made their position on this point clear at the Inter-American Conference at Mexico City in 1945, and stated it even more strongly in their attacks on the United States' plan for expanding world trade which was circulated in the summer of 1946. On the latter occasion, for example, the Colombian delegate to the United Nations Economic and Social Council was quoted in Bogotá newspapers as saying that the United States' proposal would place the industrially underdeveloped countries (such as Colombia) at the mercy of the great industrial nations (such as the United States). The president of the *Asociación Nacional de Industriales* (the Colombian equivalent of our National Association of Manufacturers) asked sarcastically whether the United States did not have sense enough to realize that the only way to expand its trade with Colombia was by encouraging that country to maintain protection in order to raise its standard of living and thereby increase the purchasing power of its people. Even the temperate Eduardo Zuleta Angel, a noted Colombian diplomat just back from London, New York, and Washington, qualified his assurance that the United States was not really trying to enslave Colombia with a reminder that in any case Colombia's delegation at Mexico City had gone on record that their country would not submit to enslavement. These sentiments are shared by leaders in Peru and Venezuela, where, if a choice must be made, their own national industrialization is preferred to the International Trade Organization desired by the United States.

What are the prospects of industrialization in the Bolivarian area? No blanket answer can be given to this question; it must be answered by industries and by countries. One thing should be made clear at the outset: the experience of the past quarter century has completely exploded the myth, once widely accepted, that Latin America, including these countries, cannot be industrialized, because of lack of coal and iron, lack of mechanical aptitude among the people, and for other equally specious reasons. Heavy industry may not develop in the Bolivarian countries for a long time to come, though Colombians and Peruvians now think otherwise; but some of them have already made notable progress in light industry, and the only question is which industries in this category can be most profitably developed, and to what extent.

Among the most important is the textile industry, which is found in all five countries but is most soundly developed in Colombia. Indeed, according to a recent authority, the Department of Antioquia has become one of the leading textile centers in all Latin America, and the capital of this Department, Medellín, has been called the "Manchester of the Andes." More than two-thirds of the total number of spindles in Colombia are concentrated here. Its two largest companies, "Coltejer" and "Fabricato," have offices in Bogotá and branches in other cities and do a nation-wide business. But Antioquia does not monopolize the industry, for active textile centers are scattered all over the country —at Bogotá and Cúcuta in the east, at Ipiales in the far south, and Barranquilla on the northern coast, and at Manizales and Cali in the Cauca Valley. It is a truly national industry in this sense and also in the sense that it is financed almost exclusively by Colombian capital. It employs some 25,000 workers, produces cotton, woolen, worsted, and rayon goods, supplies about 75 per cent of domestic requirements, and has built up a considerable export trade to Ecuador, Venezuela, and Central America. Having grown up almost entirely since 1920, it has equipment that is still classified as new despite the shutting off of new supplies of machinery during World War II. It was developed with the aid of United States technology, and Colombian mills are described as "quite as efficient and productive as the finest mills in the United States," and as having "progressed to a position where finer yarns and fabrics can now be made to compete with qualities formerly imported." They differ from United States mills mainly in the fact that, like all other Latin-American textile mills, they produce a relatively large variety of goods in small lots.

In short, the textile industry in Colombia is obviously a sound one economically and is today in a strong position to expand. Its expansion depends upon the creation of a larger home market through the improvement of the nation's very inadequate transportation facilities and a general rise in the low purchasing power of its people.

Though less well developed than in Colombia, the textile industry has also made considerable progress in the other four Bolivarian countries since 1920 and the prospect for its further growth is good. They present some interesting variations from the Colombian pattern. For one thing, they are less completely controlled by local capital. To give an extreme example, in Peru the industry is dominated by two foreign companies, W. R. Grace and Company of New York, and the English firm of Duncan Fox and Company. In Venezuela, on the other hand, one of the principal mills (at Maracay) is completely government-owned. Bolivia furnishes the only example of a monopoly in this group, for the firm of Said and Yarur has the exclusive right to manufacture cotton goods in that country. This monopoly has not stifled progress, for although only one cotton mill has been built in Bolivia (at La Paz) it is a "model of textile-production excellence" and has "served Bolivia's economy admirably."

In all these countries the textile industry has at hand important sources of supply of raw materials. Cotton is grown in all of them; that of Peru is long-staple cotton of the finest variety, comparable to Egyptian cotton. In Venezuela the mills grow and gin their own cotton, make edible oils from the seed, and reclaim the waste for the manufacture of candlewick and twine. Yarn for the new rayon mills is still imported, but Ecuador, Peru, and Bolivia have local supplies of high-grade wool provided by their herds of alpacas and vicuñas. One of the two large woolen mills at La Paz is described as a "magnificent example of what can be accomplished when modern machine technology is applied to native Andean animal fibers for the production of woolen and worsted fabrics." The problems to be overcome are much the same as in Colombia, though in Venezuela, Ecuador, and Peru they are complicated by absentee ownership and by the fact that the existing equipment is antiquated and urgently needs replacement.

At the opposite extreme from the firmly rooted and flourishing textile industry is the iron and steel industry, which is still almost entirely in the blueprint stage. But in Colombia and Peru the blueprints have been prepared and the raw materials are at hand or near by. Iron ore occurs in various parts of Colombia, which also has large deposits of coal of good quality. In 1938 the construction of a steel plant at Medellín was begun under the encouragement of a law passed by the Colombian Congress in that year. This plant is now in operation, though on a small scale. In 1943 one of the wartime "development" agencies of Colombia drew up plans for the establishment of a primary iron industry in the heart of the principal coal region (the northern Andes, in the Department of Boyacá). In Peru there are no important iron deposits, but anthracite of high quality is believed to be abundant in the Santa region. An important feature of the long-range plans for the Peruvian Santa Corporation is the establishment of a large steel plant which will ultimately not only supply domestic needs but produce a surplus for export. Venezuela, on the other hand, has very rich iron ore deposits in the Orinoco Valley, but almost no coal; its iron ore is being exploited by the Bethlehem Steel Corporation for export to the United States. Ecuador has both iron and coal deposits, but they have never been developed on a commercial scale, and in this country and Bolivia the iron and steel industry does not exist even in the blueprint stage.

It is therefore only in Colombia and Peru that there is any reasonable expectation of important developments in the iron and steel industry in the foreseeable future. Here the prospect is good enough to have aroused keen public interest. The issue is charged with high emotional content because this particular industry is basic to all industrial development and it is believed that the realization of plans for its development on a large scale would set the seal on the much desired "economic independence" of these two countries. Consequently, the issue has important political and international implications. Thus, the Colombian law of 1938, mentioned above, authorized the government to purchase up to 51 per cent of the stock of iron and steel companies doing business in that country; the Santa project in Peru is a government enterprise; and there is a strong disposition in both countries to believe that efficient aid from the United States for these new industries is not forthcoming because the United States is determined to rule or ruin them. Strong efforts to develop them on a national basis may be expected to continue, despite the formidable obstacles that remain to be overcome. Among these obstacles are the heavy capital outlay and the technological skill that are required, neither of which can be adequately supplied by either Colombia or Peru at this time. There is also the ever-present problem of transportation. Though iron and coal occur together in Colombia, the richest deposits are in a rugged Andean region that has no rail or water connections with the principal cities of the country; and in Peru iron ore will have to be imported from abroad. At present all these countries have are a few small plants such as the one built during the war at Medellín, another at Barranquilla which fabricates bridges, tanks, and small boats from imported materials, and the Cerro de Pasco Corporation's plant at Oroya, which is designed mainly to serve the needs of the Corporation itself.

For the rest, manufacturing in these five countries is confined largely to processing and to a few specialties—such as tires and pharmaceuticals—which were stimulated by the war. For example, in Colombia a partial census of manufacturing industries taken in 1940 showed that after textiles, four of the five largest industries (as measured by fixed capital investment) were in the category of food processing and beverages. These were, in the order named, beer, sugar, grain, and cigars and cigarettes. The fifth of the group was cement. These five accounted for about 40 per cent of the total investment in industry (approximately $70 million), and textiles for 25 per cent. Measured by the number of employees shown in this incomplete census, textiles stood first, with 15,317; cigars and cigarettes second, with 4880; shoes third, with 2657; and beer fourth, with 2422. These four accounted for 60 per cent of the total number of employees in all manufacturing industries (42,681).

A more complete census taken in Peru the same year showed that, by number of workers, the largest industries in that country after textiles were clothing, lumber and wood, and food products. The four together employed 85 per cent of all the industrial workers in Peru (327,284 in a total of 380,281). Most of these industries are described as "small shops and handicraft establishments operated by the proprietor alone, or with only a few hired workers." The comparatively large number of industrial workers in Peru is a measure of the considerable expansion which has taken place in that country, mainly since 1929. But this development has been due in large measure to high import duties and depreciation of the currency. The government has also in some cases granted protection against competition within the country—for example, by prohibiting the importation of textile machinery.

With allowance for minor local differences, much the same situation exists in the other countries of our group. Except in textiles, they are all at a very early stage of industrial development, a considerable part of even this modest development rests upon an insecure economic basis, and further progress will require careful planning on a broad front and more capital and technological resources than are in sight in those countries at the moment. Accordingly, since they are determined to industrialize as far as possible, their policy since the war has been to encourage the investment of foreign capital (which means largely United States capital) on the basis of participation with local capital, United States firms providing technology as well as capital but the control resting in the country concerned. This question of control is the nub of the problem and many promising enterprises may break down at this point since it involves a conflict between two powerful forces—on the one hand, nationalism, and on the other, prudent business policy. But there are many on both sides who think that the thesis of Yankee exploitation in the 1920's and the antithesis of South American expropriation in the 1930's can be reconciled in a synthesis of mutually advantageous coöperation in the years ahead.

One hopeful sign is the recent trend in these countries towards selective industrialization in the light of their individual resources and needs. In line with this trend they are pushing the development of certain industries which, though wholly or largely a product of the recent war, seem well adapted to local conditions. Examples are the tire factories established in Peru, Colombia, and Venezuela during the war, which can use rubber from the tropical hinterland of these countries and which have a growing local market for their product; the fish-canning industry of Venezuela, which is the third largest producer of fisheries in Latin America; and chemicals, including pharmaceuticals. During the war pharmaceutical laboratories sprang up in great numbers in Venezuela, Colombia, and Ecuador to meet local needs, and many of them seem destined to survive. At least one of these, a Colombian firm, has developed an export trade in biologicals, endocrines, and pharmaceuticals in general to neighboring countries—Venezuela, Panama, and Ecuador. Peru lagged behind the others in general pharmaceutical production, but even here the manufacture of quinine sulphate from Peruvian cinchona bark, which started as an emergency war measure, has become a permanent industry. Though hydroelectric power, coal, and steel have been the most highly publicized features of Peru's ambitious plans for its Santa Valley development, this enterprise is also potentially important for the chemical industries, since sulphuric acid will be one of its by-products and it is expected to produce the cheapest ammonium sulphate in the Western Hemisphere. With government aid, the heavy chemical industry of Colombia has made a good start in recent years, and already ranks sixth among the nation's industries; it is making increasing use of local materials, such as botanicals and by-products of the oil refineries.

Underlying the whole problem of the economic development of these countries—of increased and diversified agricultural production and improved transportation, as well as of industrialization—is the problem of fuel and power. The pessimism that prevailed on this score even less than a generation ago is quite unwarranted today. As already noted, the lamentations of an earlier day over the absence of coal proceeded from ignorance. Both Colombia and Peru, we now know, have large deposits of good coal, some of it equal in quality to the best Pennsylvania anthracite. Nature was not foresighted enough to put it in the right places, with the result that its maximum utility will not be realized for some time to come. But it is there, and it is already being exploited on a considerable and steadily increasing scale. In Colombia, for example, by 1935 local mines were already supplying almost all local needs, and coal imports from abroad were insignificant; and total annual production of the Colombian mines increased from less than 400,000 metric tons in the late 1930's to over 500,000 tons in 1940. Moreover, since 1920, coal has been supplemented, and in some cases supplanted, by oil and hydroelectric power. All five countries produce oil; Bolivia is the only one that does not have a surplus for export after meeting local needs. Oil and gasoline provide the motive power for steamships, locomotives, automobiles, and airplanes, and thus have helped bring about a marked improvement in transportation facilities, though much still remains to be done, especially in the way of railroad and highway construction. Many hydroelectric plants have been built and others are under construction. The largest in all five countries, the one on the Santa River in Peru, was scheduled at the beginning of 1947 for completion before the end of the year; its capacity is 125,000 kilowatts, generated at a cost of about 1¼ cents per 1000 K.W.

In short, a power revolution is in progress in this area; it has already brought about a great improvement in the basic conditions of economic life; and the end is not yet in sight by any means. Nevertheless, optimism about the near future should be very temperate. The benefits have been very unequally spread and have been confined largely to Colombia and Peru. The full utilization of the large coal deposits of these two countries will require much time and large capital investments. Though petroleum deposits are abundant and accessible in all five countries, the uses of oil as a source of power are confined largely to transportation. On paper, the water-power resources of the vast Andean area are tremendous, but the cost of harnessing this power by building hydroelectric plants is so great, and local financial resources are so limited, that progress along this line will be very slow. James S. Carson, an authority on this subject, has recently given a word of warning in regard to Latin America in general which applies with special force to our area. "It is well to repeat," writes Mr. Carson, "that if the power business in Latin America is to progress as it should then realism must govern planning. Many engineers from the southern republics have visited the Tennessee Valley and marveled at the great achievement there. Fired with enthusiasm they have talked to the press about the establishment of various TVA's in the southern continent. The funds of the Export-Import Bank are limited, however; and, even if they were not, some approximately assured markets for such gigantic power-output schemes must be in sight. The power business in Latin America has a great future if it is developed economically."

From whatever angle we examine the problem of industrialization, we have no reason to question the conclusion of George Wythe, the most careful student of the problem, that "Probably the Latin American economies will remain primarily extractive for a long time to come." As applied to the Bolivarian group, "probably" can be changed without a qualm to "undoubtedly," for none of the countries in this group is as far advanced industrially as Argentina, Brazil, or Chile, and none of them possesses in as high a degree the qualifications for further industrial progress on a broad front, such as capital, technology, and a large and accessible market.

Mr. Wythe goes on to observe that it will be to the advantage of these countries to remain primarily extractive so long as they "retain a comparative advantage in the production of their specialties and adequate markets are open to their products." From this point of view, each country in our group faces a different problem. But they all have one thing in common: all their problems are not only international but global, for all the principal products of their extractive industries enter into the world market. This will be apparent from a brief review of the situation facing each country.

Venezuela's extractive industries are completely dominated by oil. So far as resources are concerned, the country has nothing to worry about for a good many years to come, for its proved oil reserves are among the richest in the world, constituting 13.4 per cent of the world total and being exceeded only by those of the United States and the Near and Middle East. Political leaders in Venezuela profess to be greatly disturbed over the prospect of competition from the new or soon-to-be-opened oil fields of the Near East. Indeed, Rómulo Betancourt, president of the Revolutionary Junta set up in 1945, signalized his advent to power by warning his fellow countrymen that this competition was no remote danger but threatened them with national catastrophe within the next two years. Betancourt was at least badly mistaken in his timing, for at the present writing the two years of grace that he gave the Venezuelan oil industry are almost up and it does not seem any nearer ruin than when he sounded its knell of doom. It also seems a safe bet that he was mistaken in his major premise, for a large part of the oil of the Near East is controlled by the same United States and British companies that dominate the Venezuelan oil industry. They are hardly likely to enrich themselves in the Near East by ruining themselves in Venezuela.

In fact, the oil industry of the latter country is in a strong position, possibly even stronger than before the war. Because of its favorable geographical location, it was given preferential treatment by both the companies and the United States government during the war, with the result that operations were expanded and equipment maintained at the highest possible level. If United States policy continues to be decisive, Venezuelan oil will probably have a larger market than formerly, for our own country's oil reserves were so greatly depleted by the war that present policy is to conserve them carefully and encourage wider use of oil from other parts of the world.

Venezuela's extractive industries are less likely to be affected by what goes on outside the country than by the policy of its own government. In the case of oil, there is no reason to fear serious trouble unless that government yields to the temptation to go on raising the royalties from the companies—its chief source of revenue—as it might conceivably do under popular pressure to hasten the execution of its far-flung program of social reform and economic diversification. In the case of coffee, a minor but still important export commodity, there is greater likelihood of an upset because of the unhealthy condition that has grown up in this industry under a regime of protection. This has encouraged uneconomic practices which have brought Venezuelan coffee to the point where it can hardly compete in the world market in normal times without a subsidy.

What has been said about oil in Venezuela applies also, with some modifications, to Colombia and Peru, where oil is a major, though not the dominant, export commodity. Peru is a special case, because production in established fields is diminishing, and the maintenance of production depends upon the opening of new fields. This raises two important questions, one political, the other technical. The political question, already mentioned, is whether the government shall retreat from its 1943 policy of nationalization of further oil development by granting new concessions to a foreign oil company (International Petroleum). The technical question arises because some of the new oil fields lie east of the Andes in Amazonia; and the question is how to get the oil out of that remote region—whether to build a pipe line over the Andes to the Pacific or send it by barge more than 2000 miles down the Amazon to the Atlantic. The answers will determine whether Peru, the oldest and third largest commercial producer of oil in South America, is to maintain its position during the next generation.

Coffee is Colombia's number-one problem. No great difficulty should be encountered in handling this problem in the years just ahead, unless the United States suffers a depression and cuts its purchases of Colombian coffee drastically. The business is efficiently managed under centralized control in Colombia and the excellent quality of the coffee has won it a strong place in the United States, where it has been more than compensated since 1939 for the ground it lost in Europe because of the war. The recovery of the former European market should in fact put it in a better position than it held before 1939.

The long-range outlook for Peru's minerals, which are the backbone of her export trade, is on the whole favorable. Reserves of copper, the key mineral, are believed to be sufficient to maintain production at a high rate for several decades. Lead, zinc, and gold ores are abundant. The only definitely adverse factor is the exhaustion of high-grade vanadium ore, though an element of uncertainty runs through the whole Peruvian mining industry because of the complex character of a large part of its ores. As a result of this complexity, the production of copper, silver, lead, and zinc is tied up together, and the state of the industry is determined by the interplay of the world-market price of each of these minerals, of which silver is the most important for this purpose.

Ecuador and Bolivia have less reason than the other three countries to face the future with confidence. The export trade of Ecuador experienced a greater wartime dislocation than that of any other country in the group, and of the three export commodities that enjoyed a boom—rubber, balsa wood, and rice—only rice has any prospect of remaining at the high wartime level. In general, agricultural products, led by cacao, will probably continue to be the country's main reliance and soil erosion is reducing productivity in a large part of the country. Experts believe that it can be raised again by such means as education of the farmers, the more extensive use of fertilizer, and the modernization of farm machinery. They also believe that an extensive area of largely undeveloped farm land on the Pacific Coast of Ecuador has high productive potentialities. But in both cases the cost will be great and progress slow at best. The country's mining and petroleum industries were adversely affected by the war. In the case of mining, recovery will depend on the world price of gold, which dominates the whole industry; for example, profitable operation of the two large-scale copper-mining enterprises in Ecuador is made possible only by the gold that is obtained when the complex copper ores are refined. Altogether, the country's prospects for the near future are not encouraging.

Bolivia's prospects are bleak. Still in the grip of its mining complex, the country is now confronted by the renewal of ruinous competition from the tin mines of Malaysia—and the Bolivian economy is dominated almost as completely by tin as is the economy of Venezuela by oil. Several Bolivian tin mines had already been forced to close by the end of 1945, even before production was resumed in Malaysia. The industry is described as reasonably efficient, but the remaining ores are low grade, the cost of transportation is high, and labor relations at the mines have been consistently bad in recent years. A Tin Committee created by the government in 1945 to bolster up the industry at home and abroad has pinned its hopes mainly on quotas and price fixing in conjunction with the international Tin Pool in London. The demand for two other Bolivian minerals, tungsten and antimony, has fallen off greatly since the end of the war, and no large-scale recovery is in sight. As in Ecuador, projects for diversification and modernization in agriculture and industry as well as mining are on foot, but their progress will almost certainly be very slow. The financial and technological resources of the country are so limited, and the political and social situation is so deeply disturbed, that it would not be reasonable to expect any marked improvement in the sad state of the country's economy in the near future.

In all five countries one of the major economic problems of today and tomorrow is financial. Where are they going to get the money to pay for their postwar readjustment, diversification, and expansion? The bill will be a large one. Readjustment does not involve much reconversion, since there was little conversion in any of them during the war—in Peru, almost none. But heavy replacements are having to be made—of run-down railroad equipment, automobiles, and agricultural, mining, and industrial machinery. Also, as a prerequisite to any sound development, transportation systems must be improved and extended.

Except in Venezuela, which has a bonanza in royalties from the oil companies, ordinary government revenues will not help much. The classical source, tariff duties, has diminished with the rise of protectionism, and the yield from the income tax, which is in effect in all these countries, cannot be materially increased without arousing strong opposition on the home front. The foreign exchange and gold balances accumulated during the war will not go far for this purpose.

For example, Peru's balance of $50 million is half the amount that the government of that country is now seeking to borrow from the Export-Import Bank for developmental purposes. Foreign loans of this kind are one answer, but in the present state of the world they can be floated only in the United States, and, as Peru has found, they cannot be floated even here until the defaulted debts of the early 1930's have been settled. In Peru's case, these old debts amounted to nearly twice as much as the wartime accumulation of foreign exchange and gold balances. Another answer is the investment of foreign private capital (again read "mainly United States private capital") on a participating basis; but private capital is as unwilling as the Export-Import Bank to make new investments until old debts have been paid, and is scrutinizing economic potentialities with more care than was shown by United States investors after World War I.

Financial considerations reinforce the conclusion that it will be a long time before the Bolivarian states blossom forth with TVA's, mechanized agriculture, heavy industry, and a network of railroads and trunk highways. Extractive industry will continue to be their main support for an indefinite period, and there is not even any immediate prospect of a great change in the fundamental conditions under which this is carried on. Colombia, Peru, and Venezuela should continue the development of the light consumer goods industries that has been going on since the 1920's, but Bolivia and Ecuador will be fortunate if they do not lose ground on their economic treadmills in the next decade.

In view of these prospects, there is little likelihood that the near future will see any considerable development of the "open frontier" areas of these countries in the Amazon, Orinoco, and Plata basins. All things considered, such as climate, resources, and accessibility, southeastern Bolivia is probably the most promising of these areas, yet even here the difficulties to be overcome are very great. Bolivia itself cannot provide the settlers, and it is discriminating in its choice of immigrants and unwilling to admit even the best immigrants on a large scale. And, on their side, potential immigrants ask—with good reason—what outlets they would have for their products and how they would be governed.

Farther north, in the Amazon basin, heat, humidity, and jungle are a bar to colonization until one has pushed back up into the eastern foothills of the Andes. From there the voyage to the Atlantic is so excessively long that hardly any product of the region will bear the freight charges. As already noted, even its oil, which has an assured market, may have to be piped over the Andes, if it is to be exploited at all. The gathering of wild rubber, supported at high cost as a war measure, has declined sharply since the end of the war; and before the war, United States companies with the amplest financial resources failed to establish the plantation rubber system here. Tropical pests, East Indian competition, and lack of an adequate labor supply were among the chief reasons. A steady growth of Peru's substantial settlements in Loreto and along the Tingo María-Iquitos line developed during the war may be expected and the government will probably continue to support it, if only for reasons of prestige. But there is no reason whatever to expect that this region will experience a growth even remotely approaching that of our own inland empire, the upper Mississippi Valley, between the War of 1812 and the Civil War.

The destiny of the Bolivarian countries still lies in their already populated regions, the mountains and the Pacific and Caribbean coasts. Their history is already too full of expansionist forays into new areas—"waves of exploitation moving across a country, followed by abandonment and population decline," to quote Preston James's characterization again. In what is already their effective national territory, there are resources which are not adequately exploited, and there is not enough manpower now to exploit them.

The new frontiers towards which these countries should bend their efforts are neither in Amazonia nor in wholesale industrialization, but in the increased efficiency of their present economies, with a view to raising the standard of living.

4. SOCIAL AND CULTURAL PROBLEMS

Of the innumerable problems under this rubric, those that bear most directly upon the theme of this book are: education and public opinion; religion; land tenure and the closely related Indianist movement; urbanization; and immigration.

Education lies at the roots of both the political and the economic problems of these countries. Despite the noteworthy educational activity that has been going on in Colombia since 1930 and in Peru since 1945, the shortcomings of their systems are still glaring. In the other three countries the situation is still worse. The quantitative defects of the systems are only a part of the problem, though an important part. Even in Colombia, where great progress was made under the Liberal administration and primary education has been made free and compulsory, a school census of 1942 showed that there were only 653,041 children between the ages of 7 and 14 enrolled in all the public and private schools of the country, whereas the national census taken four years earlier showed that there were 2,314,979 children between the ages of 5 and 14. Only one-fourth of the children registered in primary schools go on to secondary schools (most of which are run by the Catholic Church), and only one twenty-fifth enter the universities. Qualitatively, too, the defects are serious. The great majority of school teachers are poorly trained and so poorly paid that they have to hold two or more positions to make a living. Even in the universities the full-time professor is the exception. Laboratories and libraries are for the most part woefully inadequate, though again there are exceptions, among the most notable of which are the well stocked and well organized libraries of the University of San Marcos (Lima) and the University of Antioquia (Medellín).

One of the most striking features of these systems, especially at the upper level, is their professionalized character, to the neglect of both general education and technical training. Little or no effort is made to orient the students in the modern world by giving them a good grounding in social studies, science, or even (despite the strong theoretical bent of these systems) in philosophy; much less to show them what the rest of the world is like and how they and their country stand in relation to it. Some effort is now being made to improve the systems in this respect, and again Colombia is leading the way. In 1945 the secondary school curriculum of that country was reorganized and one of the innovations was the requirement of four years of history, stressing Western Europe, the Americas, and Colombia, with a view to giving the students the kind of orientation in question. But in the universities, the future intellectual élite are trained only for a profession—medicine, law, architecture. The University of San Marcos is a rare exception to the rule. Progress at this upper level is in the direction of still greater specialization.

As a result, there is widespread illiteracy among the masses, which makes intelligent participation in the political life of the country difficult or impossible. There is also a lack of broad training for public affairs among the better-educated groups, who are accustomed at the formative stage of their intellectual development to think in a narrow occupational framework. This goes far to explain the weakness of the concept of the general welfare and the atomization of political life in these countries, and also the intransigence of political groups which we have already noted. It lies at the root of the colonialism that still marks their thought on

political and social problems despite the much advertised
nativism that has marked their literary history for many
years past. Lacking the groundwork for independent development in the field of political and social thought, they have
borrowed from abroad. Because of the cultural prestige of
France, they have borrowed mainly from that country, and
because of the predominance of the Catholic Church in these
countries they have been highly receptive to French Catholic thought. Other strong influences have been that of Spain,
and that of Germany as filtered through Spain and trans-
mitted to America in Spanish translations of German works,
which were turned out in large numbers at Barcelona in the
1920's and 1930's. Britain and the United States have not
fared well in this environment, though they have done a
great deal, through trade, investment, and technology to
give the environment its present character.

In the economic field, too, the results of the present educational system have been unfortunate. To mention only the
points most apposite to our problem, none of these countries
has the trained personnel to carry out the ambitious plans
of economic diversification and expansion which they have
all adopted, and their planning is conceived in terms of
political aspiration rather than hard economic fact. Technicians and economists are still a rarity.

Aside from the educational systems and the Catholic
Church, which will be discussed below, public opinion is
formed mainly by the press and radio. Newspapers still
dominate the field almost as completely as they did in the
United States a generation ago. Radio has come into wide
use, but its main value has been in breaking down the isolation of remote communities and making them aware of the
outside world. Except for international broadcasts beamed
from the United States and Europe, the political content of
its programs has not been high and consists mainly of more
or less slanted news reports, which are usually delivered in

a machine-gun-like staccato and seem designed to give the maximum of information with the minimum of enlightenment.

The newspapers, on the other hand, go about the business of opinion-molding deliberately, conscientiously, and as artistically as possible, using all the literary tricks of the trade and pulling out all the stops, from diapason to tremolo. Editorially, most of them are as lively and well written as the *Washington Post*, and far more violently partisan than most newspapers in the United States. The larger papers, such as *El Comercio* of Lima and *El Tiempo* of Bogotá, make extensive use of the international news services. But complaints of distortion of the news are frequent. A recent instance was cited by the Peruvian Aprista leader and university rector, Luis Alberto Sánchez, on a visit to Colombia in 1946. Complaining that many misrepresentations about the conduct of the Aprista-controlled government of Peru had been published in Colombia, Sánchez said the explanation was simple: the news was provided by press agencies in Lima controlled by the anti-Aprista newspaper *Comercio,* "which does not hesitate to adulterate the truth." "The Associated Press [in Lima] has as its manager the manager of *El Comercio,*" he continued. "The United Press is headed by this man's brother; and up to a few weeks ago Reuter's employed the director of the evening edition of the same newspaper." Moreover, outside a handful of metropolitan newspapers, foreign news items are few and brief and comment on foreign affairs is meager.

Rotary Clubs are the only important organizations for the discussion of public affairs, either domestic or foreign. Such familiar figures on the North American scene as the Foreign Policy Association and the League of Women Voters have no counterpart in these countries. There are local discussion groups of various kinds, but they are largely literary and professional. While cultural institutes are maintained in most of the principal cities by foreign nations—the United States, Great Britain, France, and the Soviet Union—these prudently stick to their cultural last. On the other hand, there is a great deal of private discussion of the whole range of politics, from local to global, in informal groups that meet in cafés and clubs. Though informal, however, these groups are more or less fixed in membership; they are composed of like-minded men (never women); and as a result their influence on the general public is negligible except in so far as the opinions of members of the group find publication in newspapers or books. Personalism and factionalism are everywhere dominant.

One of the chief problems in all these countries, therefore, is to develop better means for the discussion of public questions and to provide the basis for intelligent discussion by giving the public—adults as well as school and university students—a better-rounded view of the facts of life in the world of today.

Religion is both a domestic and an international problem in this area. This is obviously true of the central question, the relation between the universal Catholic Church and the several national states, especially when this relation is regulated by a concordat with the Vatican negotiated by the diplomatic representative of a national government—for example, Colombia and Ecuador. These concordats, which partake of the nature of international agreements, regulate such domestic concerns as the financial support of parochial schools by the national government, the binding force of canonical laws, and appointments to ecclesiastical office. For example, the new concordat concluded by Colombia in 1942 stipulated that bishops and archbishops in that country must be citizens of it and must take an oath of allegiance to it, and that prior notice of each election must be given the president of the republic so that he might have an opportunity to state his objections, if any. And, with or without a concordat, the Vatican's views on international affairs unquestionably carry considerable weight in all these countries.

Just how much weight it will carry in the near future, and what the effect on public policy will be, cannot be estimated with any great degree of precision or confidence; but it seems to be an increasingly important factor. The once bitter conflict between clericals and anticlericals, which filled the annals of these countries, as of a large part of Western Europe, in the nineteenth and the early twentieth centuries, has died down. It has not been revived, at any rate on anything like the same scale, even by the advent to power of parties which had previously been strongly anticlerical, such as the Liberals in Colombia (1930) and the Apristas in Peru (1945). It was largely a conflict within the Church, and by mutual concessions the two wings have reached what appears to be a reasonably satisfactory accommodation. The old issue has been revived occasionally, but has never proved more than a passing flurry.

The wars of religion are apparently over in this area, as between wings of the Catholic Church; and the great majority of the people are Catholics, at least nominally. But the war has ceased in one form only to take on another. Indeed, one gets the impression that the two wings have been brought together partly by the desire for mutual aid against a common enemy—or rather, enemies, for there are two of them. One is Protestantism; the other, communism. Except as a stick for Yankeephobes to belabor Uncle Sam with, it is difficult to see why the "Protestant peril" has aroused so much antipathy in these countries. For, in aggregate numbers and influence, all the Protestant churches in this area have always been insignificant, and there is nothing in the present situation to warrant the belief that they will become a significant factor in either respect in the predictable future. Reporting on the situation in Peru in 1900, a Methodist missionary wrote from Lima that "his enemies were as baffling as his opportunities for expansion were astounding." Despite nearly half a century of courageous labor and modest growth, substantially the same situation exists today. Yet in recent years the Protestant bogy has caused great excitement in the area, particularly in Colombia and Peru in 1944. In the latter country the misguided zeal shown by a missionary of one of the minor sects led the government to threaten a ban on all Protestant activities in the country— a measure for which several members of the Peruvian Congress were clamoring.

Still more recently anti-communism has achieved the proportions of a crusade. This is more understandable. In the first place, it reflects the foreign policy of the Vatican. It is also a product of the social tension that exists in all of these countries, for the label "communist" is pasted on all left-wing elements, especially the more militant labor organizations. Like anti-Protestantism, anti-communism is nourished by *Hispanidad*—the neo-Pan-Hispanic movement, which plays up both of these phobias prominently in its propaganda. Both are factors of great potential importance in the future foreign relations of these countries.

One use to which the communist label is put is to discredit reformers who are making so bold as to tamper with the oligarchical system of landownership. Sooner or later, peacefully or by violence, a change will be made in the prevailing system under which the best lands in these countries are engrossed by a handful of great landlords and worked by a semiservile peasantry. This change will not affect the United States or other foreign countries so directly as did the agrarian revolution in Mexico, for foreign landownership is far less common here than it was in Mexico. But it does have important international implications. It is bound up with the basic economic problem of raising the standard of living, and with the cultural problem of

Indianism—the problem of incorporating the great mass of Indians into the national life of this area.

The pattern of the *latifundia*, or large semifeudal estates, is illustrated by Venezuela. According to studies made in the 1930's, 84 per cent of the land surveyed in the Federal District was held by 19 owners, and the degree of concentration was almost equally high in the other Departments surveyed. Less than 1 per cent of the population owned 56 per cent of the country's total farm acreage. Most of the large owners are Venezuelans, but some are foreign oil companies which are reported to be holding the land for future oil development. Little has been done since the 1930's to change this situation. As far back as 1938 the Venezuelan government began to attack the problem, but the attack was half-hearted. It has not been pushed vigorously even by the revolutionary regime set up in 1945, which, as already noted, is making haste slowly and has declared that it will neither expropriate the great estates nor break them up indiscriminately even if their owners are willing to sell.

Substantially the same pattern exists in Ecuador, Peru, and Bolivia. Landownership is more widely distributed in Colombia, but in the past generation the operation of economic forces has diminished the significance of this fact by breaking down the traditional independence of the small farmer, particularly in the coffee-raising regions. The growing dependence of Colombian coffee on the export market has rendered it more responsive to foreign price fluctuations; the effort to stabilize the industry has led to the establishment of national controls that work out to the advantage of the large planters; and as a result many small planters have been forced to mortgage their farms on such terms as to render their ownership and independence illusory. By a somewhat similar process small farmers were forced out of the cotton belt in our southern states in the generation before the Civil War, and the way was paved for the domination of the richest part of the Old South by a system of large plantations worked by slave labor. Colombia is not headed towards the reëstablishment of human bondage, which it abolished nearly a century ago, but a considerable part of its rural population is less free in the economic sense than it was at the beginning of the present century.

In a large part of the Bolivarian area rural workers are actually held in a condition which, though not legally slavery or serfdom, is definitely semiservile. This is accomplished through debt peonage, which is enforced in favor of the landlord by sympathetic public authorities. The system is a familiar one in other parts of Latin America and existed on a large scale in Mexico before the revolution of 1910. It operates under contracts whereby the landlord makes advances of cash or food to the habitually impecunious worker and the latter is obligated to work off the entire debt before he can change employers, as well as to pay a fee to the agent who signed him up. The worker thus loses his freedom of movement, and as wages are low and most of these workers improvident from time immemorial, his freedom is lost for a long time if not for life. Moreover, on his death, the worker's debt is transferable to his children. In effect, then, a large part of the rural labor in these countries is bound to the soil almost as firmly as the serf in medieval Europe.

Because this condition reaches its peak among the Indians of Ecuador, Peru, and Bolivia, the problem of land tenure and rural labor falls within the scope of the Indianist movement, which has attracted widespread attention far beyond the bounds of Latin America in the past generation. In the United States this movement is best known because of the part it has played in the revolution that occurred in Mexico between 1910 and 1940. Actually, as we saw in an earlier chapter, Indianism was first systematically formulated by a

Peruvian, González Prada, in the nineteenth century; and in its subsequent development an important part has been played by poets, pamphleteers, politicians, and social scientists in the Bolivarian countries. Peru has furnished leading exemplars of all these types: the poet José Santos Chocano, whose eloquent poem ¿*Quién sabe?* (Who Knows?) gave Indianism its literary vogue; the philosophical pamphleteer and communist José Carlos Mariátegui, whose *Seven Essays* marked him as the Tom Paine of Indian independence; the politician Haya de la Torre, who made Indianism a main plank in the platform of his Aprista party; and the social scientists Tello, Uriel García, and Valcárcel.

The last named group and their colleagues in other lands have taken over the movement in recent years and have given it the muscle of science and realism. This was needed, for the earlier movement was largely lyrical and romantic and was in danger of degenerating into a bluestocking cult of exoticism, the "noble savage," and those quaint Indian crafts. The scientific study of the problem has developed on a truly international basis and includes, besides the Peruvians already mentioned, such notable figures as Pío Jaramillo Alvarado of Ecuador; Gregorio Hernández de Alba and Antonio García of Colombia; and the Mexicans Moisés Sáenz (who died in Peru in 1941) and Manuel Gamio. Their work is centered in the Inter-American Indian Institute, recently established in Mexico; but a large part of it relates to the Bolivarian area and several thriving local centers of study have been set up there.

The Indianist movement has acquired added significance for the future of this area because of the paradoxical fact that its outlines have become somewhat blurred at the same time that it has been made more "scientific." What has happened is that the concept of Indianism has to a large extent been supplanted by the concept of "indigenism"—*indigenismo*, which may be roughly translated "nativism." The latter is a much broader term, applying not only to those who are culturally and ethnically Indian but also to all persons in these Latin-American countries who are "natives" in the sense of having been born there, and above all to those who live the hard way of life best typified by the unfortunate Indians.

Since such a definition includes the bulk of the rural people of our area, the movement is being transformed from one of uplift in the interest of a minority group largely confined to three countries (Ecuador, Peru, and Bolivia), into a social reform movement in the interest of a large majority of the people of all five countries. It is for this reason that conservatives have pinned the communist label on the more radical *indigenistas*. Some of them have invited this attention by summoning Karl Marx to the aid of Indians and indigenes; though they themselves aver that they are not communists but socialists.

The specifically Indian problem is not being lost sight of by the *indigenistas*. Some of them are now promoting a plan for adapting the coöperative movement started in the nineteenth century by the Englishman Robert Owen to the ancient communal organization (*ayllu*) of the Indians of this area. Their thesis is that the already wretched Indians would be utterly ruined by free enterprise and rugged individualism if their communal *ayllus* were broken up; but that this ancient institution is in many ways unsuited to the conditions of modern mechanized life under a capitalist regime; and that it can be strengthened at its weakest points by features borrowed from the coöperative system. If this proposal is adopted, it will provide an extraordinarily interesting example of the fusion of ancient Indian and modern Western culture under the blowtorch of twentieth-century technology.

Whether we regard it in its Indianist or its "indigenist"

aspect, this movement is one of the boldest and most promising now on foot in the Bolivarian countries. It is attacking in a growing spirit of realism the stubbornest problem that they face, and one that directly concerns the majority of their people. It is also a matter of concern to the United States and other foreign nations, for to millions of their inhabitants—to most of the teeming Indian population of the Andes—such terms as United Nations, Pan-Americanism, and the Four Freedoms are at the present time meaningless.

At the opposite pole of life in this area, urbanization presents its public leaders with a knotty problem. According to Kingsley Davis, a leading student of population trends in Latin America, "the scattered areas of real settlement often exhibit a high density and show a remarkable tendency toward urbanization, in distinct contrast to the empty areas." Except that the degree of urban concentration is lower than in certain other parts of Latin America, the Bolivarian countries correspond to the general pattern, and even among them the cities have grown more rapidly than seems desirable. For their growth rests only in part upon a sound basis of industrialization and is in large measure a result of the flight from the soil which is going on in all these countries, and which is due in turn to a number of factors.

One of these factors—the greatly superior attractions of the city in comforts and conveniences—is familiar in the United States. Here it operates much less strongly today than it did a generation ago, because the gap between city and country in this respect has been narrowed considerably by the extension of good roads, automobiles, electric power lines, farm machinery, plumbing, movies, and radio over the countryside. In the Bolivarian area, on the other hand, the gap became wider than ever during the past generation. It was precisely in this period, beginning about 1920, that Lima, Bogotá, Caracas, and other large cities of the area were modernized and acquired those comforts and conveniences of which we are speaking. For example, the Bogotá of today has them all; but the Bogotá of the late nineteenth century has recently been described by one of its native sons as "terribly dirty and uncomfortable, without water or light," and a place where only a few favored families enjoyed the luxuries and refinements of the age, while the vast majority of its inhabitants lived under conditions that were "really atrocious."

Other factors in the cityward drift are peculiar to these countries. Among those are the desire of semiservile workers to escape from the *latifundia;* the overcrowding of the principal clusters of rural settlement; and the failure (because of lack of adequate transportation facilities, or for some other reason) to develop large tracts of good farm land—land which lies not only in remote Amazonia but also in the effective national territory in the Andes and along the coast. The disproportionate growth of the cities is thus a pathological phenomenon, a kind of giantism brought on by the injection of capitalism and modern technology into systems which were already socially and economically unsound, especially in the rural regions, where most of the people live.

All the terms we have just used are relative to the local scene. It may seem exaggerated to speak of the giantism of these cities, when the largest of them, Lima, has only a little more than half a million inhabitants, and of overcrowding in the rural clusters when the most overcrowded are less densely populated than large rural areas in the United States and Europe. Yet these terms are accurate on the local scale. There are too many people in the cities and too few in the country, where their destiny still mainly lies, since rapid industrialization seems neither desirable nor feasible.

Where is the remedy of excessive urbanization to be found? Not in persuasion or physical force; city dwellers will not go back to the soil merely because they are told that this is their civic duty, and forcible resettlement is out of the question. An incentive will have to be supplied, and this can be done only by raising the standards of economic efficiency and social justice in the rural regions. That will require much money, machinery, and technical skill. In other words, the cure for the disease seems to lie in further injections of the capitalism and modern technology which helped to bring it on—in applying their stimulus to the rural regions as well as the cities. The solution for the problem of excessive urbanization lies not so much in the cities themselves as in the country.

The many collateral problems of urbanization—such as its effects on crime and punishment, the rate of population growth, and shifts in political power—cannot be discussed here. It should be pointed out, however, that in this case as in so many others an analysis of the problems of these countries leads us to the conclusion that no satisfactory solution is possible without extensive social and economic changes, and that these require, among other things, the large-scale application of capital and technology which, in the present state of the world, only the United States can provide.

It has been suggested that, since labor shortage is chronic in this area, immigration should be encouraged as one means of solving its problems. This solution has many champions, but it has never been given a good test—not because these countries have not tried to attract immigrants, but because their efforts have failed. Not one of them has attracted any large volume of immigration at any time in the national period. The 30,000 Japanese on the coast of Peru are an exceptionally large foreign group on the scale of this area. In Colombia only about 1 per cent of the population is foreign born, although time and again since 1826 the government has offered inducements of one kind or another to stimulate immigration, both individually and in colonies.

The prospect for success would seem to be better now, because of the large number of displaced persons in Europe who are unwilling to return to their own countries and the desire of other groups to emigrate in order to escape the hard times that Europe faces for years to come. But many of these potential immigrants belong to nationalities that are not desired in the Bolivarian countries and would be difficult to assimilate. The most desirable types—those above the average in training and capacity—are also in demand in other countries, such as Argentina, Australia, and Canada, which have shown a greater capacity to attract them in the past.

Though it might be possible to attract large numbers of unskilled immigrants, strong arguments against the wisdom of such a policy have been advanced. The case has been well stated by Kingsley Davis, who writes that "masses of unskilled immigrants . . . are not needed to build up the population, for Latin America's population is already growing at the world's most rapid rate. Indeed, the fundamental problem is not lack of people, but lack of capital and skills . . . the remedy is not more people, but a new economic and social orientation. To acquire more people without having the latter is to get the cart before the horse."

5. INTERNATIONAL RELATIONS

As a result of World War II, the international role of the Bolivarian states is determined to an even greater degree than formerly by their relations with the United States. The prime factor in this relationship is still, as it has been for the past half century, the politico-military problem of the defense of the Caribbean area, and this problem is still brought to a pin-point focus on the Panama Canal. Despite the unconditional surrender of the Axis powers and the establishment of a bigger and better world organizization for the maintenance of international peace and security, it does not appear that there has been any fundamental change in the way in which this problem is conceived and handled—or that there will be any such change in the foreseeable future.

By way of illustration, look at a scene that took place in the American Embassy at Bogotá on August 6, 1946, and remember that by this time the serious tension that had developed between the United States and the Soviet Union was a matter of common knowledge. Remember also that President Truman had recently urged the adoption of an inter-American military defense system based upon standardization of arms, under United States leadership, among the American republics, and that, despite official disclaimers, this plan for tightening up the regional security system was widely regarded as a tacit admission of the seriousness of the tension and of the distinct possibility that the United Nations might not be able to cope with the situation.

The scene at the American Embassy was an interview between representatives of the Bogotá press and the members of a special United States mission, composed of high-ranking military and naval officers, which had been sent to take part in the ceremonies attending the inauguration of the new president of Colombia, Mariano Ospina Pérez, on August 7. Ambassador John Wiley was present throughout the interview. Under the circumstances, we may regard the statements made by the United States officers and the Ambassador as expressing the carefully considered policy of their government.

For our purpose, the most significant statements made at this interview were those of General Willis D. Crittenberger, commanding officer of the Caribbean defense zone of the United States, with headquarters in the Canal Zone. According to the detailed report published in *El Tiempo* the following day, General Crittenberger replied as follows (translating from the Spanish) to a question about the defenses of the Panama Canal:

"I believe that the defense of the Panama Canal requires a radius of one thousand miles in order to prevent bombers from approaching the zone. That is to say, it must extend from [the Island of] Trinidad to Florida, on the Atlantic side, and from the coast of Guatemala to the Galápagos Islands on the Pacific side, including the continental zones of Colombia, Ecuador, and Peru."

"In that case," asked a reporter, "is the coöperation of the United States Army with our countries essential?"

"I am no expert in journalism," replied the General, "and if you want to play ball with me, you will have to stay on the receiving end. So I want my statement to appear in my own words.

"The whole Caribbean area is one of the most important for the defense of the Western Hemisphere. If its defense is adequate and if it is accorded the importance it deserves, it can become the cornerstone of the defense of the whole continent and of Hemisphere solidarity. On the other hand, if its defense is inadequate and if we regard it with indifference, a glance at the map is enough to show that it would be one of the most vulnerable parts of the whole Hemisphere. . . . Consequently, all of us—the countries of Central, South, and North America—have a vital interest in the defense of the Panama Canal. The Inter-American Defense Board is well aware of all this and is studying the situation carefully . . ."

"But will the United States army furnish these countries with arms for the defense of the Canal Zone?" asked a reporter.

"Colombia is already receiving airplanes from the United States," replied the General, "and some of them are already here."

"How many?"

"I am not at liberty to say."

Then came the question that was in everyone's mind: "Do you believe that a new war is an immediate possibility?"

"I do not believe there is danger of another war soon," replied the General. After some further interchanges on other subjects, he added, "Nobody has said anything here that could be interpreted as expressing the view that war is imminent." Ambassador Wiley then brought the interview to a close by saying, "No country ought to have a monopoly of the defense of the Continent."

Despite the disclaimers of belief in the immediate danger of war, all this made no sense except in terms of war—a war brought on by aggression from outside the Hemisphere. Continental solidarity, defense of the Panama Canal, defense of the Caribbean, arms for the Good Neighbors—it sounded like the Buenos Aires Conference of 1936, the Lima Conference of 1938, and the Havana Meeting of 1940 all over again, except that inter-American coöperation was now proceeding from the more advanced ground gained during the war, and that in place of "Axis aggression" one must now read "Soviet aggression." The Soviet Union was not mentioned in this interview, but there was no other conceivable source of danger to the Hemisphere.

Otherwise the situation highlighted by this interview bears a striking resemblance to the one which existed just before the last war. So far, the establishment of the United Nations has made little difference—it was only indirectly alluded to in this interview, and the Caribbean area still possesses first-rate strategic importance despite the possibility that the next war may be fought across the Arctic. The thread of continuity runs back to an even earlier period, for while continental defense has been Pan-Americanized since 1936, the policy outlined in this interview is essentially the same as the old unilateral Caribbean policy of the

United States adapted to changed technological conditions (such as the development of long-range bombing planes) and decked out in an inter-American garb which is not likely to make any change in its essentially unilateral character.

What all this means for the Bolivarian countries is unmistakably clear from General Crittenberger's terse analysis of the situation. All of them lie well within the vital Caribbean defense zone as he described it. He named Colombia, Ecuador, and Peru as included in it. He clearly intended to include Venezuela as well, since the Island of Trinidad, which he mentioned as one of its Atlantic outposts, lies just off the northeastern tip of Venezuela, and the northwestern part of the country, including its chief centers of population and production, is within his thousand-mile radius from Panama.

The southwestern outpost of the Caribbean defense zone is formed by Ecuador's Galápagos Islands. Here the United States has gained a permanent foothold. In accordance with the general policy announced by Undersecretary of State Sumner Welles in 1943, the United States base established in these islands during the war has been turned over to the government of Ecuador (July 1, 1946), but under an agreement between the two governments the United States is maintaining some 40 or 50 technicians there. These are military and naval technicians and the stated purpose of their mission is to train the Ecuadorean garrison in order that the base may be kept in a state of preparedness. It does not appear that the Inter-American Defense Board or any other inter-American agency has any more control over the Galápagos outpost than it does over the Panama Canal Zone citadel. In all essential respects the defense of the vital Caribbean zone, which General Crittenberger described as the cornerstone of hemisphere defense, is carried out unilaterally by the United States under such bilateral arrangements with individual Latin American governments as it deems desirable and is able to induce them to enter into.

The importance that the United States government attaches to the Caribbean defense problem and the firmness of its present views on the subject are indicated by the fact that it chose to publicize them through the interview at the American Embassy at Bogotá which we have described. This policy and the publicity given it were a product of the deeply disturbed state of world affairs at that time. Since the tension still exists and no considerable abatement of it is in sight, we may expect this policy to play a leading part in the politico-military relations of the United States with the Bolivarian countries for a long time to come. From their point of view the significance of this policy is that it tends to bring them more completely within the orbit of the United States than ever before.

The most important recent contribution to the discussion of this problem is the United States' plan for the standardization of arms among the American republics and the establishment of an inter-American defense council which would have much broader powers than the Inter-American Defense Board set up at Rio de Janeiro in 1942. The arms plan was publicly endorsed by President Truman in 1946, and again, in somewhat modified form, early in 1947.

In the Bolivarian countries the response to these proposals has ranged from strong support to violent opposition. Among the temperate but outspoken critics of the plan is former President Eduardo Santos of Colombia. His opposition to it is noteworthy because he has long favored close coöperation with the United States and the strengthening of the inter-American system, and more particularly because, as we have seen in an earlier chapter, he was the chief author of the Act of Chapultepec, of which the plan is represented by its advocates as a logical outgrowth. Limitations of space forbid even a brief summary of the article, published in the *Revista de América* early in 1947, in which

Santos explained his stand on this question. We can only say that, among other things, he expressed the opinion that the plan goes far beyond the Act of Chapultepec; that the Latin-American governments' control over their foreign relations might be seriously impaired under the terms of the plan; and that it might impose upon them an armaments burden which would increase taxes, lower the standard of living, increase social discontent, and thus stimulate, instead of checking, the growth of communism in Latin America.

In general, the Bolivarian countries, like the rest of Latin America, are in a rather strong bargaining position vis-à-vis the United States in so far as the hemisphere defense system is concerned. For, rightly or wrongly, they feel that this is a question of more direct importance to the United States than to them, and it is the United States which is taking the initiative in the matter and is seeking to obtain their coöperation in it.

The roles are reversed, however, in the field of economic relations. Here the United States is in the very strong position of being the only possible source of the large-scale financial aid which those countries know they must obtain in order to cope with the many urgent problems that face them. So much has already been said on this subject in preceding pages that the reader need only be reminded that these problems run through almost every phase of the economic and social life of all these countries. Even here, of course, the advantage is not all on one side, for the United States has surplus capital to invest and, when its domestic postwar readjustment is complete, will have large surpluses of goods to sell; and it is seeking to win these reluctant countries over to its policy of a general lowering of barriers to international trade.

The latter issue is likely to be the major problem in their relations with the United States for some years to come. There has been a marked abatement of the prewar hostility to the "economic imperialism" of the United States, which had its starkest expression in Bolivia's expropriation of Standard Oil in 1937. The present trend of opinion and policy is now the other way and American capital and business enterprise are being invited to expand their activities, especially in the form of participation with local interests. A great deal depends on how private interests in the United States meet this situation; a Colombian writer recently went so far as to say that the future of inter-American relations depends upon this rather than upon anything that the United States government may do.

Culturally, the United States still labors under a handicap in these countries. Though the influence of France is still pervasive, their cultural development in recent years has been increasingly channeled into two distinct and mutually antagonistic trends, the Hispanicist and the Indianist. These conflict with each other, but neither is sympathetic to the United States. Both tend to strengthen the widespread dislike and distrust, which are deeply rooted in grievances of the more or less remote past, and in an ignorance and misunderstanding of the United States that sometimes achieves grotesque proportions. Only a few years have passed since the learned Luis López de Mesa, then Minister of Foreign Affairs in Colombia, had to read his fellow citizens a lecture on comparative cultures in order to prevent them from shaping their country's foreign policy on the assumption that Uncle Sam really is a Caliban to the Latin-American Ariel.

One of the major problems of today and tomorrow is to remove the heavy sediment of mistrust and misunderstanding that still remains. For this purpose good use can be made of one of the few cultural advantages that the United States possesses over other competitors in this area, namely, its prestige in various fields of science and technology. As pointed out not long ago by the grand old man

of Colombian letters, Baldomero Sanín Cano, it is by no
means rare for fathers who are tireless critics of the United
States in the political sphere to turn up at Colombian government offices or the American Embassy with a request
for scholarships to enable their sons to study in this country. But rapprochement on the technical level is not enough;
the main trouble lies in the realm of ideas—political, philosophical, economic—and must be attacked there. How
this should be done, it is not within the province of the
present work to say. But whatever means may be employed,
the task is so difficult and important that the effort which
has been made in recent years to promote mutual understanding through cultural relations should not be reduced
but greatly intensified. The fruits of work of this kind are
among the slowest to mature in the whole field of international relations, but they are among the most enduring.
And nowhere in Latin America is such work more badly
needed than in the Bolivarian area. Isolated and never having
received a large influx of immigrants, this area has until
recently lacked the tolerance that usually goes with cultural variety; habits of thought are rigid, prejudices are
hardy perennials; and one of the chief sufferers from this
state of affairs has been the United States. The need on
our own part is equally great, for the Bolivarian countries
have been one of our chief blind spots.

The end of hostilities in 1945 broke the virtual monopoly
of relations with these states which the United States acquired during the war, and the earlier rivalry of the great
and not-so-great powers over them has been resumed. As
compared with the prewar period, however, it is being conducted on a greatly reduced scale, and it will probably be
several years before there is any notable change in this
respect. Germany and Italy have been completely eliminated. Great Britain's trade and investment position has

been seriously and probably permanently impaired. France still has strong cultural influence, but little else. Spain's cultural influence, too, is considerable, especially through the Hispanic movement, but has been weakened both by the split between the pro-Franco and the anti-Franco Hispanicists, and by the Indianist movement. The Soviet Union is not a negligible factor, but it accounts for less than 1 per cent of the trade of the area, has a very small and badly divided following even among the more radical groups, and is cordially detested by most elements, from left of center to extreme right.

In the field of international organization the problems that face the Bolivarian states arise mainly from the policies which they have adopted as small states situated in an area where the influence of the United States is preponderant. To their way of thinking, international organization exists mainly for the purpose of protecting the small states against the large ones; burgeoning nationalism and devotion to the principle of sovereignty discourage the development of the positive functions in such organizations. In the United Nations they are continuing their attack on the veto right of the five great powers as a violation of the principle of juridical equality of states. In the inter-American system, in which this principle is already enshrined, they are laboring to maintain unimpaired the rule of nonintervention adopted at Buenos Aires in 1936. Hoping that the Good-Neighbor policy will be continued, they favor the strengthening of this system, in which there are no distinctions between large and small states and in which the Latin-American governments are not brought into contact with any communist power.

Colombia has been the principal exponent of these policies and attitudes and shows no sign of departing from them in the near future. It is in a strong position to maintain the primacy it has enjoyed in recent years. Besides Antonio López in the Security Council of the United Nations, it is represented in the inter-American system by Alberto Lleras Camargo, recently elected Director General of the Pan American Union—the first Latin American ever to hold that post. Also, Bogotá is to be the seat of the Ninth Inter-American Conference, originally scheduled for 1943, but postponed first because of the war and subsequently because of the delay in following up the Act of Chapultepec by the negotiation of a permanent Pan-American military defense pact, which it has been agreed should precede the holding of this conference.

In their relations with one another and with neighboring states, the members of our group are following the lines already plotted in the past decade or two. More will be heard of the Grancolombian movement and possibly also of the broader Bolivarian movement; and of the transborder trade agreements by which pairs of states give each other commercial privileges not accorded to other states. Though all the major boundary disputes of the area have now been settled, more may also be heard of some of these, too. The most probable source of trouble is the Leticia question between Peru and Colombia. For more than a decade Peru has abided faithfully by the definitive settlement of 1934, but many Peruvians regard it is contrary to nature as well as equity, and so sober a Peruvian writer as Alberto Ulloa has declared that it is a wrong that ought to be righted. If this idea catches fire with less sober Peruvians, the lid may blow off. Peru, though smaller than Colombia, is much stronger in the Amazonian area in which Leticia lies. Bolivia and Ecuador, too, are smarting under what they consider the rank injustice of recent settlements whereby each suffered large territorial losses; but they are both too weak to start wars of revenge and revindication, even if they wanted to, of which at the moment there is no sign.

Indeed, it may be difficult for the two latter countries to hold what they still have, and their weakness and instability constitute one of the major problems of the Bolivarian group. This situation invites constant interference on the part of larger states of the area, such as that of Argentina at La Paz. Bolivia presents the more acute problem, for it still holds large undeveloped areas in its faltering grasp. Ecuador has already been bereft of about all the territory any other nation would want except what is compactly settled, and its immediate problem is mainly the domestic one of achieving a reasonable degree of order and stability. But even this, if it is not solved in the near future, may bring on an international crisis by stimulating the existing rivalry between its two larger neighbors, Colombia and Peru.

To conclude: Under the impact of foreign capital and business enterprise, mainly since 1920, the Bolivarian republics are undergoing an economic transformation, but this is still far from complete and has so far produced a disequilibrium, both in their domestic economy and their foreign trade, which has had profoundly disturbing effects. Some of them have recently developed progressive and forward-looking political leadership, but even they have a long road to travel in this direction. All of them face manifold and grave problems which they cannot solve without foreign aid. Many of these problems are of the kind which, it seemed in the rosy dawn of the new internationalism of 1944 and 1945, might come within the purview of the United Nations or the inter-American system. Now that that sky has clouded over, it seems probable that for a long time to come, such aid will have to be sought on the old familiar terms of bargaining between sovereign national states; bargaining which involves questions not only of money but also of security and political influence, and which at times is even tempered by humanitarianism. In the present state of the world the United States is both the only power to which these countries can look for such aid on any of these terms, and also the only power that has a major interest in making it available—not for the dubious satisfaction of playing Santa Claus, but as a genuinely interested party.

Appendix. Suggested Reading

The curious reader who wishes to know more about the various questions discussed in this book has a considerable volume of materials at his disposal. He will probably find most of them accessible if he lives in a community that has a first-rate library, such as one of the larger cities or universities of the United States. But even in this case he will need to have patience, perseverance, and a reading knowledge of both Spanish and English, if he is to make full use of what is available. Some of the best material exists either in Spanish or in English alone. In neither language was much of it written with a view to aiding the student of the five Bolivarian states as a group; almost without exception it deals either with single countries or with a larger group, such as all of South America or all of Latin America. There are other difficulties, too, but they will not be recounted here, since our space is limited and anyway our purpose is not to discourage the curious reader but on the contrary to stimulate and aid him. We merely want him to know that it will probably require some effort on his part to dig out the answers to all his questions.

The following suggestions are, of course, highly selective, for the number of books and articles already published on the many topics discussed in the present volume is very large and important additions are being made to it every year. While these suggestions are confined mainly to works in English, several titles in Spanish are included for the reason given above. Their inclusion seems all the more de-

sirable because the proportion of people in the United
States who have a reading knowledge of Spanish is large
and growing—for several years past, Spanish has attracted
more students in our schools and colleges than any other
foreign language.

1. BACKGROUND MATERIAL

Lands and Peoples: Among general works on the human
geography of Latin America, Preston E. James, *Latin America* (New York: Odyssey Press, 1942), gives the best compact description of our five countries; one chapter is devoted to each country. Older but still valuable is the topically arranged volume of the Royal Institute of International Affairs, *The Republics of South America* (London,
1937). Derwent Whittlesey, *The Earth and the State* (New
York: Holt, 1939), includes a geopolitical account of Latin
America. The most comprehensive assemblage of recent
statistical and other data is provided by Pan American Associates, *The Pan American Yearbook, 1945* (New York,
1945), arranged mainly by countries. Useful trade and travel
guides are Howell Davies, ed., *South American Handbook,
1946* (London: Trade and Travel, 1946), and E. P. Hanson,
ed., *New World Guides* (New York: Duell, 1944).

The leading works on individual countries vary considerably in character and merit. Luis E. Valcárcel, *La ruta
cultural del Perú* (Mexico, D. F., 1945), Luis López de
Mesa, *De cómo se ha formado el pueblo colombiano*
(Bogotá, 1943), and Jorge Basadre, *Perú: problema y posi-
bilidad* (Lima, 1931), are genetic studies by leading authorities. Albert B. Franklin, *Ecuador, Portrait of a People* (New
York: Doubleday, 1943), is also the work of a scholar, but
is focused on the contemporary scene. Among other books
on Ecuador, which has been a great favorite in this country
in recent years, special mention should be made of Ludwig

Bemelmans, *The Donkey Inside* (New York: Viking, 1941), because it was a best seller and did a great deal to shape North American notions about that country, as did T. R. Ybarra, *Young Man of Caracas* (New York: Washburn, 1941), in the case of Venezuela. Kathleen Romoli, *Colombia, Gateway to South America* (New York: Doubleday, 1941), and Erna Fergusson, *Venezuela* (New York: Knopf, 1939), are designed for popular consumption, but give an excellent picture of those two countries. Much older works that still repay reading are the Bolivian classic, Alcides Argüedas, *Pueblo enfermo* (second ed., Barcelona, 1910), and Phanor J. Eder, *Colombia* (New York: Scribner, 1913).

The numerous Indian peoples of the Andes are the subject of Vol. 2 of the Smithsonian Institution's *Handbook of South American Indians*, edited by Julian H. Steward (Washington: Government Printing Office, 1946). A much smaller, but still significant, minority group is discussed in J. F. Normano and Antonello Gerbi, *The Japanese in South America* (New York: Institute of Pacific Relations, 1943).

The background literature in English has recently been enriched by translations of a number of works by authors in the Bolivarian countries, such as *The Knights of the Cape* (New York: Knopf, 1945), consisting of selections from Ricardo Palma's classic *Tradiciones peruanas*, translated by Harriet de Onís; and Germán Arciniegas, *Caribbean: Sea of the New World* (New York: Knopf, 1946), also translated by Harriet de Onís from a new book, *El mar del nuevo mundo*.

History and Politics: These topics are combined because information about political questions, when it can be found at all, is contained mainly in historical works, and because most of the historical works are largely political. The dearth of good material on recent developments in this field is surprising in view of the fact that at any given time it normally attracts more attention, from both nationals and foreigners, than any other aspect of life in these countries. The explanation may be partly that South American historians have found the remote past safer to write about than the contemporary period, and the wars of independence (the age of the Liberator Bolívar) far more glamorous; and partly that the short life-expectancy of political regimes in the Bolivarian area discourages serious study of the subject. Whatever the reason, the dearth is marked even in Spanish works, and in English it approaches the famine stage. The only full-length study in English is N. Andrew N. Cleven, *The Political Organization of Bolivia* (Washington: Carnegie Institution, 1940). Among occasional articles of a general character, two published in the *American Political Science Review* for June 1945 deserve special mention: Russell H. Fitzgibbon, "Constitutional Government in Latin America," and William S. Stokes, "Parliamentary Government in Latin America." For the rest, the reader must rely on what he can glean from general and special historical works. Among the former, Clarence H. Haring, *South American Progress* (Cambridge: Harvard University Press, 1934), still ranks high. Hubert Herring, *Good Neighbors* (New Haven: Yale University Press, 1942), Samuel Guy Inman, *Latin America in World Life* (New York: Harcourt, 1942), and Robin A. Humphreys, *The Evolution of Modern Latin America* (New York and London: Oxford, 1946), bring the story into the World War II period. So do the latest editions of standard textbooks on Latin America, such as those by Mary W. Williams, Dana G. Munro, J. Fred Rippy, William Spence Robertson, and A. Curtis Wilgus. All of these follow an essentially national pattern and, aside from their brief sketches, we have no up-to-date histories in English of any of these countries except Colombia. The exception, J. M. Henao and Gerardo Arrubla's *History of Colombia*, translated by J. Fred Rippy

(Durham: Duke University Press, 1938), leaves a good deal to be desired. The long reign of Juan Vicente Gómez in Venezuela is described from opposite points of view in Thomas Rourke (pseudonym for D. J. Clinton), *Gómez, Tyrant of the Andes* (New York: Morrow, 1936), and Pedro M. Arcaya, *The Gómez Regime* (Washington: privately printed, 1936).

Economic, Social and Cultural Problems: The offerings here are more abundant, but again to a large extent they have to be dug out of books about Latin America in general. Among the most useful on current questions are Seymour E. Harris, ed., *Economic Problems of Latin America* (New York: McGraw-Hill, 1944); George Wythe, *Industry in Latin America* (New York: Columbia University Press, 1945); Lloyd J. Hughlett, ed., *Industrialization of Latin America* (New York: McGraw-Hill, 1946); Moisés Poblete Troncoso, *El movimiento obrero latinoamericano* (México, D. F., Fondo de Cultura Económica, 1946); George Soule, David Efron, and Norman T. Ness, *Latin America in the Future World* (New York: Farrar and Rinehart, 1945); Mordecai Ezekiel, *Towards World Prosperity* (New York: Harpers, 1947); and Willi Feuerlein and E. Hannan, *Dollars in Latin America* (New York: Council on Foreign Relations, 1941). Three special questions of particular interest to the Bolivarian countries are discussed in A. Fabra Rivas, *The Cooperative Movement in Latin America* (Albuquerque: University of New Mexico Press, 1943); Antonio García, "El Indigenismo en Colombia," *América Indígena,* July 1945; and Kingsley Davis, "Population Trends and Policies in Latin America," in *Some Economic Aspects of Post-War Inter-American Relations* (Austin: Institute of Latin American Studies, University of Texas, 1947). A Colombian version of the "rise of the common man" theme is provided by Germán Arciniegas in *Este pueblo de América* (México, D. F.: Fondo de Cultura Económica, 1945).

For an introduction to problems of urbanization, see Francis Violich, *Cities of Latin America* (New York: Reinhold, 1944). New ground is broken by Negley K. Teeters, *Penology from Panama to Cape Horn* (Philadelphia: University of Pennsylvania Press, 1946), which includes all the Bolivarian countries except Venezuela. The story of American tropical medicine, which involves a large part of our area, is popularly told in Charles Morrow Wilson, *Ambassadors in White* (New York: Holt, 1942), and a wealth of information on the history of medicine in Latin America from pre-Colombian times to the present is assembled in Arístides A. Moll, *Aesculapius in Latin America* (Philadelphia: Saunders, 1944). Three valuable series of country studies are: *Summary of Biostatistics,* prepared by the U. S. Department of Commerce and Bureau of the Census in cooperation with the Office of Coordinator of Inter-American Affairs (Washington, 1944–1945), and the U. S. Tariff Commission's *The Foreign Trade of Latin America* (Washington, 1940) and *Economic Controls and Commercial Policy* (Washington, 1945).

Mainly historical either in original intent or in present significance are Percy W. Bidwell, *The Economic Defense of Latin America* (Boston: World Peace Foundation, 1941); Cleona Lewis, *America's Stake in International Investments* (Washington: Brookings Institution, 1938); Isaiah Bowman, ed., *Limits of Land Settlement* (New York: Council on Foreign Relations, 1937); J. Fred Rippy, *Latin America and the Industrial Age* (New York: Putnam, 1944); and the three books in the series "Studies in American Imperialism," edited by Harry Elmer Barnes, which relate to countries in our area: Margaret M. Marsh, *The Bankers in Bolivia.* (New York: Vanguard, 1928); J. Fred Rippy, *The Capitalists and Colombia* (New York: Vanguard, 1931); and Charles D. Kepner, Jr., and Jay H. Soothill, *The Banana Empire* (New York: Vanguard, 1935).

J. Lloyd Mecham, *Church and State in Latin America* (Chapel Hill: University of North Carolina Press, 1934), is the standard general work on the subject. The only special study in English for a country in our area is Mary W. Watters, *A History of the Church in Venezuela, 1810–1930* (Chapel Hill: University of North Carolina Press, 1933). A broader and more controversial work on the contemporary scene, written from the Protestant point of view, is George Howard, *Religious Liberty in Latin America?* (Philadelphia: Lippincott, 1944). On the Catholic side the best recent book is Peter M. Dunne's *A Padre Views South America* (Milwaukee: Bruce, 1945).

Much the best introduction to the literary history of Latin America, with emphasis on the social context, is Pedro Henríquez-Ureña, *Literary Currents in Hispanic America* (Cambridge: Harvard University Press, 1945), but those who can read Spanish should supplement it with recent works by leading literary historians of the Bolivarian area, such as Mariano Picón Salas (Venezuela), Rafael Maya (Colombia), and Luis-Albert Sánchez (Peru).

International Relations: For general background, see J. Fred Rippy, *Latin America in World Politics* (third edition, New York: Crofts, 1938), Arnold J. Toynbee's annual *Survey of International Relations*, and the annual *The United States in World Affairs* (Council on Foreign Relations, New York). The last-named was written by Whitney Shepardson and William O. Scroggs for several years before 1941, when it was suspended for the duration of the war. It is now being resumed with a volume on 1945–1947 by John C. Campbell. It normally contains one or two chapters on Latin America. Analyses of inter-American problems in a world setting are provided by Nicholas J. Spykman, *America's Strategy in World Politics* (New York: Harcourt, 1942), for an early stage of World War II, and by Sumner Welles, *The Time for Decision* (New

York: Harper, 1944), and *Where Are We Heading?* (New York: Harper, 1946), for later stages. The functioning of the inter-American system is best described in John P. Humphreys, *The Inter-American System: A Canadian View* (Toronto: Macmillan, 1942); its mechanics, in M. Margaret Ball, *The Problem of Inter-American Organization* (Stanford: Stanford University Press, 1944).

Broad problems in which the Bolivarian countries have had considerable interest are discussed in Warren H. Kelchner, *Latin American Relations with the League of Nations* (Boston: World Peace Foundation, 1930); Gordon Ireland, *Boundaries, Possessions, and Conflicts in South America* (Cambridge: Harvard University Press, 1938); and J. Fred Rippy, *The Caribbean Danger Zone* (New York: Putnam, 1940), and *South America and Hemisphere Defense* (Baton Rouge: Louisiana State University Press, 1941).

Among the many detailed studies of boundary disputes involving the Bolivarian countries, an important recent work is Margaret La Foy, *The Chaco Dispute and the League of Nations* (Ann Arbor, Mich.: Edwards, 1946).

For relations with the United States the best over-all accounts are Samuel F. Bemis, *The Latin American Policy of the United States* (New York: Harcourt, 1943); Graham H. Stuart, *Latin America and the United States* (third edition, New York: Appleton, 1938); and, for the Monroe Doctrine, Dexter Perkins, *Hands Off* (Boston: Little, Brown, 1941). Gaston Nerval (pseudonym for Raúl Díez de Medina), *Autopsy of the Monroe Doctrine* (New York: Macmillan, 1934), deserves mention here as a frequently cited book by a Bolivian author. Older works which are still useful for an understanding of the current scene are William Spence Robertson, *Hispanic American Relations with the United States* (Washington: Carnegie Endowment for International Peace, 1923), and Clarence H. Haring, *South America Looks at the United States* (New York:

Macmillan, 1928). Carleton Beals, Herschel Brickell, and others, *What the South Americans Think of Us* (New York: McBride, 1945), is of special interest because one of the authors, Mr. Brickell, had recently served with conspicuous success as cultural attaché in the U. S. Embassy at Bogotá. The picture it paints is somewhat too favorable. What many South Americans really think of us is better indicated by José de la Vega's unfriendly *El buen vecino* (Bogotá, 1944).

The only full-length account of the relations of any of the Bolivarian countries with the United States is E. Taylor Parks, *Colombia and the United States, 1765–1934* (Durham: Duke University Press, 1935). Dwight C. Miner, *The Fight for the Panama Route* (New York: Columbia University Press, 1940), includes a good account of the Colombian side of the story. A work of capital importance as an expression of discontent in the Bolivarian area with the policy of the United States in the early stages of World War II is Felipe Barreda Laos, *¿Hispano América en Guerra?* (Buenos Aires: Linari, 1941); the author was the ambassador of Peru to Argentina and Uruguay, 1930–1941. An important article by Eduardo Santos, of Colombia, in *Revista de América* (Bogotá) for April 1947 discusses the origin of the Act of Chapultepec in Santos' conference with President Roosevelt at the White House on January 9, 1945, points out the difference between this Act and the subsequent project of an inter-American military pact, and states strong objections to Latin-American participation in the latter.

Virtually all the literature on relations among the Bolivarian republics and between them and their neighbors is in Spanish. Among the more important works of this kind on subjects discussed in the present volume are Alberto Ulloa, *Posición internacional del Perú* (Lima: Torres Aguirre, 1941); Francisco José Urrutia, *Política internacional de la Gran Colombia* (Bogotá: Ed. "El Gráfico," 1941); Alberto

Ostria Gutiérrez, *Una revolución tras los Andes* (Santiago, 1944); Pio Jaramillo Alvarado, *La guerra de conquista en América* (Guayaquil: Jouvin, 1941); and Eduardo Plaza A., *La contribución de Venezuela al Panamericanismo . . . 1939–1943* (Caracas: Tipografía Americana, 1945). The Colombian Jesús M. Yepes has published a number of works in Spanish and French on the broader problems of international organization affecting these countries, the most recent of which is *La philosophie du panaméricanisme* (Paris, 1945). Except for studies of boundary disputes, works in English are confined to occasional articles, notable among which are three dealing with basic international problems of special significance for the Bolivarian area, published in the *Hispanic American Historical Review* for August 1943: Frank Tannenbaum, "Agrarismo, Indianismo, and Nacionalismo"; Robert E. McNicoll, "Intellectual Origins of Aprismo"; and Luis-Alberto Sánchez, "A New Interpretation of the History of America." Two recent biographical articles of international scope and special interest are Lawrence Martin, "The Ghost of Germán Busch, Dictator of Bolivia," in *Harper's Magazine* for October 1944, and Russell H. Fitzgibbon, "Colombian Gadfly," *The Inter-American,* February 1945—the "Gadfly" being Laureano Gómez.

2. CURRENT DEVELOPMENTS

Keeping up with current developments in the Bolivarian countries presents much the same problem as exploring their past. With rare exceptions, information in English will be found only in periodicals that report on foreign news in general or, at best, on Latin America in general. There is none that deals exclusively with any of these countries individually or with the group as a whole. And the many periodicals and new books in Spanish deal with single countries, not with the group.

In English, developments in the Latin-American area are reported and discussed in newspapers (especially the *New York Times* and *Herald Tribune* and the *Christian Science Monitor*), the weekly magazines of news and opinion (*Time* has a special Latin-American section, which rarely runs to much over one page), and some of the monthly magazines, notably *Current History* and the *Atlantic Monthly*, which has a regular feature, "The Atlantic Report on the World Today," that includes a section on Latin America. Occasional articles, usually of high quality, are published in the quarterly *Foreign Affairs* (Council on Foreign Relations, New York) and the fortnightly *Foreign Policy Reports* (Foreign Policy Association, New York). Annual surveys such as *The United States in World Affairs* (see preceding section) will give some help in keeping up.

Periodicals devoted to Latin America are the *Bulletin* of the Pan American Union (Washington); *Panorama, A Record of Cultural Events* (mimeographed), issued by the Union's Division of Intellectual Coöperation; and *Noticias*, a fortnightly news digest issued by the Council for Inter-American Coöperation (New York). Two scholarly journals, the *Hispanic American Historical Review* (Durham: Duke University Press) and *The Americas* (Washington: Academy of American Franciscan History), occasionally contain articles and news items of current interest. Two new journals began publication in 1947: *Inter-American Economic Affairs* (Washington), and *The Social Sciences in Mexico and News about the Social Sciences in South and Central America* (México, D.F.).

The reader should also watch the publications of various United States Government agencies, particularly the Departments of State, Commerce, Agriculture, and Labor, the Tariff Commission, the Bureau of the Census, and the Export-Import Bank. References to some of their special publications have been made in the preceding section. A regular publication of special value in its field is the Commerce Department's *Foreign Commerce Weekly*.

The regular and special publications of private business firms in the United States should not be overlooked, though they must be used with caution. The Latin-American interests of two of these firms, W. R. Grace & Company, and the Standard Oil Company of New Jersey, are concentrated mainly in the Bolivarian countries. Two of these countries, Colombia and Ecuador, lie within the area covered by the publications of the United Fruit Company's Middle America Information Bureau. The annual reports of the Foreign Bondholders Protective Council (New York) are also rewarding.

An invaluable guide to current publications relating to Latin America is provided by the annual *Handbook of Latin American Studies* (Cambridge: Harvard University Press), which fell in arrears during the war, but is now catching up. Arranged by topics (such as International Relations, Government, Economics, Literature), it includes items of current as well as historical interest.

For those who read Spanish, the New York newspaper *La Prensa* and the Mexican weekly news magazine *Tiempo* provide good news coverage for Latin America in general, though for the Bolivarian countries in particular their own local papers are essential. Among the best of these are *El Tiempo* of Bogotá and *El Comercio* of Lima. No one of them, however, covers the whole area adequately. The same must be said of the magazines and other periodicals, such as *Semana*, a weekly recently established in Bogotá, with ex-President Alberto Lleras as editor, and *Revista de América* of the same city, both of which are aimed at the general reader, and of *Revista Peruana de Derecho Internacional*, of Lima, an exceptionally stable and well-edited journal which, despite its title, covers many other aspects of international relations besides law.

The difficulty of keeping up with current developments in this area is greater today than it was a year or two ago. For the period 1941–1945 a handy guide to Latin-American developments in general was provided by the annual survey *Inter-American Affairs* (New York: Columbia University Press, 1942–1946), edited by A. P. Whitaker, but this series was recently suspended and, so far as is known, no steps have been taken to resume it. The best magazine in the field, *The Inter-American*, was recently merged with *Asia* and *Free World* to form a new periodical, *United Nations World*. One of the best general magazines published in the Bolivarian area, *Historia* (Lima), ably edited by Jorge Basadre for several years, has also ceased publication. Finally, recent events in other parts of the world have drawn public attention away from Latin America at large, and to the extent that interest in it has continued, it has been focused mainly upon the three largest countries, Argentina, Brazil, and Mexico. As a result, the Bolivarian countries, which have always been marginal in this respect, rarely appear in the news nowadays except when something sensational occurs in one of them.

In short, while current developments in the Bolivarian countries can be followed, the sources of information are so widely scattered and fragmentary that the task of assembling a well-rounded view is so difficult as to deter all but the most resolute. A great improvement in this respect will have to be made before the leaders of public opinion in this country, not to mention the general public itself, can think intelligently about our relations with those countries.

INDEX

INDEX

Harding administration, 165, 175
Hawley-Smoot Tariff, 174
Hay, John, 163
Hay-Pauncefote treaty, 161
Haya de la Torre, Víctor Raúl,
5, 32, 122, 190, 237
Hayes, President, 156
Henríquez-Ureña, Pedro, 32
Hernández de Alba, Gregorio,
237
Herzog, Enrique, 76
Hispanicism, 29–31, 34, 87, 185,
249
Hispanidad, 234
Hitler, Adolf, 119, 120, 121, 181,
201
Hochschild, 74
Holy Alliance, 153
Honduras, British, 118
Hoover, Herbert, 179, 180
Huancayo, 27, 33
Humboldt current, 28, 37–38
Hydroelectric power, 219–221

Icaza, Jorge, 5
Illiteracy, 5, 43, 45, 229
Inca Empire, 16, 26, 29, 152
Indians, 7, 14, 20–22, 26, 29, 32–35,
39, 45, 51, 62, 67, 78, 238
Indianism, 32, 236–239, 249
Indigenistas, 238
Industrial Development Institute,
95–96
Industrialization, 96–99, 107, 109,
110, 209–220, 226, 228
Institute of Inter-American Af-
fairs, 106
Inter-American Coffee Agree-
ment, 95–96, 109
Inter-American Committee for
Political Defense, 126, 137, 140
Inter-American Conference on
Problems of War and Peace,
Mexico City, 113
Inter-American Conference for
the Maintenance of Peace,
Buenos Aires, 114

Inter-American Conferences:
Washington (1889–1890), 158;
Washington (1929), 182;
Buenos Aires (1936), 113, 114,
115, 147, 189, 245, 251; Lima
(1938), 113, 115, 245; Chapultepec, Mexico City (1945), 89,
114, 115, 142–144, 146, 211; Bogotá, 252
Inter-American Defense Board,
126, 244, 246, 247
Inter-American Development
Commission, 95, 96
Inter-American Financial and
Economic Advisory Commit-
tee, 94, 95, 117
Inter-American Indian Institute,
237
Inter-American Juridical Com-
mittee, 126
Inter-American Neutrality Com-
mittee, 116–117, 126
Inter-American system, 44, 74, 87,
92, 94, 113, 114, 125, 137, 139,
141, 153, 158, 160–161, 175, 176,
184, 189, 243, 249, 251, 253
International Petroleum Corpora-
tion, 186, 202, 207, 223, 247, 248
International Telephone and Tel-
egraph Corporation, 186
International Trade Organiza-
tion, 211
Intervention, 59, 147, 176
Investments, 20, 30, 60, 207–208,
225–226
Ipiales, 212
Iquitos, 35, 39, 227
Iron and steel, 214, 216
Isaacs, Jorge, 56
Italy, 30, 59, 125, 172, 250

Jamaica, 118
James, Preston, 53, 227
Japan, 19, 30, 101, 102, 103, 108,
119, 121, 125, 130, 137
Japanese in Peru, 241

DATE DUE

APR 24 '90			
APR 13 1991			